New ethnicities and urban culture

Race and representation

A series edited by John Solomos, Michael Keith and David Goldberg

There is wide agreement that questions about race, racism and ethnicity are at the heart of contemporary social and political changes. There is, however, little clarity in the theoretical analysis of transformations that are currently taking place. *Race and representation* is firmly committed to providing a forum for the publication of innovative work in this field. We will build on recent theoretical advances by providing an arena for new and challenging conceptual frameworks, and the series will have an international and multidisciplinary focus. Our main objective is to establish a dialogue between contending theoretical and political perspectives, and to open up new ways of thinking about race and racism in contemporary societies.

New ethnicities and urban culture

Racisms and multiculture in young lives

Les Back
Goldsmiths College

UCL
PRESS

First published in 1996 by UCL Press

UCL Press Limited
University College London
Gower Street
London WC1E 6BT

The name of University College London (UCL) is a registered
trade mark used by UCL Press with the consent of the owner.

British Library Cataloguing in Publication Data
A catalogue record for this book is available from the British Library.

ISBNs: 1-85728-251-5 HB
         1-85728-252-3 PB

Typeset in Sabon.
Printed and bound by
Biddles Ltd, Guildford and King's Lynn, England.

For Vicki, Nicola and Robbie

The old river in its broad reach rested unruffled at the decline of day, after ages of good service done to the race that peopled its banks, spread out in the tranquil dignity of a waterway leading to the uttermost ends of the earth . . . And indeed nothing is easier for a man who has, as the phrase goes, "followed the sea" with reverence and affection, than to evoke the great spirit of the past upon the lower reaches of the Thames. They had sailed from Deptford, from Greenwich, from Erith – the adventurers and the settlers; kings' ships and the ships of men on 'Change; captains, admirals, the "dark interlopers" of Eastern trade, the commissioned "generals" of the East India fleets. Hunters for gold or pursuers of fame, they all had gone out on that stream, bearing the sword, and often the torch, messengers of the might within the land, bearers of a spark from the sacred fire. What greatness had not floated on the ebb of that river into the mystery of the unknown earth! . . . The dreams of men, the seed of commonwealth, the germs of empires.

Joseph Conrad, *The heart of darkness*

Far from being unitary or monolithic autonomous things, cultures actually assume more "foreign" elements, alterities, differences, than they consciously exclude. Who in India or Algeria can confidently separate out the British or French component of the past from present actualities, and who in Britain or France can draw a clear circle around British London or French Paris that would exclude the impact of India and Algeria upon those two imperial cities?

Edward Said, *Culture and imperialism*

Contents

CONTENTS

Acknowledgements

There are many people I want to thank for helping me sustain the desire and energy to finish this book. My students both at the University of Birmingham and at Goldsmiths College provided challenging environments in which to work through and establish some of the key ideas found within these pages. I owe an enormous debt to Pat Caplan, who steered me through much of this project and gave principled council – which I often did not want to hear but from which I always benefited. I will never be able to repay this arrearage but I will always cherish her example and grace. John Solomos gave endless encouragement in completing this manuscript and I learned a lot about intellectual rigour and thoroughness through working with him. I would like to thank John for all his comradely generosity, friendship and instruction in the mystical uses of the "multiple filofax". Two books gave me inspiration and radical insight during the initial stages of researching and writing this book. Roger Hewitt's ground-breaking study *White talk, black talk* provided an intellectual and empirical precedent. The areas discussed here all fall within the district that he refers to as Area B. I found out a great deal about ethnography, jazz and intellectual integrity during many conversations with Roger across his kitchen table. I'd like to thank him for too many things to mention here, suffice to say – *keep on tipping along The Stoll.* Paul Gilroy's *Ain't no black in the Union Jack* made an equal impact on me, and its breadth and vision transformed the way in which I conceived of the cultural politics of race and nation. I'd like to say a special thank you to him. During 1989 I was able to work on this research as part of a wider project on young people and social identity conducted by Barbara Tizard and Ann Phoenix at the Thomas Coram Research Unit, Institute of Education. Thanks to Barbara and Ann for their generosity and all the support and encouragement that they have given me. A range of other colleagues and friends warrant a distinguished mention for the numerous conversations that have made me think more carefully. In particular I would like to thank Nici Nelson, Parminder Bhachu, Michael Keith, Flemming Røgilds, Vron Ware, Vikki Bell, Steve Kapur, Ko Banerjea, Leslie Lyrix, Ove Sernhede, Gargi Bhattacharyya, Sadie Plant, Ann Gray, Maureen McNeil, Chris Long and Anna Arnone: love and respect to you all. Debbie and Stevie Back lovingly tolerated my altered states of mind during long periods of writing. My dearest thanks also go out to Ron Warshow, Jackie Timberlake, Richard Dinnadge, Mark "Zebra" Warshow, Pete Merchant, Dave Yewman, Adrian Collins, Paul Moody, Sim Colton, Lorna Elliot, Tim Brown and Dave Armour, whose friendship is a constant source of sustenance, kindness and strength. A special mention goes to Pete Jones who let me share his flat during the period when the bulk of the fieldwork for this book was conducted. In 1994 Pete had a terrible accident that left him paralysed. The royalties from this book will go to the Pete Jones Fund. I'd like to thank Pete for his soulfulness, humour and inspiration. Without him this book would never have been written. I would also like to thank Justin Vaughan at UCL Press for his patience and support. The largest debt of all is owed to the people of South London who allowed me to share their time.

Introduction

The growing attention given to theorizing cultural hybridity and syncretism has become the substance of a new political prudence amongst cultural critics. Much of this has been concerned with countering various forms of cultural absolutism and essentialism without falling into saccharin and relativistic versions of anti-essentialist politics. I have completed this book while trying to steer a personal, intellectual and political course through the contemporary vicissitudes of the politics of race. Equally, I have taught this new literature to a generation of students from diverse cultural backgrounds and for whom these ideas were aimed to provide a new way of understanding their social locations. What has struck me is the degree of resistance amongst my students regarding this "new cultural politics", which so many of them see as little more than the utopian musings of an older generation of critics who have lost touch with the very cultures they claim to interpret. These objections cannot be easily dismissed as intellectually callow resistance to the profoundly complex nature of our current predicament. Neither can they be read simply as proof that these ideas are of little relevance to the plight of young people. My point here is that in completing this book I have become increasingly aware of the need to remain vigilantly cautious about projecting romantic and utopian desires on to the accounts and interpretations of the culture of young people. Equally, I want to describe and valorize vernacular cultures without destroying the undeniable energy and creativity found within them. Those of us who are attempting to understand the relationship between racism and urban multiculture need to pay close attention to those dissenting voices. A kind of "discrepant cosmopolitanism" (Clifford 1992) has emerged within

1

cultural criticism through the acceptance of the visionary ideas of outernational and transcultural figures such as Edward Said, Michelle Wallace, Cornel West, Stuart Hall, Paul Gilroy, bell hooks and Homi Bhabha. My fear is that this subtly variegated and prescient new writing is leaving a generation of young scholars behind in its wake. Such a divergence cannot engender greater insight into the pressing questions of culture, identity, entitlement and belonging as we move towards the end of the twentieth century.

Renato Rosaldo, in his seminal book *Culture and truth*, argued that it is vital to take issues of recognition seriously in interpretation of cultures. The most telling feature of Chicano reactions to anthropological writing, he suggests, is that these accounts of Chicano culture seem amusing, parodic and unreal to such a degree that they are unrecognizable. Rosaldo's appeal is to take the narratives of the objects of cultural criticism as seriously as those of the critic or anthropologist (Rosaldo 1989: 147). *New ethnicities and urban culture* attempts to listen to those sceptical young voices and to outline a contingent account of the forms of dialogue that have fed the cultural creativity and expressiveness of young people in Britain's cities. It is equally concerned to explain and theorize how urban contexts also offer sites where constantly shifting forms of racism can be enunciated. It my contention that contemporary cultural theory needs to be brought closer to the experience of its youthful censors and in doing so offer an account of a cultural politics that avoids banal optimism while holding on to the possibility of transcendence. I hope this book goes some way to lessening this chasm of mutual mis-recognition.

The contexts and motivations for writing this book have changed in the five years it has taken to write it. Initially the idea was borne out of a personal frustration I felt with the forms of municipal anti-racism that were widespread during the mid-1980s. The Greater London Council's "London Against Racism" campaigns constituted the apotheosis of such strategies in the capital. Posters, badges and codes of practice proliferated, producing a version of anti-racism that rarely moved beyond sloganeering and a kind of "lapel politics". During this time I was earning a living as a youth worker in the multiethnic districts that would ultimately provide the basis for this book. What seemed clear to me was that these highly centralized and moral forms of countering racism paid little attention to the exact ways in which racism entered into the lives of young people. The model was simple. Whites were constructed as "saints" or "sinners", either singularly racist or pure advocates of rejecting racism. The consequence was that the complex combinations of racist and non-racist sentiment that were evident in the lives of young whites were simply ignored. Rather, young people were offered a moral line that they could either subscribe to or be punished by. My initial impulse was to try to make sense of what existed in the space between anti-racism as a moral dogma and the resonance that racism had within the lives of young people.

Another motivation for writing this book was to account for the truly new and challenging forms of cultural practice and identity formation that had been produced within metropolitan contexts. British anthropology and its preoccupation with a Barthian approach to the study of identity and ethnicity has been singularly out of step with the ceaselessly changing and multiply inflected forms of cultural expression that had been being galvanized within British cities (Solomos & Back 1996). Cultural Studies in contrast has provided an intellectual space in which issues of multiculture and the politics of racism received greater attention (Gilroy 1987, 1993a, 1993b; Mercer 1994). In particular, post-colonial writers attempted to face this challenge by outlining what Cornel West referred to as a "new cultural politics of difference" (West 1992). A unique dimension of the British experience during the 1970s and 1980s was the formation of an inclusive notion of blackness configured as the political colour of opposition to racism. However, by the mid-1980s the hegemony of this version of political identity came under pressure from a variety of sources. Perhaps the most significant of these pressures was the controversy that followed from the publication of Salman Rushdie's book *The satanic verses* and the subsequent political debates about this and related issues. The whole debate about religious absolutism within minority communities challenged the utility of the political category "black" in the changed social and political environment of the 1990s. In particular, the emergence of religious and communal movements within minority communities suggested that a new political alignment was taking shape.

In two important papers Stuart Hall attempted to periodize the development of black cultural politics and argued the necessity of returning to questions of ethnicity and identity, albeit in a revitalized way (Hall 1987, 1988). He argued that the coining of the term "black" during the 1970s was a means to reference a common experience of racism and marginalization. He suggested that this moment was a product of a political challenge within the "dominant regimes of representation", which included the media discourses and anthropological and sociological framework. He also argued that this definitional politics is best understood in terms of a struggle that took place over the relations of representation in which a counter-position of positive black imagery was offered to unsettle the reified images of black culture (Hall 1988: 27). Hall characterized this counter-position as the first phase in the development of black cultural politics: "In that moment, the enemy was ethnicity" (Hall 1991b: 55). The unintended consequence of this movement was a tendency to homogenize cultural, class and sexual difference within blackness.

The second phase was marked, he argued, by the end of an innocent notion of the essential black subject, and the beginning of a new politics had to work through multiple inflections. Henceforth the black subject needed always to be crossed with references to class, gender, sexuality and ethnicity. Hall asserted a politics that is composed of unities within difference. This second phase involved reinscribing ethnicity outside of the discourses of the sociology of race and ethnic relations and the rhetoric of nationalism. He argued that ethnicity needed to be de-coupled from its former associations. In his later work Hall has expanded this conception of "identity through difference" (Hall 1991a, b) and stressed the importance of placing black cultural production in the context of global networks (Hall 1992). Thus "new ethnicities" are produced in part through a productive tension between global and local influences. This way of framing ethnicity can be seen as radically different from the situational model prevalent within anthropology and the sociology of race relations, for it avoids the tendency to define ethnicity in primordial ways and acknowledges the simultaneously local and trans-local nature of identity formation. "New ethnicities" not only challenge what it means to be "black" but they also call into question the dominant coding of what it means to be British. This opens a range of issues that are related to the way notions of authenticity and belonging are defined within racist and absolutist conceptions of culture (see Gilroy 1987, Mercer 1994).

The literature on "new ethnicities" marked an attempt to recover culture and ethnicity from the clutches of the sociology of race and ethnic relations. There is little in the cultural studies literature that attempts to describe the cultural dynamics of new ethnicities at the level of everyday life. Rather the work of Stuart Hall offers a series of heuristic and informed meditations on the state of the politics of race in Britain. This work needs to be evaluated carefully alongside empirically situated accounts of vernacular culture, and *New ethnicities and urban culture* aims to fill this gap. However, my intention here is not to present ethnography as the privileged arbiter of "what is really happening on the streets", neither is it to characterize these new developments in cultural theory as removed or empirically uninformed. I want to pre-empt any characterization of this book as a form of ethnographic realism – or "strategic realism" as David Parker (1995) puts it – that is opposed to meta-theoretical writing on cultural politics. To invite such a dualism would give ethnographic authority a "truth telling" power that it does not deserve, given the trenchant critique that has been levelled at its textuality and historicity. James Clifford commented some time ago:

> Even the best ethnographic texts – serious true fictions – are systems, or economies, of truth. Power and history work through them, in ways their authors cannot fully control. Ethnographic truths are thus inherently partial – committed and incomplete. (Clifford 1986: 7)

Clifford points out that ethnography can never claim to know the whole truth or even to approach it. Such a realization need not lead to the abandonment of ethnography, but in order to return to realism we must leave it in the first place (ibid.: 25). Rather it means embracing a contingent and modest epistemology that attempts to achieve rigorous forms of reporting alongside a reflexive consciousness of the codes, textual moves and rhetoric integral to the process of writing ethnography. The anthropological colonization of veracity should be replaced with a realization that ethnography involves a series of *experiments with truth* (Myrdal 1969) that can never be completed conclusively.

Recent critical writing on the state of ethnography has stressed that in order for us to return to ethnography we need to embrace multiple strategies for writing culture. When classical modes of ethnographic reporting are applied to one's own family and friends the farcical and parodic nature of these descriptions is revealed (Rosaldo 1989). Such norms in ethnography result in an account of culture that excludes personal narratives and emotion, yet these ways of describing culture can be useful if their status and authority are viewed in a radically new way:

> There is no single recipe for representing other cultures . . .
> classic norms, used in a deliberately parodic and distorting
> manner, can at times yield forceful accounts. Normalizing
> descriptions can both reveal *and* conceal aspects of social
> reality. (ibid.: 61)

From here Rosaldo argues that it is important to recover a "cut
down" version of normalising accounts of culture and social life.
Throughout this book I have utilized these narrative modes by way
of: (a) challenging the familiarity of vernacular culture and ritual;
and (b) retaining the possibility of critical insight that is contingent
and provisional.

Within this book I use a range of textual devices to narrate the
fraught "contact zones" (Pratt 1992) that form its focus. These include extended quotation, description and monologues. All of these
devices and the accounts that are made possible through their deployment should be viewed with epistemological suspicion (Crapanzano
1986, Clifford 1988). I am arguing for this text to be read in an intellectual space that lies somewhere between the arrogance of a naïve
empiricist orthodoxy and the types of theoretical escapism that result
in little more than a reconfigured form of critical distance. I want to
brandish the responsibility for holding the pen and for the readings
and analysis that flow from it. Equally, this book is written out of a
commitment to engaging with the world of vernacular culture. This is
not to say that I am advocating a form of "heroic immersion" within
everyday life that somehow renders it comprehensible (Keith forthcoming). Rather I am arguing that, in order to escape the trap of
meta-theoretical reification, it is necessary to examine how the formation of identity, racism and multiculture is manifest within everyday life. I cannot claim to know or represent the "whole story".
Nobody can. I want this book to be read as an open contemplation on
the cultural dynamics of post-imperial London. What I have done in
the following pages is to offer – as faithfully as possible – the accounts
young people gave me of what it was like to come of age in a multicultural urban environment. If the impasse I identified in my opening
remarks is to be avoided, these muted voices must be integrated into
any understanding of the contemporary politics of culture and identity.

CHAPTER 1

The metropolitan paradox

As we move towards the end of the twentieth century, ideas about nationhood, culture and identity are increasingly seen either as in a state of attrition and fragmentation or as being reified through a language of authenticity and cultural absolutism. The choice is presented pointedly as one between viewing cultures as rooted and fixed and a vision of cultural processes as in a constant state of flux producing creative and promiscuous routeways of identification. What is omitted in the deafening row over "essentialism" versus "anti-essentialism" is the complex interplay between these two impulses at the everyday level and how forms of social exclusion and inclusion work through notions of belonging and entitlement in particular times and places. Within Europe's major conurbations, complex and exhilarating forms of transcultural production exist simultaneously with the most extreme forms of violence and racism. Urban vernacular cultures possess incommensurable political impulses that allow racism and transculturalism to be simultaneously proximate and symptomatic of what it means to grow up in post-imperial cities (Bhabha 1994). This metropolitan paradox cannot be comprehended within the binary "either/or" logic of the current debate over culture and essentialism. The central argument of this book is that multiply inflected forms of social identity are being expressed within cities such as London but these are equally being met by multiply accented forms of popular racism that sometimes operate inside urban multiculture and at other times prey on these fragile forms of dialogue from outside.

If we are to think again about the vexed question of multiculturalism it is vital to avoid any slippage into the false comfort of simple cultural archetypes that reify "minority" and "host" cultures respectively. Imperialism and the racist discourses that have flourished in its wake insist on what Roland Barthes (1973) called the "simplicity of essences". However, cultural processes themselves confound the idea that cultures exist as hermetically sealed absolute unities. Urban cultures, in particular, are highly promiscuous in their endeavour constantly to re-make and invent traditions in the present. Edward Said attempts to name this process by insisting that one must view the politics of culture within "overlapping territories" and "intertwined histories" (Said 1993). The key question thus becomes how to render explicit the multiple influences that resonate within metropolitan contexts such as London, Amsterdam, Paris, Hamburg and Berlin.

The politics of multiculturalism is a matter not of somehow simultaneously understanding and tolerating "foreign cultures" but of facing an imperial history that has brought people from around the globe into intense and sometimes terrible contact. In this sense the history of Europe is profoundly multicultural (Gilroy 1993a). It is for this reason that throughout this text I have taken the hyphen out of this formulation in order to stress the polyglot and intensely pluralized quality of urban multiculture. Yet European racism has equally insisted that the distinction of the European be established and maintained in the face of the barbarism and inferiority of the native, the immigrant or the ethnic minority. The relationship between racism and the construction of identities is not simply a matter of making non-Europeans inferior within some pseudo-biological logic. One of the cultural contradictions of racism is that the Other can be seen as an object of desire, simultaneously a "noble savage" and a "violent avenger" (Hall 1988). This syndrome is signalled by Franz Fanon, who argued with great power that the European romance with the difference was equally as devastating as the venom of racial hatred to subaltern peoples. A multiculturalism that simply celebrates the Other – albeit with liberal intentions – runs perilously close to this syndrome. Crude models of "the traditional" or primordial ethnic definitions are of little use when applied to the ambiguous social ground inhabited by multi-ethnic communities of young people in metropolitan settings. The social semantics of race, nationhood and belonging have undergone important transformations at the local level. It is the nature of these transformations that the book attempts to explain.

"England, half English": youth, racism and cultural syncretism

Racism is a notoriously difficult concept to define. Early writers concentrated on criticizing the legitimacy of the "idea of race" (Banton 1970) or they accepted the existence of "races" and focused on the way in which they were constructed in congenitally superior/inferior relationships (Benedict 1983). I will refer to racism as an ideology that defines social collectivities in terms of "natural" and immutable biological differences. These are invested with negative connotations of cultural difference and inferiority, whereby the presence of other "races" can be correlated with the economic and social health of either a specific region or the nation as a whole (Miles 1989). Racism is defined within particular historical and social contexts where past racial ideology can be used alongside new elements (Fanon 1967, Hall 1980); thus there is no one monolithic racism but numerous historically situated racisms.

During the 1980s Conservative ideologues woke up to the political necessity of reconstructing a unified British culture. This resulted in a British or English nativism extolled by such New Right commentators as Ray Honeyford (1989) and enshrined within the 1988 Educational Reform Act. Here culture, rather than pigment, became the key referent. The texture of British identity, stripped of its Celtic and regional components, is dominated by a cultural aesthetic of "Englishness". At the beginning of the new decade, the Conservative Member of Parliament Norman Tebbit appeared on the BBC's programme *Newsnight* and warned that "Many youngsters leave school totally confused about their origins and their culture". It is this shift that has prompted commentators to identify a new period in the history of English racism. The "new racism", or what Fanon (1967) referred to as "cultural racism", has its origins in the social and political crisis afflicting Britain (Hall 1978, Barker 1981, Gilroy 1990). Its focus is the defence of the mythical "British/English way of life" in the face of attack from enemies *outside* ("Argies", "Frogs", "Krauts", "Iraqis") and *within* ("black communities", "Muslim fundamentalists").

Paul Gilroy points to an alarming consequence of new racism where blackness and Englishness are reproduced as mutually exclusive categories (Gilroy 1987: 55–6; see also Wallman 1978a: 210–12). This is neatly captured in the cultural quotation used in the title of his influential book *There ain't no black in the Union Jack*, which referred to a racist slogan used during the 1970s and 1980s. Gilroy alludes to a new kind of cultural politics that defies the new racism and develops a political and cultural aesthetic that is both black and English. Stuart Hall, returning to the flag metaphor, refers to a shift in his own thinking:

> Fifteen years ago we didn't care, or at least I didn't care, whether there was any black in the Union Jack. Now not only do we care but we must. (Hall 1988: 30)

This is not simply a matter of building a series of cultural extensions on to the edifice of Britishness. Rather it involves an excavation of the diversity of traces found within British social formation so that the colours of the union flag develop a wholly different corona. The anti-road movements of the 1990s have further carnivalized the political semantics of the flag in the production of the vibrantly multicoloured "Union Jill". The forms of cultural politics that are practised through the art of subversion and recovery point to the "opening up of a self-conscious post-colonial space in which the affirmation of difference points forward to a more pluralistic conception of nationality and perhaps beyond that to its transcendence" (Gilroy 1993b: 62). In the encounter between black young people and their white inner-city peers, "Black culture has become a class culture . . . as two generations of whites have appropriated it, discovered its seductive forms of meaning for their own" (Gilroy 1990: 273). Young whites in this situation may have more in common with R. Kelly[1] than John Bull, with the result that it is impossible to speak of black culture in Britain separately from the culture of Britain as a whole (Jeater 1992). Beyond this it is impossible to speak of British culture without understanding these "overlapping territories".The perspective that I develop with this book recognizes the presence of new, and indeed old, racisms, but equally it is concerned with exploring the degree to which the emergent "new ethnicities" are reworking the terms of racial inclusion and exclusion.

It is important to counter the idea that socio-cultural groups – including nations – are essentially unchanging and atavistic entities. This phenomenon, which Paul Gilroy (1987: 59) appropriately calls "ethnic absolutism", ossifies the complex and changing nature of social and cultural life in Britain. He writes:

> The absolutist view of black and white cultures, as fixed,

mutually impermeable expressions of racial and national identity, is a ubiquitous theme in racial "common sense", but it is far from secure. (Gilroy 1987: 61)

In addition to Gilroy's work there is emerging a small but significant literature that documents the cultural creativity of young people who reside in multiracial areas (Hewitt 1986, Jones 1988, Rampton 1989). The detail of this process promises to transform the way we understand the politics of "race" and the paradigms that have been utilized to analyze multiracial contexts within British cities. Consequently, it is important, on the one hand, to view cultural meanings as in a constant state of negotiation and evolution, and, on the other, to be sensitive to the political, historical and ideological context in which this process takes place. The fundamental starting point of this analysis is that it is impossible to divide the British social formation into neat cultural compartments.

The earliest attempts to discuss negotiations taking place between black and white young people in British cities are found in the work of Dick Hebdige and Ian Chambers (Chambers 1976; Hebdige 1974a,b, 1979, 1981, 1983). Chambers saw that black cultural forms provided a resource on which white youth could draw, thus undercutting and contesting the dominant cultural hegemony (Chambers 1976: 160). A more developed statement on black/white dialogues is provided by Hebdige's account of "style". He suggests that within the development of youth styles it is possible to see a "phantom history of race relations":

> The succession of white subcultural forms can be read as a series of deep-structural forms which symbolically accommodate or expunge the black presence from the host community. It is on the plane of aesthetics: in dress, dance, music, in the whole rhetoric of style that we find the dialogue between black and white most subtly and comprehensively recorded, albeit in code. (Hebdige 1979: 44–5)

Here Hebdige claims that we can view a dialogue of emulation and accommodation. We see a history of "England, half English" encoded within these spectacular youth styles. As Hebdige points out, the impact of black culture on white young people was not uniformly progressive. For example, skinhead style incorporated Jamaican forms of

music (such as ska and bluebeat), yet at the same time it also proclaimed white power and white pride. In this case, like a photo-
graphic negative, black culture was an emblem of white chauvinism
(Mercer 1987, 1994). However, there are problems with Hebdige's
provocative and programmatic analysis.

Hebdige, true to his post-structuralist method, tends to read off
meanings from style formations without paying any attention to the
interactional components of racial dialogue at the level of everyday
experience. Writers working within the cultural studies paradigm
have for the most part not attempted to develop detailed ethnographic recordings of youth styles but have relied predominantly on
textual reconstruction. A notable exception here is the work of Paul
Willis (1977, 1978), who is perhaps the most rigorous ethnographer
to emerge from the Centre for Contemporary Cultural Studies. However, his work does not deal in any systematic way with working-class
racism (Marcus 1986). Hebdige views the interaction between black
and white youth in urban contexts as "ghostly" or "encoded", without addressing lived manifestations of the process of conflict and accommodation. Although Hebdige's work serves as a useful platform,
there is a need to look at these dialogues within specific ethnographic
contexts (Jones 1986: 89).[2]

Jones (1988) develops this approach in his analysis of white experiences of black youth culture. In his study of a section of Birmingham's youth he shows how reggae music provides a site where
dialogues between black and white people can occur. He reports:

> They are visible everywhere in a whole range of cross racial
> affiliations and shared leisure spaces; on the streets, around
> the games machines, in the local chip shop, in the play-
> grounds and parks, the dances and blues, right through the
> mixed rock and reggae groups for which the area has become
> renowned. (Jones 1988: xiv)

Here, the national chauvinism so prevalent in Britain during the
1980s, he argued, is simply redundant. Although one should be careful about viewing these dialogues through the lens of a utopian ro-
manticism, the fact that such phenomena existed at all pointed to the
emergence of a youthful social sphere in which racism – however
fleetingly – could be organized out of social life.

Another social location where exchanges take place between black and white young people is in language use (Hewitt 1982, 1986, 1988b). There exists a growing literature on the development of a specific British Creole that is distinct from the Creole spoken by first-generation Afro-Caribbean migrants (Sutcliffe 1982, Sebba 1983a,b, 1986, Sebba & Wooton 1984, Wong 1986). But by far the most comprehensive account is Hewitt's (1986) book *White talk, black talk* – an analysis of two contrasting London neighbourhoods, one ethnically mixed and the other predominantly white. He points out the different factors acting to censure Creole usage amongst the youthful black population. Hewitt interprets London Creole as a prestige form of speech and locates it within anti-racist struggle and a reaction to the "mundane face of racial discrimination" (Hewitt 1988b). He shows that in the multi-ethnic neighbourhood Creole usage is also adopted by white young people. This takes two forms: first, ethnically unmarked use of the Creole lexicon, and, secondly, fully marked Creole usage. In situations where friendship and trust are developed, whites may use this form of speech in the company of black peers. However, there is a constant monitoring of this usage and limitations are placed on what will be tolerated by black friends.

Hewitt's analysis is refined and methodologically grounded in recording observed behaviour. The result is a compelling analysis that is located in a particular historical and ethnographic context. However, there are some limitations in his discussion. He focuses exclusively on interactions between black and white youth, to the exclusion of other minority groups in the area. The difficulty with such an approach lies in the focus on a set of interactions, which is then used as an indicator of levels of adolescent racism. Kelly (1987) has shown that the concentration on black–white relations can give "interactional politics" a false significance. As I will show, dialogue between Afro-Caribbean and white working-class youth may have little or no impact on the use of racist discourses that are applied by whites to other minorities.[3]

I want to emphasize the importance of locating this analysis in specific social contexts. There is a need to investigate the practices that emerge within adolescent communities that give meaning to "race". I am suggesting something more than the term "culture contact" can adequately capture (Hewitt 1988b, 1991). Rather, what is needed is an approach that looks at urban multiculture in ethnically and racially plural contexts and takes on board the dialogue, transmission and hybridization of ethnicities (Bhachu 1991, Rampton 1987, Wulff 1988). This approach seeks to report sensitively the processes whereby British youth of various lineages work out and give meaning to their heritage in the context of daily experience. Also, it is vital to see how ethnicities are made through associations, friendships and cross affiliations.[4] The picture that is already beginning to emerge (Hewitt 1986, Rampton 1987, Jones 1988, Røgilds 1991) is infinitely more complex than the polemical black–white race relations model, and its complexity constitutes a new challenge for those interested in understanding the truly multicultural and multiracist character of Britain's youth.

Imperial London in a post-colonial era

The history of the capital is integrally connected to imperial expansion and trade. At its height during the eighteenth and nineteenth centuries London emerged as "a kind of Emporium for the whole Earth" (Joseph Addison quoted in Porter 1994). Peter Linebaugh comments in his seminal study of eighteenth-century London society:

> The Thames was the jugular vein of the British Empire. London, the largest city in the western hemisphere, containing by 1800 nearly a million souls, was both the capital of England and the centre of the empire that embraced the workshops of Bengal, the plantations of the Caribbean, the "factories" of West Africa and the forests of North America . . . Through these waters passed the wealth of the Empire. (Linebaugh 1991: 409–10)

Along with the flow of commodities came migrations of people from various hinterlands: Jews came to London from Poland and Germany and French Huguenots came fleeing religious persecution. It is also little known that from the middle of the eighteenth century there were 5,000–10,000 Africans living in London; some of them were seamen but in large part they were transported to Britain as servants and chattel (Fryer 1984). London provided the financial centre from which Britain's slave trade was financed and it was developed economically from the fruits of slavery. From the late eighteenth century, London's population, and in particular its working classes, may be likened to a popular drink of the time called "All Nations": this intoxicating mixture sold in "dram shops" was made up of the dregs of different spirits (Linebaugh 1991: 358).

The great trading companies of the imperial era established themselves on the banks of the Thames. To the north, the West India Company built large dock complexes in the last years of the eighteenth century. It was from here that sugar – the fruit of Caribbean plantocracies – was unloaded and popularized amongst London's citizens, regardless of class. Indeed, so prized were these Caribbean spoils that a River Thames Force was established in the late eighteenth century as the first force in London's history to command centralized state authority; it was responsible for the payment of the West India Fleet's "lumping gangs" and dockside workers (Linebaugh 1991: 433). South of the river, the East India Company – founded in Deptford – traded silver to Chinese merchants, and brought home, among many other items, tea, which became a favourite English drink in the eighteenth century (Rediker 1987: 39; Dews 1971, Steele 1993). Some of the most quintessential icons of Englishness – like the cup of English tea – barely dissolve the sweet traces of an imperial legacy (Hall 1991b, 1992). It is crucial to stress here that the development of the English social formation has depended on flows of commodities and labour for at least three hundred years. Even fish and chips, the most evocative culinary emblem of "native London life", conceals a hybrid cultural history. Popularized in the late nineteenth century, fish and chips were the result of the fusion of French styles of preparing fried potatoes and an east European Jewish tradition for frying fish (Malvery 1907).

The point I am trying to make through these examples is that the issues I am going to talk about with regard to contemporary London are not part of a kind of "Other England". The relationship between imperial expansion and Englishness is central to the story of what it means to be part of English society in general and London in particular. Equally, the historical denial of the long-standing presence of Africans and south Asians has meant that their contribution to English society has been ignored. London has a multicultural past to be recovered but the historical traces of this history have been bleached from public memory. English culture, whether embodied in the "afternoon cup of tea", the Friday night "fish and chips supper" or the "jovial London Bobbie", is intertwined with the history of imperialism and intercultural contact. Yet imperialism also brought the children of empire "up river", and this process has intensified in the post-colonial era.

The book focuses on two neighbourhoods that have contrasting ethnic compositions. The two areas are located little more than a mile away from one another in the northern half of a South London borough. This area consists of a mixed housing stock, but the overwhelming feature of the district is a series of post-war council estates and high-rise tower blocks that dominate the skyline. This study focuses on two of the council estates in this area. Before going on to discuss these areas in detail I want to sketch out the historical processes that have affected the economic and social fabric of this district.

The historical and social setting

The population of this district is currently around 60,000 and the economic activity that has been associated with this area has largely been the result of its location on the banks of the River Thames. The local economy has been dominated by a combination of dockyard activity and industrial manufacturing. Significant dock complexes were dug south of the river and the major traffic was in timber and grain. In the period of industrialization during the nineteenth century, the region also became a focus of intense railway construction. There were also locomotive works in the locality. In addition, glass works and distilleries took advantage of the raw materials brought to them via the river and the railways.

As well as the shipyards and docks, a flourishing metal trades sector developed, taking advantage of the low rental on the river. This district became the centre of London's heavy metal trades and the area was dubbed by locals "Birmingham by the water". The metal industries were divided into a number of sections that included large-scale capitalized factories specializing in boilers and marine engineering and locomotive production and medium-sized metal-working firms specializing in shutter production and brass, zinc and tin working. Petty commodity producers, who included smiths, zinc and tin workers, wire workers, locksmiths and bellsmiths, set up small workshops. Also important in the Victorian economy were building, artisan and retailing trades.

The economic expansion that took place during this period was paralleled by rapid population growth. Between 1841 and 1891 the population of the area increased more than fivefold. In the mid nineteenth century it was doubling every ten years and by 1901 it had grown to 110,000. This figure remained constant for the next 30 years. Urbanization on this scale had severe social consequences and significant patterns of residential segregation occurred within the district, echoing and reflecting the extreme social inequalities produced by industrial capitalism.

The majority of the industrial working class lived on the alluvial flood plain adjacent to the River Thames. However, on the terraces and undulating hills above, a middle-class suburb developed. By 1901 a complete class division had emerged, with the middle classes occupying the elevated areas in the south, and, as one progressed north, the housing stock was graded from terraced streets occupied by artisans and clerks to riverside slums occupied by the industrial poor. A Victorian observer noted in the local newspaper, "[those] living on a stagnant flood plain, had, close at hand, a high hill from which the loveliness of the world may be seen". Social homogeneity within the middle-class suburb was maintained by the high rents. The private developers built houses for "respectable" workers and thus established a band of working-class housing that served as a buffer between the middle-class hills and the riverside slums. Within this belt the company often turned down potential tenants because of "doubts in their personal integrity".[5]

In contrast to the "labour aristocrats" who lived in the "buffer zone", workers in the riverside areas lived in the most appalling conditions. Rent-farming practice (multiple letting of decrepit property) was rife and this area became renowned for street crime and prostitution. The importance of these divisions is that within this area a significant differentiation existed between, on the one hand, a community of skilled workers who worked in industrial manufacturing and, on the other, an unskilled labouring class that depended on casual labour in the docks. At the turn of the century Charles Booth described the district in his famous study *Life and labour of the people in London*:

> The bulk of the population are waterside workers . . . They are a careless, hand to mouth class; heavy drinkers, rather rough, but not criminally disposed . . . An extract from our notes on one of the streets, the worst, will help to show how great the fall has been: "Rough women are on the doorsteps, one of them with a bandaged head, others with black eyes. Shoeless children run about, and an old harridan sits smoking a clay pipe. The prevailing dirt makes itself felt by a faint

foetid smell, only over-powered in places by disgusting
stenches." This is the bottom. Above this lie various degrees
of badness, and also much that is quiet and respectable.
(Booth 1902: 7)

This account reflects the moral imperatives adopted by the nine-
teenth-century "social explorers" who enquired into the lives of the
poor. Urban poverty was an "internal Orient" to be discovered and
tamed. Connections between these urban voyages and colonial exploration were made clear by social commentators such as William
Booth. Similarly, George Sims in *How the poor live* – published in
1883 – spoke of his enquiry as a voyage of discovery that delved "into
the dark continent that was within walking distance of the General
Post Office". In view of this it is hardly surprising that Joseph Conrad
begins his novella *The heart of darkness* from riverside London, and
Marlowe, Conrad's protagonist, looking back on London from the
lower reaches of the Thames, comments that "this also has been one
of the dark places of the earth" (Conrad [1899] 1990: 138). For
Conrad the river provided both the literal and the metaphorical
means to float dreams of Empire.

These journeys have a range of effects on the social and political
development of this part of London. The important point to stress
here is that imperial exploits went hand in hand with the mastering of
urban poverty. These twin processes involved the promotion of particular ideas. Edward Said has stressed that imperialism was above all
about consolidating a vision of the world and how it ought to be (Said
1993). One might also say that poverty was domesticated through the
deployment of a communal morality. The large, skilled elite provided
the backbone of community organizing in this area. Much of the language and symbolic meaning of "community" was the product of a
collaboration between skilled workers and local professionals, and in
many ways this was forged through a moral consensus. In this area
community-conscious organizations such as the Mechanics' Institutes
and Friendly Societies asked local professionals to become honorary
members. This was reflected in the alliance that developed between
artisans and Liberal politicians.

It was not until the economic recession of the 1930s that a broader
and more radical manifestation of class consciousness developed. Economic adversity led to the welding of communal and class consciousness. It is important in view of what I will discuss later to make it clear

that this social order had a relatively shallow historical depth. The "golden age" of working-class communalism lasted little more than two generations. The cultural and social order referred to in much of the sociological literature (Young & Wilmott 1957, Hoggart 1958, Jackson & Marsden 1966, Jackson 1969) must be understood to be the result of a temporary moment of social and economic stability.[6]

From the 1920s onwards, outward migration took hold as slum clearance programmes were initiated. Over the 20 years from 1930 to 1950, the local population dropped by 25 per cent. This period was characterized by economic decline within the area's manufacturing industries (Hewitt 1986: 13) and the district fast became a "twilight zone" (Rex & Moore 1967), an area of slum clearance, falling house rents and economic decline. This process accelerated in the mid-1960s. However, the decline in population was partially arrested as international migrants from several countries settled in the district.

The largest single group came from Jamaica and other parts of the Caribbean. Roger Hewitt comments:

> In the late 1950s and early 1960s a "Caribbean quarter" developed, as West Indians bought up houses, initially in a single street, and sublet them to other West Indians as well as to whites . . . Shops and market stalls mushroomed, while black churches, social clubs, educational and other self-help projects came to co-ordinate and give visible identity to the black community, and in some respects to superimpose new networks of kinship and association on the older, fading, white working-class patterns. (Hewitt 1986: 13–14)

The settlement of black people within the area did not go unopposed. In 1948, agitation from the National Union of Seamen to stop black people working on British ships provoked a violent confrontation. A year later, black immigrants were again under attack from white racists. In this situation the local council was caught between a sense of duty regarding the plight of black people and the groundswell of anti-immigration feeling; some local politicians became apologists for the attacks on black people. A councillor in July 1949 commented in a local paper:

> The recent disturbances were unfortunate but the fault was not all on one side. From time to time coloured people come

> here . . . and we've got to do something with them. They are
> happy go lucky people who come here to what they regard as
> the land of the free. They look for a job and whether they
> like it or not there are some people who do not want to work
> with them.

There was also hostility to black people within the local labour movement. The result was the emergence of a far right-wing political splin-
ter group that commanded considerable electoral support in the area
throughout the 1960s and 1970s.

During this period the number of black people in the area grew
steadily. By 1981 black people constituted 25 per cent of the overall
population of the borough and in some of the districts in the north
between 40 and 50 per cent. This population was also youthful. The
area divided into a white population that was ageing, as young white
people moved out, and a disproportionately youthful black population. In 1971, 45 per cent of people aged 15 and under were black.[7]
In addition, small numbers of people settled from Pakistan, India, Africa, Greek and Turkish Cyprus, and during the 1980s a large number
of Vietnamese people arrived.[8] Equally, during the later part of the
1980s and in the 1990s a significant number of West Africans took up
residence in this part of London. However, these migrations occurred
towards the end of my period of fieldwork and as a result they are not
explored fully within this book.

The district was subjected to economic decline throughout the
1970s and 1980s. The situation was particularly acute for young people of school-leaving age. By 1981 the local rate of unemployment
was over 30 per cent and the situation for young black people was
worse still. A study of school leavers in 1977 showed that young black
people were three times more likely to be unemployed six months
after leaving school than were whites. By the mid-1980s the situation
was even more acute. The unemployment level among the adult male
population was 25 per cent in the borough as a whole and in some
districts it was estimated at 45 per cent. Youth unemployment was
again estimated as being much higher, in places up to 60 per cent.

Although the ethnic composition of the area has changed, the poverty and unemployment that were a symptom of the early twentieth
century remain the same. In fact Charles Booth's description of the
area in 1905 is applicable to the situation in the mid-1980s. As
Hewitt comments:

It remained what it had been for most of the century, a de-
pressed lower working-class district, albeit one with a strong
sense of identity. (Hewitt 1986: 15)

There exist, however, important variations within this area. It is to
the nature of these variations that I now turn.

The neighbourhoods and the methodology

The research was conducted between 1985 and 1989 and entailed
participant observation on two post-war council estates within the
district. The first, which I refer to as Riverview, is located next to the
River Thames and is predominantly composed of white working-
class residents. The second, which I refer to as Southgate, contrasts
with Riverview because it is a multi-ethnic neighbourhood. The
names of these districts and the identities of all the people quoted in
what follows have been changed to protect their anonymity.
Throughout the research period I lived in or at close proximity to the
research area. During 1986–7, I rented a room in a tower block on
Riverview Estate and I used the flat as a base from which to do
research in both districts.

I chose youth club settings to initiate contacts with young people
in these two neighbourhoods. There were a number of reasons for
this. First, I wanted to explore the kinds of environments and communities they experienced in the neighbourhood. Secondly, I wanted
to establish links with young people outside of school. In addition, I
chose the youth club setting because I felt a commitment to get
involved as far as possible with developmental work within the community. This led to other problems. I came to realize that youth clubs
themselves were far from indigenous community institutions. However, throughout the research period I did a combination of paid and
voluntary youth work within clubs in these districts. Starting out with
Southgate, I was connected with a youth centre on the margins of the
neighbourhood. This was renowned for being a black youth club and
had a long history of self-organization within the area's black community. Through contacts established in Southgate Youth Club I was
offered a part-time job in Riverview Youth Club. The reasoning
behind my appointment was that the senior youth worker wanted
people who had experience in combating racism. The youth club had
a local reputation for being a haven for white racist youth.

21

My role as a youth worker often placed me in an ambiguous relationship to the young people I was trying to work with, and on a number of occasions I was placed in the impossible position of having to act as an authority figure. However, inside and outside the youth clubs I met with young people from the area, developing relationships and collecting ethnographic material in the form of informal discussions and interviews. Additionally, I conducted semi-structured taped interviews with key informants as well as group interviews. The interviews were conducted either in the young people's homes, in my flat, or in a local college with which I had connections (see Appendix 1).

The rationale behind this methodology was to try to get an appreciation of the way young people articulated their notions of identity and ethnicity, but also the way identity was acted out within the context of adolescent interactions. This was particularly important in relation to the ways in which racism entered into the lives of these young people. Accounts given within the context of interviews would often be contradicted by actions and statements in other settings. Through using a flexible methodology I developed a close appreciation of both what young people *said* with regard to race, ethnicity and racism but also what they *did* in the context of interactions with peers.

Angela McRobbie has commented on the silence on the part of male academics with regard to how they chose their research subject:

> Although few radical (male) sociologists would deny the importance of the personal in precipitating social and political awareness, to admit how their own experience has influenced their choice of subject matter (the politics of selection) seems more or less taboo. (McRobbie [1980] 1991: 18)

Although I agree it is necessary to give some account of the "politics of selection", I think there are some important issues beyond giving honest justifications for the choice of any particular intellectual project. I think the most important of these revolves around the way this process may lead to an elaborate, often completely fictitious, form of credentialism. In terms of the way in which the research was conducted it is important to stress that my own personal biography played some role in the kinds of access and negotiations that took place. I was born in South London in the early 1960s of white working-class parents. Later my mother and father were moved to a large council estate outside of the inner-city areas and for most of my life I lived approximately 10 miles from where the research was conducted. During the 1970s I became acutely aware of the popularity of far-right political parties like the National Front among my peers and the community of which I was a part. The area where I lived had only a small black population but because of its disproportionately youthful nature there were large numbers of young black people in schools. The tension between the prevalence of racist ideas and the relationships I had with black friends was highly formative. Thus the two experiences from my youth that have remained a guiding influence on my interests and politics are the already mentioned dramatic transformations that occurred in working-class life and the intensity of racist reactions within working-class communities during the 1970s (Back 1993). My background did not, however, mean that the division between self and other was dissolved. I have become increasingly suspicious of those – particularly in discussions of working-class culture – who claim "insider status" through invoking a kind of radical credentialism. It seems to me that such rhetorical moves are little more than micro-political gestures determined by the politics of the academy. More disturbingly, invoking insider status can result in intellectuals and ethnographers claiming a privileged right to speak for "the people". This merely dresses bourgeois ethnographic authority in the new clothes of ersatz "radicalism".

In one anthropological review of my previously published work I was constructed as a "native anthropologist" (Jahan Karim 1993). Reading this disturbed me profoundly. Here I was represented as a stricken soul caught between anthropological selfhood and native otherness. Yet, such a dualistic model of inside and outside makes little sense in the "contact zones" (Pratt 1992) from which this book was written. I agree with Rosaldo that empathy, translation and understanding within ethnography do rely on an interplay between personal experience and the accounts given by others of their lives (Rosaldo 1989). However, the re-inscription of a privileged, or unique, line of sight from the "native ethnographer's point of view" seems to me to suppress the multiple aspects and social features that affect fieldwork relationships. What is thus invented is a novel intellectual hyphen that in effect represses such complexities through a homogenizing discourse of nativism. The nuances and multiplicities in the researcher's experience are corralled, organized and simplified. There are some who have embraced this strategy. However, I feel that

such credentialism results in little more than an elaborate masquer-
ade that makes the uncomfortable experience of social dislocation
easier to bear. Within anthropology, the neat hermetics of such an
intellectual division make it easier to dismiss, and arguably
marginalize, the work of "native" writers as in some way compro-
mised, biased or partial. In Britain, a central issue in the debate on
research practice in the sociology of race has been the ability of white
researchers to understand and empathize with black experiences of
racism (Lawrence 1981, 1982). Although it is profoundly true that
whites cannot fully comprehend the experiential consequences of
racism, we do experience the transmission of racist ideas and formulae. This is an important distinction in research within multiracial
contexts. My whiteness and the way it was constructed within fieldwork relationships was an important feature of the types of trust and
dialogue that were established. A question that is often raised is what
one does in situations where racist ideas are communicated to the researcher. To say nothing in response to them points to the legitima-
tion of these ideas through silence. Particularly in contexts where
forms of racial abuse were used, I felt compelled to counter them, but
more generally there was a real dilemma in doing this research with
regard to what one should say in reply to people who used racist ideologies and discourses.

Equally, my relationship with black young people in these areas
was not unproblematic simply because I openly stated that expressions of racism were wrong. Indeed the real issue was the degree to
which racism structured the relationship between researcher and respondent. Although young black people shared their experiences
with me, it would be foolish to say that our relationships were completely free from the effects of racism. As such, the trust that black
people offered me was always contingent and in need of renewal. In
fact, the negotiations that I recorded in black–white friendships were
often re-enacted in fieldwork relationships with black people. In a
similar fashion, gender was also an important social feature to be
considered in terms of the quality of field relations in these settings
(Back 1993). For example, I could meet with young women openly
and freely in groups within the youth club but if the conversation
centred on one or two individuals I would be open to accusations
from young men of making sexual advances. On numerous occasions
I was accused of "fancying" or "chatting up" particular young
women. In the course of doing fieldwork it became clear that such

contact placed young women themselves in a vulnerable position. This meant that I often met with young women outside of the view of their male peers. This produced other sets of issues and dilemmas. The interview context opened young women to the kinds of exploitation that feminist critics have levelled at male researchers. Reflecting on these events, I think a variety of dynamics occurred. In similar fashion to my relationship with black young people, I do not think that all of my interactions with women were totally limited by the sexism that was so widely prevalent. But neither did these relationships fully escape the effects of gender inequality. On some occasions the young women replicated in the interview situation modes of resistance they operated vis-à-vis their male peers.[9] Equally, young women would not always be willing to discuss areas of their private lives, and in many ways the question was how far we could negotiate our differences.

Judith Stacey raises similar issues when she discusses the possibility of conducting feminist ethnography (Stacey 1988). She shows in an honest and sophisticated way the limits of empathy and mutuality in feminist scholarship. She ends her discussion by suggesting that there can be a partially feminist account of culture enhanced by the application of feminist perspectives while recognizing that "conflicts of interest and emotion between ethnographer as authentic, related person (i.e. participant), and as exploiting researcher (i.e. observer) are also an inescapable feature of the ethnographic method" (ibid.: 3). In this context, rather than hide behind fictional credentials, perhaps it is more important to open up the structure of ethnographic texts to a plurality of readings and to refuse to embrace an absolute notion of ethnographic authority.

The point that I want to emphasize is that the following study should be read in the context of research relationships developed by a white male ethnographer. In this sense it is necessary for me to position myself within the field relations that facilitated the study. I am asking the reader to judge the "truth claims" (Clifford 1986) made in what follows in this context. Throughout the study I have tried to point to situations where my social identities may have been particularly important in interpreting the meaning of a particular event or interview extract. A position that I develop throughout the book is that the accounts quoted here constitute interactive samples and are the product of a particular social circumstance – be it an interviewer–interviewee relationship, a group discussion or a dramatic event involving numerous people (see Ch. 3). Although I offer my reflections on these events by way of guiding the reader through an analysis, it is equally my aim to provide enough material – albeit in an edited and managed form – to open up the possibility of other interpretations. I present these arguments through a single narrative but I invite you "to read against the grain of the text's dominant voice" (Clifford 1988: 53).

The book is divided into three major parts. The first (Chs 2–5) focuses its attention on the predominantly white working-class neighbourhood – Riverview. The three chapters within this section are devoted to the nature of "community" (Ch. 2), youth social structure and identity (Ch. 3) and the local impact of popular racism (Ch. 4). The second part looks at the ethnically mixed neighbourhood – Southgate. The thematic structure of this section follows the issues raised in Part I to facilitate comparison. Chapter 5 looks at community discourses within this district, Chapter 6 at young people's social identities, and Chapter 7 at black young people's experience of racism. The final part places the analysis of the local settings in a wider context. Chapter 8 focuses on the musical cultures that are being created by young people in South London. I show that the processes of cultural syncretism occurring here have to be viewed as being nested within international networks of cultural transmission and in particular the cultural exchanges occurring throughout the African and south Asian diasporas. Chapter 9 pulls together the central issues addressed within the book and summarizes its major conclusions.

I now turn to the predominantly white working-class district of Riverview and discuss the history of this neighbourhood and the notions of community found there.

PART I

Racism, community and youth culture

CHAPTER 2

"White flight": locality, nostalgia and the preservation of privilege

Introduction

In this chapter I provide a contextualizing account of the neighbourhood composition of Riverview Estate. I argue that "community" in this area is constructed on at least two levels. First, there is a notion of community encoded within the spatial design of this unit of housing. Secondly, the history of settlement on this estate and changing access to this housing resource has prompted a number of reconstructions of community.

The theoretical questions that I am raising here follow from Benedict Anderson's (1983) famous notion of "imagined community". The use of the term "community" refers to the way communities are talked about and constructed by residents and it does not refer to a structurally defined social system or subsystem. The local ideology of community is multi-faceted and it consists of a number of discourses that lay claim to a vision of who is included in the community and the quality of neighbourhood life. In short, community is a discursive construct that is utilized as an ideological resource in situations where inside/outside definitions are discussed (A. P. Cohen 1985: 21).

In the following analysis I use the concept of *community discourse*. Such discourses have organizing themes and a consistency in meanings. The result is a formulaic construction of social reality. Discourse is preferred to the concept of ideology because discourses are by their very nature less stable in terms of their semantic consistency and they are not formalized in the way that ideologies can often exist. As I shall illustrate, these constructs may also form part of a more complex meaning system. In this analysis, ideas about "community" are understood to consist of a series of organizing principles (community discourses) that are interrelated and mutually reinforcing (a semantic system).

This notion is not dissimilar to Sandra Wallman's concept of "local style" (Wallman et al. 1982, Wallman 1984, 1986). However, where my approach diverges from that adopted by Wallman is that (a) I view the notion of "community" or "local style" as the product of competing social definitions, not homogeneous, and composed of a variety of community discourses and (b) although I accept that in some contexts particular definitions – or versions – of community predominate, all community discourse should be treated as having equal significance. I want to explore the social functions that these discourses and semantic systems serve with reference to the local manifestation or rejection of racism.

It is impossible to decipher the ethnography that will follow without mapping out the management history of this unit of housing and the processes whereby people from various socio-cultural backgrounds have been located in this neighbourhood. Here I draw on the conceptual framework developed by Manuel Castells (1977) and in particular his notion of collective consumption, defined as those resources that are provided to ensure the reproduction of the labour force. These are the social costs of reproduction provided by the state, i.e. housing, health services, transport and education.[1] What follows is a description of the way in which a geographically well-defined urban resource (a council estate) was allocated and managed, showing how this can explain some of the racialized conflicts that are found there.[2] To push Manuel Castells' notion of collective consumption further, I will show how changes in the provision and allocation of collectively consumed resources provide the underlying impulse for the development of a local racism.

"Official communities": urban life idealized

The Riverview Estate was opened in the mid-1960s. As a showcase of post-war reconstruction, it constituted an attempt to improve the plight of the respectable dockland working class by constructing a phoenix-like planned society that would emerge from the rubble of slum redevelopment. In the early years it lived up to this expectation, and the development of a nascent community provided the evidence of success. The beloved structure of urban dockland neighbourhoods seemed to have been successfully translated into the modernist landscape of post-war public housing. However, 20 years later this image had been transformed; it had become a pathologized problem area, subject to its own urban mythology and referred to as a haven for neo-fascist politics, constituting a white microcosm in an increasingly multi-ethnic landscape.

Riverview was built by the Greater London Council (GLC). From the initial design concept, the Riverview Estate was to be a model for urban life. Drawing on ancient metaphors, the estate was constructed in the image of a medieval walled city. There was a commitment to giving this project an aesthetic of its own, unlike many of the mass-housing developments of the period. Generally, the rents on this estate were higher than those for comparable council property. During the 1960s most of the low-rise flats were around £5–8 per week depending on the number of bedrooms. However, some of the renovated buildings on the estate were as much as £12 per week. This was significantly more expensive than other council property. Thus, the development offered a higher standard of housing provision for those who could afford it.

Encoded in this built environment is an image of urban community. The focal area was to be in the centre of the estate, which was connected by a complex of elevated walkways converging on a small elevated shopping centre that included a grocer, butcher, hairdresser, pub, and fish and chip shop. Adjacent to the shopping centre, a community centre and youth club were built. The Tenants' Hall and Youth Club building was constructed with a pointed roof intended to look like a church spire. This may seem bizarre, but the architects – who later received an award for the design – intended the central area to provide a focus for this "urban village".

The walkways were designed to promote a sense of unity as the blocks would be joined together in a matrix of elevated access points. The external network was enhanced by internal corridors connecting the low-rise tower blocks. This strategy aimed to encourage neighbourliness. The corridors were called "Coronation Streets" – after the popular working-class soap opera – in the hope that they would become informal meeting places. This approach may have been informed by the work of social democratic writers (Hoggart 1958) in many of whose post-war studies (Young & Wilmott 1957) the notion of a traditional working-class community appears as sacrosanct. Yet, as I showed in the previous chapter, the history of this particular manifestation of working-class community in South London is a relatively short one. The planners sought to resurrect a neighbourhood mentality transposed from the "back to backs" to the tower blocks. This desire, at least initially, appeared to be realized.

"The golden age of community": allocation, vetting and institutionalized racism

The allocation of housing in this area was based on what was referred to as "selective tenancies". The principle was simply to make sure that the household head could afford to pay the high rents. Although the official title for allocation was selective tenancies, local people referred to the process as *vetting*. Basically a housing official would visit prospective tenants in their current homes to collect information on income and, some tenants suggest, to see if they "kept a clean home". Through this process of selective tenancies the metropolitan authority created a hierarchy in the allocation of public housing. As blocks were opened, families were settled once they had proved they could pay the higher rents and gradually the population grew.

Most of the new settlers were married couples or people with families. This new population was youthful and producing children. Jean, a heath visitor during this period, remembers how fortunate people felt to be moving onto Riverview:

> People were fighting to move onto Riverview and the lucky ones felt privileged. They were proud to be part of a show case – spotlessly clean and well looked after.

Ron, the local police officer between 1966 and 1981, recalls the positive way most people viewed their new homes:

> It was a good time to be living on Riverview. The accommodation was good and most people were happy to be here. The feeling of community spirit grew up quickly because the estate was filled gradually and people joined in activities that were going on.

The Riverview population had been controlled and allocated through the selective tenancies procedure. Penny remembers:

> It made us laugh because it was . . . five years before the first black family was moved onto the estate. It was five years I think. It was mainly white families.

The allocation procedures operated by the metropolitan authority were institutionally racist (Carmichael & Hamilton 1968). Black people were in effect excluded from being residents of this estate. A former GLC housing officer explains:

> Well, it wasn't as simple as – "We don't want black people living there". It was more subtle than that. It was more like an assumption that black and white would rather live separately from one another. So as you go down the Old Kent Road you can see that some estates are white and others are black or mixed. It didn't happen by accident. Housing officers just didn't allocate black people to Riverview.

Riverview was handed to a relatively affluent, white working-class population.

The allocation of the tenancies was slow enough for the new members of the estate to get to know each other. In particular, the corridor was the site of social networking; it acted as the place of introduction for the new migrants. This led to a high degree of neighbourliness, as Penny explains:

> Well, you can't 'elp it when you are living on a corridor anyway. You get to know people sort of thing. Some you like, some you don't, but most people were friendly and open. We used to take it in turns to 'ave parties at Christmas time and other times. We used to 'ave parties and they would leave the kids "indoors", leave the flats open and now and again a couple of women, or men, would go round all the houses and check on the kids. I remember my mum doing the same. (Penny, resident, 1965–87)

Within a few months of the opening of the estate the tenants decided to organize some form of social club. The beginning of the Social

Club marks the rise of the community organization on the estate. The pinnacle of community self-help was the annual Palaver celebrations that were organized by the Social Club and started in 1971. A Tenants' Association emerged alongside the Social Club to give a framework for community organization. Both of these bodies were well attended and supported and were the infrastructure that organized the Palavers. The celebrations lasted two days and were on a scale incomprehensible today. The events included a race to the top of a tower block, performing bands and market stalls. Jenny remembers:

> It was like a holiday. They used to be around July. You had music going on from nine o'clock in the morning to twelve at night. There used to be groups playing and there used to be stalls out. We used to have fireworks and all that; it was really good. The whole estate would come out for this one day, everybody would come out from everywhere. There was a beer tent. It was like a summer festival I suppose, but it was just for the estate. I was only a kid then and it was brilliant for us kids.

These celebrations were so successful that the GLC made a documentary film about the Riverview Palavers. This was intended to show what can be achieved on council estates, but the amount of energy and commitment necessary to maintain the event proved to be its downfall. Later Palavers were cut to just one-day events and they soon became just a sports day. With the movement of a community arts project onto the estate in the early 1980s the Palaver was reinstated, but they never managed to capture the verve and excitement of early festivals.

What is interesting is the role that the naval metaphors played in the construction of this local identity. The neighbourhood philosophy was explicitly nationalist. This was taken to quite extraordinary lengths. The Tenants' Association "adopted" a naval frigate and naval officers visited the estate and residents went on return visits when the ship was docked.

The early period of settlement is often romanticized by the tenants who have experienced 20 years of Riverview residency. They were in effect the "golden years" of community. During the first ten years it appeared that this designed "urban village" had rescued the pre-war working-class community. Indeed, the building of inner-city developments "close to the social group to which they already belong" (Young & Wilmott 1957: 198–9) seemed, on the surface, to have solved the problem of the decline of working-class communities. However, its nascent parochialism was not simply the salvaging of antiquity. Its origins lay in the particular nature of the contemporary allocation of housing as a unit of collective consumption and the dynamics of the dockland areas south of the river.

A segment of the working class – a particularly affluent segment – had been brought together and handed a residential space. This segment was also predominantly white. As late as the 1981 census, 1,802 of the 2,500 household heads were born in the United Kingdom and a further 143 were from the Irish Republic. Here a public housing "residential aristocracy" was maintained through the process of selective tenancies and high rents. However, it is somewhat ironic that in the year that Riverview Estate opened, an adjacent railway dockyard closed. The general economic decline that the area suffered in the following decade placed serious pressures on the metropolitan authority to change its policy.

Crisis-management, change and collective consumption

The effect of the general economic crisis of the late 1970s was exaggerated in the former dockland areas of South London by the large-scale economic transformation that had been occurring since the end of the Second World War. The economic and social order that owed its origin to the riverside industries and dockland activity started to crumble. The borough itself had only a small economic base and the loss of 10,000 jobs in the period 1975–85 reduced its capacity even further. In less than five years between May 1979 and January 1984 the number of people registered at the employment and careers offices trebled.

The Riverview Estate lies in an area that since the mid-1970s has experienced a deterioration in physical environment and a growth in social conflict and tension. Racist explanations of these circumstances correlated the presence of black people in the area with the deteriorating economic circumstances. In 1977, the National Front carried out a widely publicized march through the streets of the borough. The Riverview Estate was seen in local lore as being a haven of the National Front, neo-fascist politics and racism. An analysis of the

1981 census returns does little to refute the idea that the estate constituted a white microcosm in an area that was becoming increasingly
"race conscious": 77 per cent of the estate population was born in
England and only 8.6 per cent of residents were from the New Commonwealth; out of the New Commonwealth residents, 41 per cent
were from the Caribbean, 25.9 from Africa (excluding East Africa)
and 12.3 per cent from the Mediterranean (see Appendix 2).

The image of Riverview as a white stronghold, essentially hostile
to black and minority populations, survives. As a young black Briton
from a neighbouring area described:

> I just don't go down them areas; it's not safe for someone
> like me in them areas. A black man like me just don't go to
> those area, I don't know what it is but I just don't feel safe.

Whatever the actuality of the situation (some former residents
strongly deny the reputation with which they have been labelled), this
lore exists and is a powerful component of the folk taxonomies and
social geography demarcated in the minds of members of neighbouring minority communities.

The 1981 census material shows that the population of the estate
was economically better off than those in the surrounding area: only
13 per cent of all economically active males were unemployed in
1981, compared with figures exceeding 18 per cent for the district
generally. The majority of the unemployed were young: 52 per cent
of the male unemployed were aged 16–29. There were a considerable
number of self-employed men, reflecting occupations such as building trades, mini-cabbing and commercial haulage. The high rent levels on the estate meant that it was imperative to maintain relatively
high incomes to keep pace with the cost of residency. The residents of
this estate were thus relatively affluent and better able to deal with the
economic recession that had hit with a vengeance by 1981.

In 1979 a qualitative break took place in the allocation of housing.
The management of the estate passed from the Greater London
Council to the local borough. The changeover was marred by industrial disputes that slowed the transition period. Tenants were extremely dissatisfied with the provision of service and matters
worsened. The borough fully realized the effects of the past letting
scheme, as a prominent council worker – interviewed in the
Riverview community newspaper in February 1986 – notes:

> Like most London boroughs, [we] started providing council
> housing in the fifties for families – in practice that meant
> white working-class families, generally skilled manual work-
> ers. Now, however, the authority has had to realise that there
> are other kinds of people in housing need, people who do
> not fit that category.

Although the emergence of an alternative housing allocation process
was piecemeal and slow, between 1979 and 1983 the borough attempted to construct a system that concentrated on need as opposed
to ability to pay. This change in housing strategy must also be seen in
the context of a housing crisis. The turnover of council housing is
very low on the estates that are more desirable and the authority's
programme for rehabilitation and rebuilding had ground to a halt.[3]
This means that the housing supply in general has contracted from
3,849 properties to let in 1982/3 to 2,845 in 1983/4. This decrease in
housing provision was taking place in a period when housing demand
was very high. The council attempted to deal with this crisis by offer-
ing properties according to five priority groups.[4] Having laid down
the official priority groups, available housing was offered to each
group starting with those in highest priority. The situation was aggra-
vated by a reduction in central government funding. In 1985 the
amount of money given to the borough council was reduced by 30
per cent.

The image of the estate slipped from that of a model development
to a seed-bed of problems and a nightmare for the local authority. It
was during this period that rumours of fascist affiliations amongst the
estate's young started. Equally, the young were identified as the per-
petrators of crime, particularly car theft and breaking and entering.
This happened in a period when youth unemployment was reaching
crisis proportions. The crime rate on Riverview between 1981 and
1985 attained very high levels, peaking at 49.1 crimes per 100 households per year in 1982. The figure in 1985 was still very high, with
25.6 per cent of all households getting broken into each year.[5]

The effects of the introduction of "scag" (heroin) at relatively
cheap street prices exacerbated the growth in crime:

> It's kids doing all the burglaries. Kids! Yeah! Most of it's kids
> and the "scag" and that. You never heard of any drugs or
> thing like that when I was young. It's just in the last few years

that you start to hear about it, I suppose it was kept quiet before and nobody said anything. The thing was, when we was kids, was to have "puff" [marijuana] behind the blocks sorta thing. You'd never let your mother know but that was just like ordinary cigarettes with a bit of a kick but now it's all drugs and everything. They are even on the stairs in the blocks and my kids have to walk through that. On the stairs you see the tin foil, where they smoke it in tin foil and everything you know. There are dealers on the estate, there are enough dealers on the estate – almost one in each block. (Penny, resident, 1965–87)

There seemed to be a connection between street youth, drug abuse and crime. Most of the break-ins were attributed to a gang of estate kids who came to be known as "the chip shop mob". It is significant to note that these young men (there were only a few young women associated with the chip shop mob) were born on the estate and were the children of the first residents. For them, the estate and the surrounding area were their whole social universe, their domain and territory.

Youth in this period was identified by the residents as a major social problem. However, they were not the only group who were pathologized. The newcomers and residents who were being moved onto the estate according to the new policy of allocation according to need were also seen as the cause of the general decline:

When they moved the problem families in, that's when you got a lot of trouble and that . . . They started off with just that one block. Now it's all round the estate. (Jane, resident, 1967–88)

What we see during this period is the emergence of a youthful population that was undergoing economic and, to some degree, social marginalization, on the one hand, and the growth of a population of high need, mostly poor newcomers from minority backgrounds, who were classified by many established residents as "problem families". These changes were taking place within a community of "respectable" and relatively affluent workers, who have become increasingly hostile to the newcomers. The level of dissatisfaction is reflected in the high rate of transfer applications. In January 1982, 25 per cent of the householders were on the transfer list.

"Estate people" and "problem families": social taxonomies and community discourse

So far I have identified the changes in management that led to new populations being settled on the Riverview Estate. What I plan to do now is look at the ways in which a new social cartography was constructed and the nature of social life on the estate in the 1980s.

The original or long-standing residents are often referred to as "estate people", those who have a long-term stake in the area. The term is widely used, both within the group and by those outside. They were the first to mark a claim in the area. Many of them remember the estate in its early years – the "golden age of community":

> When I first lived here I was in the tower block . . . If I 'ad to go to the shops it would take me a couple of hours to get through there and back [the central shopping area is only a five minute walk from the tower]. You'd walk down there and I'd literally know everyone and go from one natter to the other. I think I must 'ave spent most of my time in those days "jawing" [talking]. Now I walk down there and I 'ardly know anyone. (Mary, resident, 1970–86)

The "estate people" are the established families, those who have kin settled close by, with children who have grown up in the area. Their response to the "crisis" has taken two avenues: either to leave, applying for transfer or buying out into the private sector; or to retreat into the established centres of community organization. For many residents who were adequately housed, the housing transfer bureaucracy gave them lowest priority. Here two cases illustrate the point.

Mary and her family have lived on the estate for close to 20 years. She was a child when her mother moved here from Bermondsey. She married and stayed local, being moved into a tower block. Now she lives close to her mother in low-rise accommodation. She desperately wants to move.

> If I tried for a transfer now they say that we are in what they call "adequate accommodation". We have got three bedrooms and two kids. I would have to have another two kids before they would move me out.

Les: So if you wanted to move on, you'd have to do it on your own?

Yeah definitely. Well, we tried! I have had my transfer in for about four years now. We have been thinking about moving for a long time. I got a letter back from the council and they said that were are "adequately housed". They won't move us.

Les: How do you feel about living here in the eighties?

Well, I'm fed up, I really am. Put it this way, we used to play out and go all over the place – all over the parks and all over the estate. I wouldn't let my kids do that now. It's not safe. Whereas before your mum was quite 'appy to let you go out, they knew exactly where you were. Now you let your kids go out and you don't know what is going on. We lived here nine years before there was a burglary on the estate. We never heard of burglaries. Now its burglaries all the time. I think the whole site has gone down the drain. I want to get away for the kids really, I don't want them growing up in this.

Most people rationalize the desire to leave by referring to their children and a wish to give them a better environment. Mary's husband Ron, who works in a local plastics factory, went as far as the Isle of Man to look for new work and a new life. In fact, six months after this interview the family moved to the Isle of Man.

The second case is Jane, who lived on the estate for ten years and has recently "moved off" and has a mortgage on a private property in a nearby neighbourhood. She has two children and her husband – John – is a bricklayer.

When we went to the housing office they asked us where we lived and we told them we lived in Ivory House. They said, "Ah, you've got no chance, they're all 'problem families' in that block". I told 'em we were no problem family, I've never missed a day's rent in all the time we lived there. That didn't matter, as far as they were concerned everybody in that block was tarred with the same brush. We was on the exchange list for God knows how long and the rents were still high. We were paying over £50 for one of the penthouse flats on the top of the low rise. Then we sat down and realised that, paying that kind of money, we could have a mortgage – a place of our own. I suppose everybody ultimately wants that and within a year we'd found a place and moved off.

This second case is typical of those who have taken the opportunity offered by the central government's change in philosophy over the provision of housing, allowing those who can afford it to buy out of the public sector, assisted by the explosion of bank and building society mortgage provision. Bill describes the logic of this:

Well, who wants to buy round here. I mean look at it. The place is run down, people with all kinds of problem, blacks, Vietnamese, it's a real fairyland down here now. So we took the chance, bought a place, took out a mortgage and got away.

With the change in political climate the very population that the estate was designed for started to move out.

For the "estate people" who remain, their major response has been one of withdrawal and the defensive occupation of what community provisions remain. The Tenants' Hall and Tenants' Association have become the last refuge of the diminishing population, although commitment even to these organizations has started to wane.[6] The Sports and Social Club controls the bar in the community centre complex in the centre of the estate: this is principally the refuge of the "estate people" (mainly men) who use the facility. Members are allocated a plastic card key and non-members are excluded. As one resident noted:

That's where all the people who have been here a long time hide. Look at it. It's like trying to get into a bank. Really, it should be a place for everyone on the estate to get a cheap drink but it's really for those who belong to the club. (Pauline, resident, 1980–88)

For the long-standing residents, their embitterment is essentially the result of what they feel is a broken promise. They were handed a residential space, which they took as their own, and now they feel as if that space is being invaded by "foreign" newcomers and a council that is essentially unsympathetic to them. Opposition by established residents to the settlement of ethnic minority tenants manifests itself in a racialized form (Miles 1989). The cultural and racial "difference" of new tenants is construed to explain the falling standards of housing provision and the decline of general living conditions. The logic of this discourse revolves around the assertion that the degeneration of public housing is explicable in terms of the "lower standards of hygiene" and "lack of responsibility" of ethnic minority tenants. Racist formulae of this type are widely circulated and can be heard in almost every context where established residents congregate. The development of this ideological response is linked to an engagement with their economic circumstances (Phizacklea & Miles 1980, Cashmore 1987). As Hall states:

> Racism represents the attempt ideologically to construct those conditions, contradictions and problems in such a way that they can be dealt with and deflected at the same moment. (Hall 1978: 35)

In addition, they feel betrayed by the council, which does not have the facilities to cater for their needs, but does provide for those in greatest need – "the problem families". Their estate, of which they were so proud, has been turned into a "human dumping ground":

> It's like [this area] is the end of the road, the toilet of society and we get all the dregs. A place is only as good as the people who live there. (Bill, 75 years old)

The criteria for the classification of a "problem family" are difficult to identify. Such families are often merely newcomers. Many complaints are made about "noisy", "irresponsible" tenants, those who don't pay their rents and don't care about communal space. In many ways the problem families are scapegoated for all ills. There is an underlying driving force that fuels these conflicts. The borough has changed its allocation procedure and thus brought an established group into conflict with an ill-organized and economically impoverished collection of newcomers. In the borough's attempts to give those in need priority, they have made "estate people" and "newcomers" adversaries.

Many of the highest-need residents were single parents – principally mothers. The introduction to Riverview for these people has been, at times, harrowing, as one single mother remembers:

I remember when I first moved here on an inter-borough
exchange from Tower Hamlets, I'd left my husband with my
four kids and was living in a small flat in a tower block. When
they offered me a place in a ground floor flat on Riverview I
jumped at the chance. But you see when I arrived I was seen as
a single parent – another "problem family". I remember how
unfriendly people were, they just didn't speak and every time
I walked out of my door I felt like I was running a gauntlet.
People slowly come round. But it took me over a year to feel
safe going out. All I did was stay indoors.

So, for many newcomers their outsider status was reinforced by the
fact that they deviated from the assumed moral code (i.e. the sanctity
of the family and community) shared by many of the established residents. Also, many of the "problem families" were dependent on
social security and were seen as living "off the state". In fact, many
could afford to live on Riverview Estate – which still had higher rent
levels than surrounding estates – precisely because social security
would automatically pay, regardless of the rent level.

The estrangement and hostility were reinforced in situations
where new ethnic groups were settled on the estate. A number of
black people, particularly the young, had negotiated a place in the
localist ideology despite its generally racist nature. Black people who
were "like us", meaning no different from those who already
"belonged", were essentially part of the parochial culture. They
spoke in the vernacular of the estate and they were accepted. This was
not the case, however, for the refugees from Vietnam who were offered accommodation on the estate.

The borough agreed to take a population of refugees from Vietnam in the early 1980s. The very way that their settlement was han-
dled inflamed many of the established residents, as Dave, a
community worker, points out:

Basically, there was an informal rule of thumb that new people moved onto the estate would be settled in the tower
blocks first, then moved into the low-rise blocks later. Well,
when the Vietnamese were moved onto the estate, the council moved them straight into the low-rise blocks. This caused
a lot of animosity amongst the people who had been on the
housing list for two, three, four and five years. There were

many horror stories about attacks on the Vietnamese, remember this was at a time when National Front stickers appeared in the local youth club and a couple of local young men were active in the National Front and British Movements.

By the middle 1980s over 100 Vietnamese refugees had been settled on the estate and there were repeated cases of racial harassment. Burning torches were pushed through their letter boxes, and on one occasion a vicious Rotweiler dog was dropped into an enclosed area where Vietnamese children were playing. In a report written by the Riverview Improvement Project it was suggested that:

> One explanation for tenant antipathy to the new arrivals from ethnic minority groups is that tenants resent the allocation of desirable properties to outsiders when they have been waiting several years for a transfer.

The effects on these migrants, who had already endured so much, was catastrophic, as Tran, an Outreach Worker with the refugees, recounts:

> This family, they went to do their shopping in the supermarket. When they come to the lift, because they live in high block, four or five people come and attack them. She get hurt. Also they ask her for money. She say, "Sorry, I have no money". They hit her and now she is frightened, now she stays home all the time. It is not happening so much now [1987], but still refugee[s] will not let their children go to the youth club.

Les: Was it worse before?

> Oh yes, in 1982–3. Things like this were happening all the time and families were getting hurt. Six or seven of these families still live on the estate. Now, when it gets to six and seven o'clock in the evening they never go out on their own, they always travel with three or four people. They are frightened, they are too scared. Some, like one family, who lives on the Riverview estate, they tell me that whenever they go shopping they always phone their friends first to see if her friend will go shopping the same day as well, to go with her. We get a lot of pressure.

Much of the "pressure" was a response to outrage that many felt towards the council's policy of allocation.

On every corner of the estate the "death of community" was mourned by those who could remember it. What we see are discourses on "white working-class" social life and the "traditional" that purport to explain the nature of how things should and "used to be". There are a number of meanings to "community" within this context. These community discourses imagine, claim and characterize this area. The symbolic materials that these constructs utilize consist of fragments of national ideology and images of communal working-class life. With the shifts and changes within the allocation of the housing estate the cultural construction of Riverview community is used to define insiders and outsiders. This construct affects the way in which racism gets expressed. The "death of the community" is attributed to being swamped by variously defined racial others. I will end this chapter by explaining the relationship between community discourses and the material circumstance to which they relate.

Conclusion

Under the GLC, the Riverview Estate was a prestigious development. A nascent parochialism developed alongside a strong sense of nationalism. When the borough council took over the estate it was no longer willing to maintain the privileged position enjoyed by the initial residents. Parochialism turned into hostility towards outsiders, and nationalism was translated into racism and harassment. The proliferation of community discourses in this area has to be viewed in the contexts of these changes.

The result is the development of a series of social constructs that define the quality of community at different periods. Here I am drawing on Michael Keith's (1993) discussion of how variables of race, crime and public disorder interact in what he described as the discourse of *lore and disorder*. A central part of the notion of locality within Riverview is a discourse that outlines a "golden age" of community. Here images of pre-war working-class dockland community are applied to the modern context of a post-war council estate. This is not a nostalgic idea about pre-1939 working-class life, but the re-invention of community within the post-war context. So within the Riverview case the "golden age" existed between 1966 and 1975.

In contrast to the "golden age" discourse, there exists a construct that reports and explains the decline of community within Riverview. I refer to this as the "death of community discourse". This construct has two elements: (a) it marks the end of community on the estate and (b) it explains the demise of the area as being related to the settlement of "problem families", black people and Vietnamese refugees. Another component of this discourse correlates the settlement of new populations with the emergence of crime (drugs and house-breaking) and the general decline and disrepair of the estate.

Lastly, a recurring theme is that the decline of the estate has forced the long-standing residents to leave the area. This notion is repeated with such frequency that I refer to it as "the white flight discourse". A metonymic relationship exists between these three discourses. Here, denoting one of the discourses automatically triggers meanings associated with the other two at the level of connotation, a process that Stallybrass and White refer to as *transcoding* (Stallybrass & White 1986). The result is that these discourses are located in a triangular relationship to one another (see Fig. 2.1). These formulae are used by the established residents frequently when an appraisal of the estate is required. The patterns of these discourses here take on a life of their own and constitute a resource that residents can operate. The nature of these discourses has important implications about the way racism is expressed locally. Notions of community are infused with racial meanings. The "golden age" of community coincided with a period when the estate was almost exclusively the preserve of white workers; equally, the passage of that era identified in the "death of community" discourse correlates with the settlement of black people and Vietnamese refugees. Here we see the expression of racism through the language of community.

Riverview shows many of the characteristics of what Wallman (1986) calls a closed resource system, that is, the workforce is

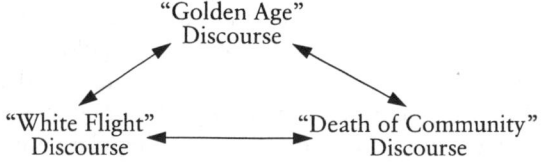

Figure 2.1 "White flight" semantic system

dependent on local industries, there are low levels of mobility and accommodation is dominated by the public sector. In many respects this explains the nature of the community discourses I have documented. However, these versions of community are not the only ones articulated. As I have mentioned, there also exists a poorly developed discourse that claims that harmonious relationships are emerging in the area. The simple point that I want to make here is that these discourses are to some degree in competition with one another, and as a result it is not possible to speak of *one* local style. What in fact exists is a number of community discourses that claim to represent the locality. As I will show in the next chapter, young people in this area are developing this notion of inclusive harmony, and they are fostering what I will refer to as "neighbourhood nationalism". I have attempted to point towards some of the factors that affect the "parental voice" – the kinds of processes that underlie consciousness of nation, neighbourhood and race. The extent to which the "youth voice" constitutes a translated and re-assembled version of this narrative is the next question I want to explore.

CHAPTER 3

"Neighbourhood nationalism": Youth, race, nation and identity

Introduction

In this chapter I aim to discuss the way in which notions of self and identity are formed in the adolescent community of Riverview, with particular reference to concepts of race. The principal aim is to show that, within predominantly white constituencies, racism and chauvinistic types of imperialist imagery are not reproduced crudely or mechanically. I attempt to outline the cultural context in which neighbourhood definitions are also at times of equal or even greater importance. The identities of these young people exhibit complex and multiple reference points. In this sense I try to show how meanings and identities are mediated within this particular context by a set of historical conditions and socio-political circumstances.

Social context and identity

The central concern of the following analysis is to discuss the ways in which social context affects identity formulations. The notion of social context utilized here falls into three broad areas. The first relates to the immediate context of the interaction, including the interviewer/interviewee, group discussion, groups of friends and potential onlookers, and the situational circumstances and events that prompt the account. The second notion of context includes the "referent informational influences" (J. C. Turner 1987). These comprise the immediate set of class, race, gender, community and other cultures, ideologies and discourses into which individual subjects place themselves. These may be highly localized phenomena, or they may call into play national discourses on "race" and nation. The third notion of social context refers to the socio-economic circumstances, including demographic composition of the neighbourhood, local labour and housing markets, history of population turnover and minority settlement patterns.

The relationship between self and society is viewed as a dynamic and integrated process whereby individuals work within, and contribute to, defined social realms of association (Tajfel & Turner 1979, 1986). For example, to define oneself as "black" or "white" is to say something fundamental about who one is as an individual, but the meaning of "black" and "white" is a social product that cannot be reduced to a single individual and may have local, national or even international variants and heritages. Additionally, an informant might view her/himself as white and articulate whiteness with nationhood and a concept of racist closure and exclusion. Conversely another informant may accept "white" as a descriptive marker, while rejecting racist positioning as a determinant of inclusion within national terms. In both cases the assertion "I am white" is being made, but the meaning attributed to this identity register may be complex, contested and need placing within wider social frames of reference. On a macro scale, national race discourses may furnish these meanings, or, on a micro level, close friendships with peers from other cultural backgrounds may stimulate reflexive modifications of the notion of whiteness. In both cases there is a need to *socialize individuality* (Reicher 1987) in order to tease out the significance and subtleties of subjective responses.

This approach moves away from the search for "essential" identities towards a perspective that views social identity as a multi-faceted phenomenon that may vary through time and place (Benson 1981, Breakwell 1986) and call upon many influences. For this purpose, ethnography is concerned with illuminating the way in which social selves emerge from specific contexts. This methodology starts with recording everyday talk with young people at a street-corner level, continues in the form of group interviews, moves to individual interviews with young people and finally interviews those in early adulthood who reflect on the passage of youth. It is a closely reflexive endeavour that builds into the analysis an interrogation of the status of each account.

National identity, locality and youth

In the previous chapter, I outlined the economic and political processes that result in the local expression of racism within the adult population. The central concern of this section is to map out the youthful constituency in which young people operate and the extent to which these adult definitions impose on, or affect, the adolescent community. The picture that I will construct outlines a cultural space in which "race" is temporarily and superficially banished as a meaningful concept. It must be kept in mind that this process by which common sense is forged takes place in a world where there is a numerical predominance of white young people. However, there exists no simple notion of community–race closure with which the voice of racism is usually associated. In fact, the young people themselves would often say that it was "out of order" to talk about people's colour.

The ejection of "race" from peer group common sense – the notion that we are "all the same" – allows these young people to draw on a diverse range of linguistic and cultural resources. The points of contact with the raw material of this youthful bricolage vary from the immediate experience of black language forms heard in the localities and at school, to mediated forms of cultural practice in general circulation via mass-produced film, music and television. The South London landscape provides a rich corona of cultural production, including the symbolic storehouse of the African diaspora from at least three continents (Africa, America and Europe). This vibrant hall of symbols is accessible to white and black youth within this predominantly white neighbourhood. This results in the reworking of symbols within a context where they have a particular and creative expression and provides the terms and means of cross-racial communication. This is the landscape of interaction and negotiation.

The language of these communications draws on ethnically unmarked forms of black language, for example: "na mean" (you know what I mean), "rasta", "facety" (cheeky), "safe" (good, sound, OK, certain), "innit" (isn't it), "tief" (thief), "cuss" (to insult), "shame", "bad", "wicked" (meaning good). These terms are not utilized in strategic switches, as in the case of the previous accounts of black code switching (Hewitt 1986). Neither are they examples of the conscious white inhabitation of black forms; rather the use of these terms exemplifies a process whereby lexical items filter through into a shared speech community.

51

These forms are available in the immediate social milieu: "black voices" are heard on street corners, in the playground and at every public registration of the black presence within this area. The lack of marked enunciation strips these words of their heritage and gives them a new place within a specific location. Rather than linguistic mixing (Rampton 1989: 19), this language takes on a syncretic expression (ibid.: 18), and the resulting vernacular should be conceptualized not as a mixed bag with discrete parts, but as a collection of linguistic forms, articulated by particular speakers, that exhibits such a great degree of "fit" that it must be considered as one single form. It is a matter not of "mixing heritages" but of making a new heritage.

In addition to these black speech forms, lexical items from the white working-class vernacular are also used – phrases such as: "get out of town" (meaning don't be ridiculous), "mucker" (friend), "geezer" (man), "na" (no) and items of non-standard grammar, e.g. the use of "like" as an emphasizing tag. The points of inheritance may be from the parents, they may be located at school or they may emerge from neighbourhood extra-kin relations. What is significant is that such voices are not automatically deemed to be the logical point of identification. Rather they are one of many resources available for play and youthful linguistic assemblage. The language created is neither black nor white but combines lexical and grammatical forms from a variety of different sources. Similar mixed languages have been reported by Hewitt (1989: 139) and Rampton (1989: 18).

In addition to the linguistic processes I have briefly outlined, there exists a highly diverse mixture of popular cultural forms. Particularly significant is the adoption of Afro-American and Afro-Caribbean genres of popular music: *Afro-Caribbean* reggae, sound systems, rub-a-dub and MC-ing; *Afro-American* soul, hip hop & rap, house. These forms have been given new meaning as they take their place within the context of contemporary London in general and within this neighbourhood in particular.

In short, then, within this adolescent community there exists a process of reworking charged symbols.[1] Rodney, a white working-class boy who lives in the area, represents this process. Here is an extract from my field notebook that documented our first meeting.

Rodney is 15 years old. He lives in Nelson Tower with his mother and father who are both of white British extraction. He has blonde hair and is about 5 feet 2 inches. We met over the pool table and exchanged conversations in between shots. Initially we talked about music. He was listening to a Saxon Studio tape, and we discussed reggae, MC-ing and rub-a-dub. I asked him why he liked the music and he said that he didn't know. Papa Levi was the MC chatting over this particular cut and I asked him if he understood the lyrics. He said he could. I mentioned that I liked rub-a-dub and Rodney looked at me curiously and laughed. Rodney was wearing a Millwall Football Club T-shirt, on it was a Lion in Rambo-like battle dress holding a rifle standing in front of a Union Jack flag. Above this figure Millwall was proclaimed. I asked him about the shirt and we started to talk about football. He said he liked Millwall because they were "harder" than other teams. The conversation ended quickly because Mark (a friend of Rodney's) arrived.

The lasting impression I have of our first meeting was one of complete confusion. I could not understand how Rodney could on the one hand like and admire music that is invested with black political messages and on the other ally himself to the discourses on nation that were evoked by the "Rambo" images of militant nationalism he also sponsored. Although these symbols may appear to be in opposition to one another, for Rodney there was no contradiction. The important point to grasp is that the subjectivities of these young people are multiple (Henriques 1984) and reflect the diversity of ideologies and discourses that they both consume and engage with.

My concern here is to try to present and describe a domain within which race is temporarily deconstructed. As Teresa, age 17, puts it, "Colour don't come into it. We are all the same round here." Although this "commonality claim" will be questioned in what follows, I maintain that there is an interactional level of reality where the salience of "race" is denied. In the Riverview situation, patterns of multiethnic friendship are to some degree facilitated by this de-racialized discourse.

In a sense, the rejection of the significance of "colour" constitutes an attempt to shrink the definition of inclusion and exclusion to a size that mirrors their immediate set of social relations. The nation is thus shrunk to the size of the neighbourhood, resulting in the emergence of a kind of "neighbourhood nationalism". The syncretic culture I have briefly discussed acts as the symbolic capital that furnishes this identity, an over-arching reference point that is made more resonant by the shared experience of school and street and the culture that emerges from these locations. The inclusive definitions that are promoted within this concept stand in opposition to racialized versions of national belonging. This does not result in the complete rejection of what I referred to in Chapter 1 as the "new racism". Rather, within common sense there exists a tension between competing ideas resulting in a process by which the meanings of "race" are split for white young people.

"She's alright – she's different!": white identity and the definition of insiders and outsiders

> Na Carol's alright, she just like – the same as anybody else. I mean it not right to judge people by their colour, it's just those other people – like up Southgate and that! (Janet, aged 15)

Although I have argued that young people in this area tended to shrink the definitions of inclusion to the size of the immediate neighbourhood, there are also processes whereby inclusion is measured and identified. This reflects the conditions in which boundaries are constructed. Images of racialized nationality are dialectically opposed to the neighbourhood nationalism. The social identity of young whites has to be located within these competing definitions.

During the 1970s two contradictory strands of thought referring to white youth and race were offered. First, writers interested in race identities, particularly Peter Weinreich (1975a,b, 1979), viewed white youth as being "more stable" than other ethnic groups. Secondly, during this period discussions of racism were dominated by the importance of neo-fascist youth groups and extreme expressions of racist rhetoric and action (Daniel & McGuire 1972, Pearson 1976, Billig 1978, Murdock & Troyna 1981, Cashmore 1984). This literature provides an incomplete account of how ideas about "race" enter into the social worlds of young whites.

In a different field of study, Richard Dyer (1988) has shown that film representations of whiteness have an "everything and nothing quality". Here white ethnicity is implicitly present but explicitly absent. The result is that whiteness is equated with normality and as such it is not in need of definition. Thus "being normal" is colonized by the idea of "being white". However, white young people within Riverview are forced to break this spell of "white invisibility" through their association with black peers.

The meanings of "race" are split. A tension exists between a racialized construction of Englishness/Britishness circulated nationally and a "neighbourhood nationalism" that attempts to banish the racial referent and replace it with a simple commitment to a local territory. In the following extract, Scott gives an account of the estate in relation to the "Others" who live there in which one can see in operation the processes of splitting. The incident occurred on the stairway of a tower block located on the estate.

Look at this place, Les. It is disgusting innit. It never used to be like this. See all this graffiti [referring to hip hop signatures – called tags – painted on the walls]. Tony Costings did most of that. It used to be beautiful. I mean I like hip hop and all that but this is going too far. You know like this estate used to be lovely when it first opened.

Les: Why do you think it has changed?

Well it was when they moved the problem families in, yeah that's when it all started to go wrong. You know what I mean? People just don't care any more and it ain't right – people moving in from outside.

Les: What kind of people?

All kinds of people. But you know my mum was walking down there the other day [pointing towards a small shopping centre in the middle of the estate] and she saw this big black geezer coming along and she put her head down and walked past – you know – holding her bag. And it was Lloyd, you know Lloyd, he's lived around here for years, he used to be mates with my brother. He said, "Alright it is only me". You know what I mean, it is out of order but it makes you like that. I've known Lloyd all my life but I've got to the stage now when I start to feel threatened – it makes you like that.

Les: What makes you like that?

You know mugging and all that stuff, you see it on the telly and you hear stories about people. I mean I had my gold ring stolen up Elephant and Castle. Now I think twice.

Les: You talk about black things but do you think of yourself as being white?

Na, I mean – I'm not racist in that way.

Les: What way?

I mean, you know, skinhead and all that business, that's completely out of order.

Les: But what about Lloyd?

That's different. I don't know, I just feel wary.

Scott was born in 1972, eight years after the estate was opened and around the time when it is reputed to have started to go downhill. This evaluation cannot therefore be grounded in actual experience, rather, it relies on accounts that are in general circulation within his family and the adult population. What we see here is an expression of the "death of community" discourse referred to in Chapter 2. The account is concerned with closure and the definition of "insiders" and "outsiders". Here Lloyd, a black insider, is instrumental. Lloyd is "alright" but it is the rest of "them" that are not. One gets the feeling that Scott is tripping over the threads of racist logic – "it's out of order". But in the end, "it" makes you like that, "it" being the fear that is fed by criminalized images of black youth presented in the media and local folklore.

Scott uses "race" markers in the context of racist talk when applied to "others" but when applied to the self it is denied. Scott evokes race and uses racist social constructions while maintaining that this process is "out of order" in general terms. However, this split causes a contradiction between an idealized racist construction that has no meaning outside of its own logic and the relationships and immediate social knowledge of black friends who are the objects of racism. In Scott's case the division is between racist discourse that portrays black people as criminals and his social knowledge of Lloyd as an individual. A way out of this contradiction is to suggest that individuals such as Lloyd are exceptions to the rule. However, this strategy is becoming harder to validate in commonsense terms given that Riverview is fast becoming a more heterogeneous space; simply, there are so many exceptions that the "rule" becomes harder to sustain.

The ambiguity of these accounts and the phenomenon of "splitting" race registers must be understood within an environment where

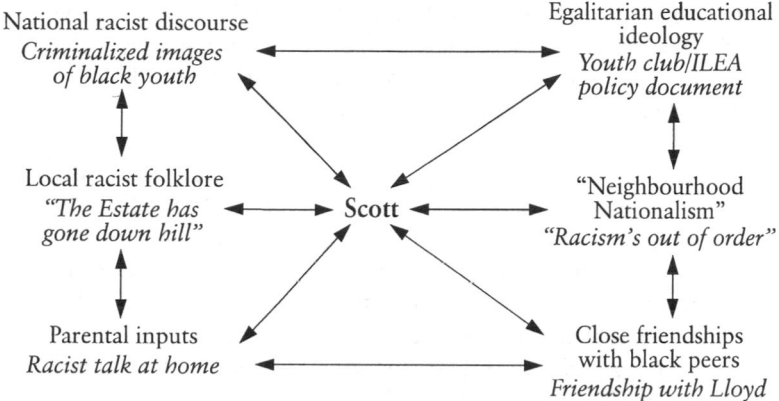

Figure 3.1   The conflicting semantics of "race" and "whiteness"

the semantics of "race" are struggled over and subjected to competing social forces. In Scott's case these forces divide up (see Fig. 3.1) into those practices that promote the transmission of racist constructions (i.e. national discourses, local variants, and racist reproduction within the family) and those that make the operation of racism problematic (egalitarian ideologies at school, multiracial peer group common sense, and inter-racial friendship).

The tensions between these meanings form the social ground where Scott has to locate his own notion of "race". It is within this framework that the phenomenon of "splitting" race registers must be located. In this sense young whites are caught within the paradoxes that emerge from their use of racist discourses and their lived experience.

Blackness, "neighbourhood nationalism" and the position of Afro-Caribbean youth

I have offered two contradictory images of black–Afro-Caribbean youth held by white youth: one is of the black insiders who become partially included within the concept of neighbourhood nationalism and the other is of black outsiders, a view that relies on a new racist ethos that defines black youth as culturally "foreign". So, for young white people, the degree of racial inclusion was defined in terms of their shared experiences with black peers in the neighbourhood. Two

57

important questions are raised here: first, to what degree do young black people identify these shared experiences, and, secondly, how do they locate themselves in reference to an idea of black identity?

Phil Cohen, in a programmatic essay, comments:

> Passports to success are by definition not issued, and those that are link origins (place and date of birth, nationality, distinguishing features) to quite other destinations. Racism forges all our identities by such means . . . Under these circumstances immigrants have little choice but to "ape" the manner of their "masters", albeit often exaggerated in such a way as to leave no doubt as to who is closer to the animal concerned. (Cohen 1988c: 12)

This perspective on "(mis)identification" with a racial oppressor is not a new one (Clark & Clark 1947, Fanon 1968, Davey & Norburn 1980), but the implications of these ideas are particularly relevant when placed in the Riverview ethnographic context. In some of the accounts given by black informants there was reference to how young black people tried to lighten their skin, and equally some talked of young black men who were involved in far right political movements in the 1970s and voiced open hostility to Afro-Caribbean and Asian youth. I did not meet young people who adopted these practices. However, the terms in which Afro-Caribbean youth identified with the concept I have called "neighbourhood nationalism" cannot be simply used as evidence to refute Cohen's claims. In all cases the young Afro-Caribbean people from this area recognized and identified the notion of "blackness" as a salient part of their identity, but this concept was located within other forms of identity that they shared with their white peers. Consider this quote from a 17-year-old girl of Barbadian parentage. Here she is being asked if she considers herself to be black:

> Yes I am black, but because I am black doesn't necessarily make me different from everybody else, you know what I mean. I mean there are people round here who are racist and talk about colour and all that, but when they see me in the area they know where I come from and they know my family. I suppose I've got as much in common with them as I have with my mother's relations in the West Indies. I mean I think

that is wrong . . . like they assume because you look a certain
way then they expect you to carry yourself that way.

The point that this young woman is making is that she can place herself within this constituency without distancing herself from a notion
of blackness. She does not see herself as a "white shadow" or as a
mirror of her white friends. Her very presence contributes to the
terms in which the meaning of the locality is constructed in adolescent common sense.

A contributory factor here is the prestigious position of black
youth cultures and styles in this area. In this sense the "master's man-
ners", to use Cohen's phrase, are not fully of the "master's heritage".
Young black people are involved in this process of culture building
and are often cultural innovators. I am not suggesting that power relations can be "magically suspended through the direct exchange of
experience" (P. Cohen 1988c: 13); but, rather, these definitions and
power relations are struggled over. The identification of black youth
with a local identity in no way denies their "blackness".

As I have described elsewhere (Back 1991a), the claim by young
whites that it is wrong to refer to people's colour did not prohibit incidents of racist name-calling (see Ch. 4). I want to discuss some of
the implications that the proximity of racism in this dramatic form
had for the understanding of young people's identity in this area.

The incident I am about to describe happened during a disco that
took place inside the youth club. In the course of the evening a
number of incidents of racist name-calling occurred. As the evening
drew to a close the lights were switched on in the youth club and I
noticed that the user population divided into a white/black segmentation. The separation that occurred in this period is not accidental. I
remember feeling that lines and boundaries were being drawn,
prompted by the dramatic manifestation of racism that had occurred.
I was standing close to the canteen with Valerie (black youth worker),
Evonne (15, black, Jamaican parentage), Amanda (16, mixed parentage), Christine (19, black, Afro-Caribbean, Jamaican parentage) and
Kenny. I should note here that Kenny looks "white" and visibly indistinguishable from the other white kids. The following exchange
occurred:

Valerie [looking at Christine]: You know Kenny is black, yes he has
black family.

Christine: Is it?

[Kenny walks over to the canteen area and walks into the canteen]

Valerie: Kenny, are any of your relatives black?

Kenny: My mum's from the West Indies . . . Barbados, she's a singer – you know what I mean.

Valerie: I thought so, I – there was something about you and I thought to myself I bet he's got some black family.

Kenny: Yeah, you can always tell a black person in a dark room!

Valerie: Yes, yes! [Laughs]

Christine: You know what I mean! [Laughs]

[Amanda laughs]

In this extract identities are explored. Kenny is being placed, and places himself, within a notion of "blackness". Although Kenny may move within sets of social relationships that deny that "race" or colour are meaningful, in this situation he is positioning himself with black peers and articulating a notion of black identity. This is a profound comment about the subtleties of registrations of identity, and in this situation a notion of self is triggered by the proximity of racist practice.

John is a young man of "mixed parentage". He lives with his mother who is white, and is father is Afro-Caribbean. I first met John when he was 12, and at this period he had a limited understanding of black language. However, over the four years I have known him his knowledge of black language and his interest in black cultural forms, particularly music, have grown steadily. He, along with Scott, a white friend (mentioned earlier), and Tony, a black friend, run a small sound system. In this John has acted as a cultural innovator within the neighbourhood while consciously probing connections with a black collectivity through language and culture.

Black young people living in Riverview are sometimes characterized as being "white on the inside" by people who live in areas with strong black communities. The terms used are various and include "coconut" and "Bounty" (after a chocolate bar that has a coconut filling). Such terms can be accusations and insults that imply that in some sense black people have been co-opted to white norms.[2] In these terms, "blackness" and "black culture" are understood as having some essential character. This constitutes a kind of ethnic absolutism that separates cultural and racial absolutes from the historical circumstances that give them meaning (Gilroy 1987: 43–71).

Young people like John and Kenny may be accused of being "Bountys". To classify these young people in these absolute ways reveals little of their complex position. Neither of these young men would identify themselves as wanting to "be" white or as shadowing the practices of their white friends. Indeed, their relationship with a wider black collectivity is constantly being probed and explored in the same way that their relationships with white peers and the locality are tested and defined. So, to fix the identities of these young men is to misrepresent their dynamic and negotiated character. In both cases these young men held prestigious positions within the adolescent community. They were both popular and respected. In the process of being so they became "partially soluble" within the boundaries of the neighbourhood, while maintaining the potential to develop connections with the wider black collectivity. The degree to which these two avenues of identification are in conflict with one another is open to question, but I would maintain that their identities cannot be characterized as ones that exhibit "crisis" in the sense that the term is used in the sociology of race relations.

The young black people that I have worked with in this area understand the ambivalence of their links with their white peers. In the following extract, two young women talk through their relationship with each other. Julie is 15 and of black Nigerian parentage, while Sue is the same age and has white British parents.

Les: Do you think that colour can be important to friendships?

Julie: Yes, I think it can come into it. I mean I have got friends where it doesn't matter. I mean Teresa is one of the few non-racial people I know.

Sue: But I don't think colour comes into – do you think that I am a racist then?

Julie: Well, what about that time when you called me a black bitch!

Sue: Yeah but I wasn't being serious then – I mean I didn't mean anything by it, I was just mucking about. I think it is stupid to be prejudiced.

Julie: But the difference is right, Teresa wouldn't even say something like that – not even mucking about, [looks at Les] you know what I mean?

Les: What do you mean?

Julie: Well, like people would see my colour as important and make a joke out of it, or say something – but truly non-racial people would see my skin and not take any notice of it, it wouldn't be important.

There are two very important things being said in this exchange. First, Julie is making the statement that colour is often important in friendships and that being "truly non-racial" means not investing skin colour with any meaning. To refer to colour, even in play, is to make it meaningful and consequently to be "racial". Secondly, Sue defends her "race talk" as being nothing more than play. This response was repeated on numerous occasions where incidents of racist name-calling took place. My point here is that "race" may be negotiated out of the terms of friendship but this is an ongoing process. There is always a potential for racist materials to be utilized strategically by whites as a means of gaining an advantage or hurting black peers. As a result, the location of black peers as "insiders" is always contingent upon the absence of racist talk and practice.

The position of Vietnamese youth

In contrast to the dialogue that occurs between black and white people, the situation for Vietnamese youth is very different. These young people are left out of the relationships that occur within the youth club, and the Vietnamese do not participate in these peer relationships. In the following extract, two Vietnamese boys pointedly show how they have been forced to engage with the meaning attached to "race" and their experience of racism within Riverview. The incident involves Trong, who at the time was 16, a Vietnamese refugee of Chinese-speaking parents, and Pasha, 16 years old with one Chinese parent and the other of Turkish origin. The incident also involved two youth workers and myself. Mel is an Afro-Caribbean youth worker and Tran a Vietnamese youth worker. This particular night the activities in the centre were divided in half: downstairs, Chinese classes were being held for Vietnamese young people between the ages of 10 and 14 and upstairs a general club session open to anybody over 14 was in full swing. Trong and Pasha came in, paid their money and walked towards the room where the Chinese language classes were being taught. What follows has been reconstructed from memory, but I am quite confident that I have captured the correct sequence and content of these accounts.

Mel: You can't go in there!

Trong: Why!

Les: The language class is just for the younger kids tonight.

Trong: Why t[h]at? Why can[t] we go in there? [Getting angry]

Mel: Because you are too old.

Trong: Why can[t] you have a nigh[t] where you have all Chinese people. In Chinatown they have one day when all Chinese people – no one else, just Chinese people!

Les: It's just that we need to have the people in the class about the same age.

Trong: Come on, le[t]'s go. [Looks at Pasha]

Mel: Why can't you go upstairs and mix with the other kids?

Trong [turns back and looks at Mel]: White people don't like Chinese people!

Mel: But . . .

[Tran comes walking down the stairs. He has been trying to set up a camping trip to take 20 kids from the club on a holiday]

Tran: I have worked ou[t] how say the trip an[d] we are going to take ten whi[t]e and ten yellow ki[d]s.

Mel: What do you mean "white" and "yellow". You mean [that] you are going to take a mixed group.

Trong: Wha[t] you yellow!

[Mel has a light skin colour]

Mel: What do you mean?

Trong: You half cas[te]!

Mel: I am black West Indian!

Pasha: Well, where do I fit in then? My father is Chinese and my mother is Turkish.

Mel: Well, if you identify with the Vietnamese then that is where you belong.

Tran: No but we are all the same – all human race.

Mel: Look! [with emphasis] I identify with black West Indian – which I have a right to do. Isn't that right Les? [Looks at Les]

[Les nods and says nothing]

Mel: I respect you for being what your race and you respect me as being black. Of course we are all the same!

Tran [pauses and begins to reply]: But . . .

Trong: Ten white, ten yellow!

[Trong and Pasha leave and walk upstairs]

Trong points out the segmentation in this adolescent community and he explains it in "race" terms – "white people don't like Chinese people". This is offered to explain the lack of participation in the club and in peer groups generally. Secondly, this exchange is interesting because it provides an example of where identities and classifications are being interrogated through lived exchanges. With the entry of Tran, a series of claims and counter-claims are made about self-definition. Mel criticizes Tran's "white"/"yellow" terms of reference. Trong attempts to place Mel within these terms and Mel resists this process by articulating a notion of black West Indian identity. Pasha enters into the discussion and asks how he fits into these categories. Here Mel makes the claim that identity is a matter of participation – "If you identify with the Vietnamese then that is where you belong". Tran tries to bring the pattern of definition–counter-definition to an end by suggesting that we are all members of the "human race". However, this strategy has no meaning for Trong and he vividly shows the salience that "race" has for him. He leaves the exchange reiterating the primacy of racialized definitions – "Ten white, ten yellow!"

I included this extract primarily to point out the position of the Vietnamese young people in these areas. In many ways they operate outside of the linguistic and cultural exchanges that take place within multiracial peer groups and constitute a subordinate youth group, or what Roger Hewitt (1990: 141) has termed a *sociolinguistic under-class*. The Vietnamese youth rarely ventured into the club on mixed sessions. Provision for the Vietnamese was a constant issue for the members of staff who were concerned that they should be catered for. Usually, the result was to hold special sessions for them either on the weekend or at special discos run privately.

Many of the white young people justified the absence of the Vietnamese young people by asserting that they "liked to keep themselves to themselves" and that they "won't mix". Their lack of participation in friendship groups was the result of the kinds of constructions that were mobilized against them by whites. In the course of fieldwork I noticed that a Vietnamese boy – Tanyi – started to come into the club with two white boys – Cliff and Jack. Cliff and Jack were from established "estate families". Cliff's father, in particular, was reputed to have been a supporter of the National Front in the 1970s and vehemently opposed the settlement of the Vietnamese on the estate. The three boys were said to "hang around together" which usually meant that they spent time together on the estate and in the youth club.

The three boys would come in the club and spend their time playing football and pool. Occasionally, Tanyi's Chinese–Vietnamese origins were mentioned in "wind-ups" (see Ch. 4) and play exchanges. The most recurrent reference point was the association of Tanyi's background with a stereotype of "Orientals" who are proficient in martial arts. On one occasion the three boys were playing pool and Cliff rolled the pool cue over his shoulder and adopted a fight stance in front of Tanyi. He then withdrew saying, "I'd better watch it. Tanyi would make Bruce Lee [a famous martial arts hero] take up pool." All three boys laughed at this. Although Tanyi was accepted as part of the peer group, his "difference" was often referred to in these exchanges, making it apparent that his presence was always contingent on Cliff's and Jack's approval. It was clear that the three boys used their masculinity as a common register around which to build friendship. In this sense the masculine forms of play that they were involved in were expressions of this process at work (Back 1990). However, these friendships did not last long.

After two months I started to feel some tension between Tanyi, Cliff and Jack. On one occasion at the entrance to the club a new worker asked Tanyi to spell his name; Cliff, who was standing behind him, said, "Just put Tony". This process of Anglicization of names is common amongst British Asian young people who move in white peer groups. Within this area the Vietnamese young people would justify this by claiming that the whites could not pronounce their names properly. On this occasion I think that Cliff's "naming claim" was of greater significance. It signalled an increasing resentment towards Tanyi's "difference". This change also manifested itself in their interactions within the club. Cliff challenged Tanyi in duelling play more often and subsequently the boys spent less time together. Three weeks later Tanyi stopped coming to the club.

When I asked Cliff and Jack about this they told me that Tanyi had decided to "go back to his own kind". A few days after this discussion I saw Tanyi on the estate and I asked him why he had stopped coming to the club. He said:

> I was jus[t] sick of the way they treat me. You know, yellow this yellow that, "Chink" this "Chink" that. Then I decided that I was not going to come to the club any more. I decided that I didn't want them to use me as something to play with. See they say we don't come to club because we don't want to – but would you want to be treated like that? I go to the club when they have Vietnamese disco and the club on Sundays but no more in the week.

Clearly, the manifestation of racist practices was the most important factor in the breakdown of this friendship group. So, rather than being a matter of voluntary absence, the lack of a Vietnamese presence in the club was the result of an informal exclusion.

Vietnamese youth were also subject to racial harassment and attacks. There were several instances reported by the Vietnamese refugees of harassment on their way to local shopping facilities. There were also stories of young men urinating into the letter boxes of Vietnamese residents and of burning torches being placed outside their homes.

In the face of this kind of harassment it is hardly surprising that the Vietnamese young people were reluctant to use the youth club or to enter into close relationships with other young people in the area. The question that emerges here is why can young black people gain access to a contingent insider position while the Vietnamese cannot?

The shifting terms of racial inclusion and exclusion

The notion of "neighbourhood nationalism" that states "it is out of order to talk about people's colour" is not an empty gesture but the product of a long struggle over the inclusion of black people within this parochial identity. It is not a benign ideology facilitating cross-racial "harmony" but a product of lived struggles between black and white young people over belonging.

For Vietnamese youth, however, their exclusion is more acute. It is in this sense that the Vietnamese are actively prevented from entering this "multi-ethnic constituency". Perhaps it is the Vietnamese who pay the price for the dialogue that occurs between black and white young people. The simple fact that Vietnamese young people are prevented from entering the nation, as defined within the neighbourhood, means that they incur the full wrath of the new racism that defines "outsiders" in terms of cultural difference.

In the following extract, Cliff articulates this process in an exchange that took place in the youth club between Cliff and myself and another white youth worker called Jane. Jack was present but he did not contribute. The prompt for this account was the issue of whether the Vietnamese should be allowed to have special provisions within the youth club.

Cliff: This club is racist because you have nights when the Vietnamese come and we are not allowed to.

Les: But if we didn't have a Vietnamese night they wouldn't come in. You know what happens – new people come in and they . . .

Cliff: That rubbish – no one's stopping them coming in here. They don't want to come here, all they want to do stick with themselves. What about people like John and that, they are coloured and they come in and mix – nobody says anything to them. I hate the Chinks, you should see them. Their cooking stinks and you see them going up the shops with their shopping on their heads – the next time I see one on the street I am going – I'd like to give them a good kicking.

Jane: What about Tanyi? You used to be friends with him.

Cliff: Yeah, look what happened to him – went back to them. They stick together don't they – don't want to know anybody else.

Les: Don't you think that's probably to do with the way you treated him.

Cliff: That's bollocks – I treated him the same as everyone else.

Les: Come on Cliff, I've seen you winding him up.

Cliff: That don't mean nothin' – just 'aving a laugh.

Jane: Maybe he didn't think it was funny.

Cliff: It's always the same with you lot – one law for them and another for us. If they say something we musn't say a word – if we say something then we're in the wrong.

[Cliff bends down and picks up a small Union Jack that was left
   over from a youth club activity. He turns to Les and stretches
   out his hand with the flag in it]
Cliff: Here, give that to the Vietnamese! Come on Jack.
[The two boys get up and leave the youth club]

In this extract Cliff points out the terms that justify his exclusion of
the Vietnamese. He claims that they have no desire for participation,
that they are different and that they are not like the "coloureds" who
have been accepted. It is in this sense that racialized nationalism
becomes a resource that excludes the Vietnamese. This is profoundly
manifested in the presentation of the Union Jack – "give that to the
Vietnamese". Cliff sees "coloured" people as being accepted and
included because of their commitment to contact. However, the
boundaries of these divisions are always ambiguous and can be
opened and closed at will by whites where it is to their advantage
(Back 1990).
   Where young whites are identifying with black culture it is important to question the constructions of blackness that they find attractive. For young white men this may be located around racialized
definitions of masculinity. In this sense the image of black masculinity
as invulnerable, "hard" and "bad" is alarmingly similar to racist
notions of dangerous or violent "black muggers". At the moment
when racist ideas are most vulnerable, in situations where there is
intimate contact between black and white men, stereotypical ideas
can be reproduced "dressed up" as positive characteristics to be emu-
lated. This kind of identification can find itself locked within the discourse of the "noble savage" that renders blackness exotic and
re-affirms black people as a "race apart".
   In an associated way, gender and racism interact to construct Vietnamese young people within this masculinist discourse. Here the Vietnamese young men are constructed as generally weak and feeble.
Although there were on a few occasions references to an imagined
relationship between "Orientals" and prowess in martial arts, the
Vietnamese young people were viewed as vulnerable, soft and effemi-
nate. Thus black people are constructed within this discourse as hard
and respected while the Vietnamese are labelled as soft and are vilified.
   The contours of these racialized hierarchies were apparent in an
account offered by a young man called Chas. When I met Chas in
1987 he was 14 years old and lived in Riverview. He is white but was

intimately involved with the musical cultures of black London. He had taken on the full blazonry of black style forms. One of his front teeth was gold capped, he had "tram lines" shaved into the sides of his blonde hair and he wore a medallion with the symbol of Africa coloured in red, gold and green. We would talk about the relative worth of black British musicians such as Soul II Soul compared with the American rap aces Public Enemy. He was unequivocal about the issue of colour. "It's pure wickedness to cuss people's colour – you know what I mean? Like my black friends have as much right to be here as I have." For a short time Chas "went out" with a black young woman from the area. However, the politics of this posturing was not extended beyond his identifications with his particular image of blackness.

On one occasion we were walking through South London sharing discourse on the state of dance music when his model of racial hierarchies became clear. We passed a Vietnamese refugee and her son walking back from a shopping excursion. Chas turned, "There is one thing though – I can't stand the chinks. Their cooking stinks and they keep themselves to themselves like. They don't want to mix." I asked "But isn't that just as bad as saying that all black people are muggers." He replied, "Na! That's not the same at all! My black mates wouldn't let people walk over them the way the Vietnamese do – do you know what I mean? Black people have nuff respect for who they are. If you said things to dem you'd get nuff licks [physical retribution]."

In this short extract we see the articulation between gender and racism rising to the surface of consciousness. Here a dualism develops that connects racialized boundaries with gendered characteristics. In the framework of white working-class masculinities, black and "Oriental" youth are characterized in terms of a set of dualistic oppositions. The terms of inter-racial dialogue are set by this process of *race–gender othering*. An image of blackness is defined in the context of white commonsense that is in turn viewed positively. This results in the definition of black young men as contingent insiders. In contrast, the Vietnamese young men are castigated within a kind of Orientalist discourse and are attacked and excluded. What follows from this discourse is that particular minorities are designated as being "hard" and assertive, whereas others are designated as being "soft" and vulnerable.

The configurations of "white masculinity" are inextricably linked with the processes of constructing various Others. Franz Fanon

(1968) showed that in colonial and neo-colonial societies the division between Self and Other is often a crude simplification of the complex psychological legacy of racism. His aim was to deconstruct the white masks that racism imposed on black people, or, as Homi Bhabha puts it, "the white man's artifice inscribed on the black man's body" (Bhabha 1990: 188). Bhabha himself suggests that the division between Self and Other is always partial with the result that neither is sufficient unto itself (ibid.: 193). Appropriating Fanon's metaphor one might pose the question of how white young men are adopting black masks. What I am suggesting here is that white masculinity does not involve the assertion of a monolithic racialized Self. Rather it embraces and rejects differently positioned images of masculine Otherness. On the one hand, white young men identify with particular constructions of blackness, and in doing so they appropriate these images as part of *their* selfhood; while, on the other hand, they reject any form of identification with images of the "Oriental" as being anti-self. Complex configurations of identity emerge in a situation where "[t]he shadow of the Other falls upon the Self" (ibid.: 203).

A range of masculine identities is being embraced by white young men. The essential point is that these notions of identity are harnessed to sets of racialized constructions. In this situation the identities that are rejected, or from which individuals distance themselves, are as important as the ones that are embraced. In the process of saying "I am not like him/her" the subject is saying something about who they are and how they conceive themselves. In view of the issues discussed here this manifests itself in a process whereby particular combinations of masculine identity are embraced while others are rejected. My point is that all of these forms of masculinity are racialized. I have argued in this chapter that in order to understand the contingencies of folk rejections of racism we have to cross our analysis of racism with the politics of various masculinities. It is only here that we can begin to decipher why it is that Vietnamese young people – male and female – in this part of South London are so viciously harassed.

However, the complex racialized hierarchies referred to here are also part of a wider set of social relations that can be participated in by both young men and women. The exclusion of the Vietnamese and the contingent inclusion of black young people can be explained by, first, an understanding of the way "race" becomes split in the identities of white young people, and, secondly, the struggle that young black people are engaged in to maintain the legitimacy of their inclusion. In this sense divisions within this adolescent community are the result of the practices of the numerically predominant white group.

Conclusion

In summary, the social identities and social structure within this community exhibit a number of features. First of all, there exists a significant level of reality that actively denies racial terms of reference. This manifests itself in a concept of neighbourhood nationalism that is inclusive of young people according to shared territory. Also, a process of cultural syncretism results in the crossing of black youth culture and language into a new shared youth language and argot. At the same time, there exists a racialized nationalism that is in circulation both in the parent culture and in the national media discourse. In this sense the identities of young whites must be understood as the product of a conflict between competing definitions. Thus, although "neighbourhood nationalism" may curb the expression of racism, it does not banish the prevalence of racist practice. Black young people both maintain a commitment to the concept of neighbourhood nationalism and also probe the possibility for identification with a wider black collectivity. Vietnamese young people are actively excluded from these territorially defined identities. This is explained by the attitudes of the numerically predominant whites, who locate the Vietnamese within a discourse that defines them as cultural outsiders who have no legitimate claim for inclusion.

Throughout this discussion I have maintained that significant negotiations are taking place within this adolescent community that, to a limited extent, threaten to dislodge some of the tenets on which nationalism and the new racism are premised. In short, identities are being forged between black and white young people. This assertion is not a new one and the central point is that shared locality offers an alternative identity option to divisive and exclusive notions of "race" (Wallman et al. 1982, Wallman 1983, Hewitt 1986, Jones 1988). Some have gone so far to suggest that, "in some areas, the culture and politics of young people exhibits a seamless and organic fusion of black and white sensibilities" (Jones 1988: 232). Crucially, this calls into question the idea that black and white cultures exist as mutually autonomous phenomena. To use Hall's (1987) phrase, identities are not "armour plated against one another".

Yet whereas black young people within this area have won a degree of inclusion, another racialized group (i.e. the Vietnamese youth) is excluded and marginalized. Why? I think the answer lies beyond any simple ideas about correlating the decrease in racism and exclusion with duration of migrant residence. As I have tried to show, contact between young people of various origins does not take place in a context that is autonomous of local and national ideologies. Young people are not the passive recipients of these ideologies but neither can they escape their effect. In this sense the locally achieved inclusion of black young people can exist alongside new racist ideas about "culturally different" black people in other parts of London and Vietnamese young people in the area. The result is the muting of the expression of particular racisms while others flourish. In places such as Riverview, racist ideas are unevenly developed but undeniably present.

The creative cultural dialogues that I have identified in the early part of this chapter constitute a working-class youth culture that is shifting the meaning of race and the terms of racial inclusion. The taking on of black symbols by white and black young people alike may have transformed the sight and sound of neighbourhoods such as Riverview, but this clearly has not led to the formation of an unambiguously inclusive working-class youth culture. The emergence of de-centred subjectivities (Hall 1992, Bhabha 1994), while providing important sites for cultural contest, does not necessarily produce progressive outcomes. I have argued that the range of identifications elaborated by young white men in particular points to the complex intersection between plural forms of racism, masculinity and multiculture.

In the next chapter I want to explore exactly how racism violates the tenuous cultural bridges that are being built between black and white young people. Here I will focus on racist name-calling.

CHAPTER 4

Social context and racist practice

Introduction

In the previous chapter I showed that within Riverview black young
people have negotiated a contingent form of inclusion. Here the
meaning of "race" as a divisive social parameter is denied. I also
showed that there exists a complex process of social definition
whereby young people of Vietnamese origin are excluded from the
dialogues occurring locally and black people from areas outside of
Riverview are also seen as a stigmatized group. In this chapter I will
show how the local identities I have referred to as "neighbourhood
nationalism" become violated by the use of racist materials by young
whites.

The chapter focuses on incidents of racist name-calling in multi-
ethnic peer groups. What I will produce is a picture of the meaning,
ambiguity and paradox of "race" in the public lives of these young
people. The fundamental question I ask is, how can young people
deny the importance of colour yet at the same time practise racist
name-calling?

Interaction and ritual duelling play:
"cussing" and "wind-ups"

In the preceding chapter I have described a relatively unselfconscious
space in which communication takes place in multiracial peer groups
outside of racially circumscribed boundaries. Even so, such interactions do exhibit a dynamic quality. It is not simply a matter of the

existence of a volatile multiracial social structure, because the young people themselves are constantly negotiating the terms of this structure. Play is instrumental in this process, for it is in play that young people are involved in *their* passage through youth and social learning. It is not simply that young people "learn to belong"; they are also involved in an active process that explores the meaning of belonging. It is thus impossible to understand racist name-calling without first developing an understanding of play and its significance.

Bateson's essay "A theory of play and fantasy" (1978) outlines the processes by which meaning is transformed by meta-communication in play. Bateson uses material gathered from animal behaviour to show how an act of aggression – such as a bite – can have its meaning emptied in the course of play:

> Not only does the playful nip not denote what would be denoted by the bite for which it stands, but, in addition, the bite itself is fictional. (Bateson 1978: 155)

In this process, comments, practices and actions that are invested with non-play meanings are subverted and inverted by collusion. Through playing, a negotiated alteration of meaning takes place that dislocates practice from what it "stands for" in wider usage.

This perspective on play is applicable to the kinds of activities that occur in this adolescent community. I use the term "duelling play" to describe the kinds of interactions that take place in this context. This is referred to in the peer group as "cussing someone out" (which has overtones of an insult) and "wind-ups" (that is, the process of getting another person angry then ridiculing their anger by exposing its illegitimacy – "I was only joking" – "only winding you up"). In operating this kind of play the sensitive lines of significance are policed. On one side of this line is the meaning that the word or exchange stands for in wider usage, on the other is a meaningless denotation guaranteed by play. The tension in this kind of early and late adolescent play is centred around the issue of whether these acts mean what they stand for or not.

Duelling play is a process whereby young people test out the boundaries of interpersonal relationships (i.e. how far play can be extended and pushed). Like joking relationships in other societies these "sham conflicts" actually reflect friendship and extra-kin association (Radcliffe-Brown 1940, 1949). These exchanges have greater significance than just play for play's sake. They not only mark the boundaries of tolerance within dyadic friendships but they also mark those who are included in the peer group: those who are "alright" and who you can joke with, and those who are excluded – "wallies". As Apte points out, the "[a]cceptance of a person's joking is an indication that he or she is part of the social group" (Apte 1985: 54). In the following extract a play exchange is recounted between two young women who are in early adolescence (they are both 11). Prior to this exchange they had been involved in a game of "back slap and chase" (this is a descriptive term, not one that the young people use themselves) in the youth club. The game involves slapping an opponent on the back then running off; the recipient then tries return the blow. This particular evening six young people were involved, divided into two teams.

Kelly [to Mary]: Did Scott get you?

Mary: Na. 'e's too slow. [Both girls laugh]

Kelly: But you can't get away from me though, I'm way too fast for you. I could get you any time – you ain't that fast.

Mary: Yeah but at least I'm not slow in the head.

Kelly: You calling me stupid.

Mary: Na, but you can be a bit of a div [idiot or fool] sometimes.

Kelly: You can't talk.

Mary: You can't talk. [Both girls laugh]

Kelly: You idiot! [Still laughing]

Mary: Don't cuss me, I ain't done nothin' to you – divy.

[The tone of the exchange gets more intense]

Kelly: Oh, shut up you wally [said loudly in a confrontational manner].

Mary: Don't tell me to shut up. I'll say what I like if I want to.

Kelly: Well don't say it around me then.

Mary: You're . . .

Kelly: Shut up you wally. [Kelly turns and walks away]

This extract is an example of "cussing". It emerges out of a particular play context (i.e. the aftermath of a back slap and chase game) and during this exchange a number of claims and counter-claims are being made about athletic and intellectual prowess. Kelly starts this by stating she is athletically superior to Mary. Mary then counters this by "putting down" Kelly's intellectual ability. However, during this banter the exchange remains at the level of play; the meanings invested in these prowess claims are not escalated to insults. This meta-communication breaks down when Kelly calls Mary "You idiot!" Mary then accuses Kelly of "cussing" and cusses her back, calling her a "div". From here the exchange is escalated into open confrontation and the play state is abandoned. Kelly tells Mary to "shut up" and accuses her of being a "wally". Mary protests the right to criticize: "I'll say what I like if I want to." This resource is often employed in "cussing" exchanges; it is used as a legitimization for any comment that may be critical or adversarial. Kelly recognizes that Mary can say what she likes but she qualifies this by abandoning the exchange – "don't say it around me then". This marks the total breakdown of the play state and Kelly turns and walks away.

The significance of this exchange is that the boundaries of what can be accepted in friendship are being marked. The drama tests the status of their friendship. Up until the abandonment of play meanings, both young women have colluded to make these play insults meaningless. But at a crucial point, this agreement breaks down, throwing the status of their relationship into crisis. Although their friendship does not break down irreparably, the boundaries of what can be agreed within this friendship are plotted.

Although cussing is equally apparent within male and female friendship and peer groups, the phenomenon I have referred to as "wind-ups" is a predominantly masculine one. Whereas the previous extract looked at "cussing" as a form of dyadic negotiation, "wind-ups" are usually associated with public gaining and losing of face. Often what is communicated in a "wind-up" is the status of individuals vis-à-vis the peer group. In the following extract, two young men are involved in a "wind-up". Steve, who is 16 and of white English parents, is the main actor. Robert, who is 15 and of Irish parents, is the "wind-up subject". Tony, 16 and of mixed parentage (Afro-Caribbean and white English), is the audience–foil.

Steve: 'ere Tony, 'ave you seen the size of his hands [pointing at Robert's hands while stirring his tea]?

Tony: Yeah, come here Robert, let's 'ave a look at those hands.

[Robert walks over. Steve puts his hand on the table for comparison with Robert]

Steve: Put your hand down there next to mine [looks at Robert].

[Robert looks at Steve and puts his hand down. Steve takes the spoon out of his tea and puts it on the back of Robert's hand]

Robert: Agh – you wanker!

[Steve and Robert laugh]

Steve: What a wally.

[All three boys laugh]

There are two things I want to point out. First, the teaspoon wind-up initiates Tony into a group where "wind-ups" are not taken as insults. Tony enters a space, or more correctly agrees to enter a space, where wind-ups are not a form of conflict. The play state is maintained. Although insults are hurled by Robert and Steve, their meanings are impotent. Secondly, although the collusion that takes place within this interaction prevents any escalation in conflict, status positions are defined. Steve and Tony establish themselves as the agents who act upon Robert – the subject – who is thereby shamed. Robert is included in the peer group but at the same time relegated to a secondary status (at least in the context of the interaction). This process is constantly being repeated within these peer settings. The actors may be agents of "wind-ups" in one situation but relegated to subjects in others. It is in this way that peer status is contested and continuously modified.

Although I am presenting these rituals in their youthful manifestation, they are by no means confined to these kinds of setting. In fact, the practice of "wind-ups" must be located within male working-class occupational culture in general (Roy 1953, 1960, Willis 1977, Vaught & Smith 1980). This was made clear to me in a conversation I had in the youth club with Darren, a 17-year-old bricklaying apprentice, about his work.

Everyone gets the piss taken out of them but they are alright. It's like when you are new they suss you out – make you look stupid. There was this one geezer today and they told him to go down to the stores and get a bag of "glass nails" and he fell for it – you know what I mean. They are always laughing and joking with you but that's the way it is.

Les: Do they do the same to you?

Me, not really. I remember once they sent me to the stores for a "rubber hammer" [laugh]. And another time, they wanted me to get inside a piece of scaffold pole to measure its diameter. I mean there ain't no way anybody is going to get inside a scaffold pole is there [laugh]. Another time they tried to get me to go down to the stores, to get some holes for a bag of nuts – all stupid things like that. But if you don't know what kind of things come out of the stores how are you going to know any better?

There are striking similarities between the content of occupational "wind-ups" and those used in male adolescent peer groups. Darren says that "everyone gets the piss taken out of them", implying that these practices define a notion of group, a group that "plays". Again there is a suggestion that this is a rite of passage: "when you are new they suss you out." Through various "wind-ups" (glass nails, rubber hammer, scaffold pole, holes for a bag of nuts) the apprentices are made "to look stupid", conferring on them a non-adult/junior/subordinate status. Interestingly, Darren both recognizes this and resists it for himself but accepts its wider legitimacy.

In both of these cases the "wind-up" defines belonging and also marks status. Those who endure the "wind-ups" and learn to act within them are seen to be "alright" (insiders). But this is not to say that the "wind-up" never breaks down into open conflict. In some cases the "wind-up" may go wrong, occasionally resulting in fighting amongst young men.

Working in close proximity to young people it is always difficult to gauge the line between play and non-play behaviour. In the extract below, I recount an exchange that took place around the door of the youth club. The incident involved Tony (15-year-old white English youngster) and Peter (15-year-old black youngster of African parentage). Just before the exchange between Peter and Tony occurred, Tony had been involved in another incident, having been "offered out" (asked for a fight) by a friend – Mark – in the club. The two boys acted out the scene. They squared up, shoulders pushed back, heads tilted to one side as they exchanged challenges. Then the boys attacked one another, rolling around on the floor. But from the first clash they started to laugh uncontrollably. Clearly, this was play by Bateson's definition – the confrontation did not denote what it stood for. Alison James (1986) has described similar forms of play fighting, called fun fights or funning, amongst groups of young people in the north-east of England. However, the interaction documented in the extract below exhibited a very different result.

Tony: Well come on then.

Peter: Yeah, do you want to know [laughing].

Tony [stops, pulls back his shoulders, raises his voice]: Right now.

Peter: Agh go away Tony.

Tony: Come on.

Peter: Yeah? [Turns and faces Tony]

Tony: Yeah?

[Tony pushes Peter. Peter takes a punch at Tony, misses, but a scuffle breaks out]

Les: Hey come on guys.

[Les intervenes, grabs hold of Peter and takes him outside of the club. Tony stays in the club]

Les: Cool down Pete, it's not worth it, you're fighting over nothing.

Peter: He ain't taking liberties with me.

[Peter stops struggling and stares back into the club at Tony, still trembling with intense emotion. Tony walks upstairs and out of sight. The incident is over]

This exchange started off as a "play fight". But crucially this broke down, leading to a fight situation. Play was abandoned and a scuffle ensued. Being close to this scuffle I could not understand what was at stake in this conflict. There seemed to be little at issue. The initial play confrontation was fictitious: there was no overt conflict and no justification was given afterwards. But powerful emotions were being articulated and the tussle that resulted was very real. Peter says at the end of the conflict: "He ain't taking liberties with me." Implied in this remark is a notion of self, the "me" in the sentence. From this viewpoint it is possible to prise some meaning from this event. At the level of "face" both boys are presenting themselves as equal adversaries. In addition they are both identifying themselves as masculine. At the point that Peter states that Tony is not going to "take liberties" with him he is answering Tony's challenge, defining himself as "hard" and not vulnerable to challenge. Encapsulated in that moment is an unselfconscious registration of masculine identity.

Duelling play – as characterized here – can dramatize notions of status at a variety of levels. First, "cussing" can plot the boundaries of familiarity and friendliness within male and female dyads or groups. Secondly, duelling play in the form of "wind-ups" takes on a predominantly masculine expression. This may be explained and echoed in the kind of transitions young men are in the process of navigating, a passage to the occupational cultures of working-class male life. The result is an apprenticeship in both inclusion and status. So here we see the development of clearly gendered forms of play where both young men and women indulge in "cussing" exchanges, while "wind-ups" remain in most cases the province of young men.

Racist name-calling and conflict situations

In this section I document a series of conflict situations where race is evoked as a powerful and potent register in name-calling. In the previous sections I have tried to sketch out the context from which these events emerge. In order to grasp the full meaning of the incidents it is essential to place them within the negotiated peer space that temporarily banishes race as a meaningful concept. The incidents of racist name-calling lead to a flight from multi-ethnic peer space and result in moments of heightened "race" consciousness. What I am particularly interested in is the way that young whites justify the use of racist social constructions.

All of the incidents that will be discussed here took place in the Riverview Youth Club. Racist name-calling was a regular occurrence. Over a six-month period I recorded 32 incidents where racist discourses were used in "cussing" or "wind-up" exchanges and I am sure that many more took place. These incidents would usually occur in cycles: sometimes two weeks would pass without event and then three or four episodes would happen during one session.

The youth club followed the policy directive of the Inner London Education Authority (the wages of the workers were paid by ILEA) which explicitly took an anti-racist stance, prohibiting racist name-calling in ILEA institutions. This policy was made known to the users of the club, and the senior youth worker drew up a list of rules that were given to each member. Racist and sexist name-calling was placed second behind drug use on the list of prohibited activities. The club rules, circulated in September 1985, stated:

> Derogatory terms, i.e. racist and sexist comments, or foul language amongst members or directed at staff will not be tolerated. If a member continues to disregard this rule then action will be taken that could result in banning.

This kind of proscriptive statement took no account of the lived cultures of the young people who were subject to these rules. The conventions of "cussing" and "wind-ups" were simply labelled as "bad" behaviour that led to ideologically unacceptable expressions of racism and sexism. This response, based on reaction and suppression, was also suggested by the National Union of Teachers in their booklet, *Combating racism in schools* (1981). As I will show, proscriptive anti-racism was fraught with difficulties when it came to dealing with incidents in the youth club. I want to make it clear that I still support the view that rules are necessary to state openly that racist abuse is unacceptable. However, the central point I stress is that proscription alone is not enough.

I have chosen four incidents to try and exemplify the complex set of processes that are in operation in these conflict situations. Although quantitative evidence of the frequency of this kind of abuse exists (Kelly 1987), little is known about the micro-dynamics of these encounters. All of the 32 incidents I recorded had unique characteristics. Here I refer to only five examples in order to try to understand the kinds of social forces that are manifested by particular episodes of racist name-calling.

Incident A. Cussing and race name-calling

This exchange took place during a general youth club night. It involved John, Bob, Dave, Debbie and myself. John (15 years old) and Debbie (16 years old) are brother and sister. Their mother is white English and their father is Jamaican. Bob (15 years old) is white English and Dave (15 years old) is white Irish. All the young people involved in this exchange are from Riverview Estate. My role in this interaction was as a youth worker. In many ways I was responsible for maintaining the rules of the centre. The incident begins with a comment about Dave's hair, which had been cut that day.

Bob: Alright Dave, who did it to you?

Dave: Leave it out Bob.

John: Don't mock the disabled.

[Dave walks away leaving Bob and John playing pool]

Bob: He ain't right with that hair.

John: I don't know what you're saying – with a face like that [referring to Bob's skin complexion because he was suffering from quite acute acne].

[Bob walked around the pool table and whispered something to John. John stopped playing pool, looked at Bob]

John: What did you say?

[John swung the pool cue at Bob. Les grabbed the pool cue and took it away from him. John then picked up a chair. Les stopped John from hitting Bob with the chair. Bob moved back, away from the pool table. There was more shouting. John's sister – Debbie – and another black girl ran over to the scuffle. Les was holding John, thereby stopping the fight]

John: You come near me and I'll kill you. Don't say anything about my sister or my colour right?

Bob: I didn't say anything about your sister.

Les: I think you've said enough Bob.

[John's sister and her friend took John over into the corner of the youth club. Bob stood alone by the Space Invader machine in the club. Telephone rang – Les went into the office to answer the call]

John [shouting at Bob from the corner of the club]: You wait until my brother hears about this, nobody says anything about my colour, right?

Bob: I never said nothing about your colour.

[John struggles to get away from Debbie]

Debbie: Leave it John, he's not worth it.

[Les comes out of the office and walks over to Bob]

Les: Bob, what did you say?

Bob: I never said nothing – all I said was "passage to India".

Les: That kind of comment will not be tolerated here, Bob.

Bob: So it is alright for him to cuss me out but I'm not allowed to cuss him back.

Les: No it's not alright but . . .

[John walks across the youth club floor looking at Bob and Les. He approaches, pointing at Bob]

John: I'm going now and when I come back I'm going to be with my brother.

[John storms out of the youth club]

Debbie [following John down the floor of the club with her friend]: Don't you call my brother a "Paki".

Bob: I didn't call him a "Paki".

Debbie: Yes you did, don't deny it.

Bob: But he's not a "Paki", is he?

[Debbie looked back, said nothing and walked over to the canteen, where she sat down with her friend. There was a pause. Bob stood alone by the Space Invader machine. The head of centre suggested that Les talk to Bob about the incident]

Les [walks over to Bob]: Bob do you want to come in the office?

[Bob looks back, says nothing and reluctantly follows Les into the office]

Les: What you said was wrong. You shouldn't bring John's colour into any argument.

Bob: But it is alright for him to say anything about my skin [his voice is trembling with intensity].

Les: No, it is not alright for him to say anything about your skin, but you've got to understand that it is not the same – and that you are putting him down because he's a different colour. You are judging him on his skin colour alone.

Bob: Alright, I'm sorry about that – I shouldn't have said anything about his colour but I was just try to get him back for cussing me.

This extract starts with both Bob and John "winding up" Dave about his new hair cut. Dave leaves and then John "cusses" Bob about his complexion. Bob's comment "passage to India" implies that John is of Asian descent, calling into play a racist construction – "Paki". Here Bob is trying to "cuss" John back by using racist discourse to hurt him as he has been hurt. After the initial moment of confrontation, the youth club divides into two camps – black and white. John, Debbie and her friend go to a corner of the youth club to calm John down. Bob stands alone close to the Space Invader machine and doesn't talk to anyone until I approach him.

In this case, Bob is using heavily loaded racist materials in order to hurt John. Although Bob did not call John "Paki" he evokes a discourse that constructs the British Asian population as a stigmatized group (Cohen 1988b: 28). John resists this process. He says pointedly, "Don't say anything about my sister or my colour". Here he is not simply rejecting the applicability of the term "Paki" but also rejecting Bob's right to give his colour meaning within a racist discourse.

Twice in the course of this exchange Bob complains that it is unfair that John can "cuss" him but he cannot cuss him back. Bob protested later on in the evening that it was "alright for John to say anything about me but if I say anything about him I am automatically in the wrong". The important thing to grasp is that Bob is using racist resources in a context where meaning and significance are often inverted and transformed, i.e. in duelling play. Bob repeatedly denies the repercussions of what he said: "I never said nothing about your colour"; "I never said nothing" ; "I didn't call him a Paki". But perhaps the most revealing exchange is between Bob and Debbie.

Debbie opens the exchange and warns Bob not to call her brother a "Paki". Bob denies calling him the name. Debbie repeats the accusation. Then Bob accepts and qualifies the accusation with "but he's not a 'Paki', is he?" Here Bob is justifying the "cuss" because it uses illegitimate terms of reference. He does not reject the use of a racist construction (i.e. the term "Paki") but simply maintains – in his defence – that in this case the term is not applicable.

There are two strands in Bob's account. The content of the cuss is supported by racist notions that are intended to hurt John. Bob denies that this cuss is meaningful because these terms of reference are illegitimate in John's case. This is the same style of discourse that is operated in both cussing and the wind-up. The important difference is that, in using racist materials, Bob has also violated peer common sense (i.e. "it is out of order to cuss someone's colour"), and this results in Bob being ostracized by all of the club members. My intervention shows the limitations of a proscriptive strategy. Initially I acted as a controlling force preventing retribution. Then, after the incident had been recounted by Bob, I reprimanded him in line with the policy of the club. In the dialogue that developed, I simply stated that comments about colour are illegitimate. All of my responses were located within a "politics of skin complexion", that is, it is unjust to judge people on skin colour. The meaning of race in its wider political sense and the racist constructions used (i.e. the term "Paki") were not touched upon. There are two important failings here: first, there was no understanding of the social process within which this incident took place, i.e. a cussing exchange; and, secondly, the racist linguistic materials that were being used were not identified. I am not suggesting that, if I had been able to work through this deconstruction, Bob's use of racist forms would have been "punctured by a superior logic" on the spot (Cohen 1988a), but, had I been able to identify the racism invoked in this incident, Bob might have entered into a critical dialogue. Instead, manifesto anti-racism was offered and, although Bob left the conversation grudgingly accepting "the rules", he was also ambivalent and confused.

Incident B. The chip shop mob and picture drawing

In the previous example a white youth used a phrase that evoked a racist construction in order to hurt a black young man in a cussing exchange. The following incident shows the variety of images of black people that are held by a young white man and represented in a series of sketches. The point I want to stress is that this white youth possesses a repertoire of images that symbolize black people and that can be strategically operated against a black peer.

This incident involved a group of young men who were members of the gang already referred to as the "chip shop mob". These young men were between the ages of 19 and 21 and were users of the club facilities until they were banned from involvement. Most of these youths were, at this point, still excluded from entry. Danny (18, white English parents) and Jack (19, white English parents) were both members of "the mob" but they were no longer banned from participation in the club. Lloyd (17, white English mother and Barbadian father) was not fully involved in the mob's activities but he was associated with them.

This particular evening Danny, Jack and Lloyd collected in the lower part of the club close to the canteen. I sat with them for about 20 minutes and during that time a succession of "wind-ups" took place along with general banter. It was at this point that Danny, who was particularly good at drawing, started to sketch a figure of a "skinhead". I was called away to work with a group of younger kids in the upper area of the club. For the rest of the evening I glanced over at the three boys but was unable to record any of the exchanges that took place. After the session finished I chatted with a white youth worker who was working in the canteen and she informed me that Jack was "winding Lloyd up" over something but she was not sure what the issue was. However, she noticed that all three young men left together.

Figure 4.1 Danny's drawing

On clearing up I picked up Danny's sketches; these included drawings of prize fighters and the drawing reproduced in Figure 4.1. Other sketches were scattered around the table, including the one reproduced in Figure 4.2. I asked the youth worker who had drawn this and she told me that Jack had drawn it when he was trying to "wind Lloyd up".

Danny's drawing represents three "urban stylers". Significantly, all these examples of working-class experience are male. Far left is a skinhead fully equipped with "bovver boots", swastika/National Front tattoos, shaved head and ripped jeans.[1] Next to the "Skin" is a dreadlocked "Rasta". Lastly, there is a posturing "Teddy Boy" with elbows quarter bent and wrists pointing down to the floor. His hair is styled in a DA (duck's arse) cut, he's wearing a drape jacket, bootlace neck tie and "brothel creeper" shoes and he is smoking a cigarette. Danny had also started to draw a fourth picture of a "punk" but this was unfinished and I have not included it here. These three characters are examples of masculine "urban cool" idealized in caricature.

The images do not directly reflect Danny's experiences or describe his peers. But they do give some insight into the many ways in which race is symbolized. The two white characters – Skin and Ted – have a different posture within this drawing. The Skin is more threatening. His shoulders are pushed back, his neck lunges forward and he brandishes a hammer ready to strike out at the reader. The Ted's pose is less confrontational. He is smoking a cigarette, hands hanging down,

Figure 4.2 Jack's drawing

surveying the scene. This is interesting when one thinks of the histories of Teddy Boy and skinhead movements that attacked and opposed the black presence in Britain with equal vehemence (Hebdige 1979: 44–5).

The "Rasta" is the only black figure. He is represented alongside and not necessarily in confrontation with the two white stylers positioned on either side of him. Although the Skin is threatening and aggressive, his bravado is not directed towards the Rasta. The Rasta is portrayed here as a prestigious masculine figure. On other occasions in the youth club I have heard white young men talking about "Dreads" in a positive way, expressing admiration for their style. I think this reflects the attraction that young whites – principally men – feel towards the variety of black cultural modes of resistance. Yet such attitudes towards black culture do not prohibit the use of racist representations. Young whites can switch from apparently positive evaluations of black images into the most crass use of racist rhetoric. In Figure 4.2 we see such a switch.

Jack, who on other occasions has talked about the "coolness" of Rastafari, draws a picture that includes a full armoury of racist symbols. Lloyd is represented as a "smelly, thick-lipped and bone-nosed primitive". It is a racist construct actualized within a "play" context, i.e. the wind-up. The raw materials of this "wind-up" bear the hallmarks of the heavy ideological load that constructs people of African descent as "primitive animals". This unabashed racist image is unbelievable even to Jack. Sartre (1965), in his classic essay on anti-Semitism, showed that extreme forms of bigotry are not even believed by the bigot. What has to be comprehended is the effect that the deployment of these images has. In this case, racism is being used to undermine Lloyd's position within the peer group.

I think this incident shows that white young people can both hold attitudes that construct "blackness" in a prestigious way while at the same time using crude forms of racist imagery. Multiple attitudes towards black people and their culture are held by white youth (Cochrane & Billig 1984) and used strategically against black peers.

Incident C. The interrogation and rebuttal of racist name-calling

In the two incidents discussed above, racist materials were used in the context of "cussing" and "wind-up" exchanges to hurt black peers or to lower their status. The incident reported here is one where racist name-calling is rebutted by a female peer group. The young people involved include: Esmin, 15, Turkish-Cypriot parents; Sarah, 15, Greek-Cypriot parents; Martin, 15, white English parents; Lynne, 15, white English parents. The girls gathered outside the youth club, talking, laughing and sharing stories. Martin walked towards the entrance. I sat close to the door of the youth club and watched the following exchange unfold.

Esmin [looks at Martin approaching]: Look what the cat's dragged in.

Martin: Shut up you Paki!

Esmin: Fuck off you racist bastard.

[Martin walks in the building and pays his money. Esmin, Lynne and Sarah follow Martin into the building]

Esmin: Who do you think you are?

Sarah: Yeah, Martin, Martin.

[Martin walks quickly upstairs]

Sarah [follows him upstairs then shouts upstairs]: You white shit!

Lynne [following Sarah]: Martin – white trash!

Here Martin uses the term "Paki" and applies it to Esmin. This name is illegitimate within the commonsense terms of this female peer group. Esmin rejects this racist definition. Then all three girls mobilize against Martin as they bring into play counter-insults. These three young women mobilize against an accusation made by a male peer. Here gender intersects race, constructing an alternative form of alliance. Esmin, Lynne and Sarah are united in opposition to Martin's racist "cuss". Interestingly, all three girls make reference to Martin's whiteness. Yet such names do not have the same currency in racist discourse and cannot hurt in the same way.

It is tempting to read, and applaud, this extract as an example of "folk" anti-racist praxis. However, there are two important factors to take into consideration. First, "Paki" is recognized within this adolescent meaning system to be illegitimate when applied to people of Greek or Turkish Cypriot origin. When I challenged Martin about the use of this term he dismissed my criticism by saying, "Well, she isn't a Paki is she!" This repeats the strategy adopted by Bob in incident A.

Secondly, this kind of mobilization is not always applied to people outside of this friendship group. I have recorded other accounts where at least two of the young women reported here made derogatory comments about Vietnamese (within the area) and Afro-Caribbeans (from outside the area) utilizing racist constructions. On one occasion I was sitting in Lynne's house watching television with her family and an image of a young black man walking across a street in South London appeared on the screen. She immediately launched into a tirade about "lazy", "ignorant", "violent", "criminal" blacks who lived in other areas.

Young white women expressed contradictory attitudes towards black people in the same way as did their male peers. However, the young women did not use racist insults as often. Over the six-month period when I monitored racist abuse in the club, 24 out of the 32 incidents were perpetrated by males. This can be explained in terms of the prevalence of "wind-up" play amongst young men. These masculine cultural practices acted as the platform on which racist name-calling was utilized. It would also be true to say that there were more young men using the youth club. This may have contributed to the higher frequency of racist name-calling amongst males but the youth club was not exclusively a masculine domain. It was clear that ritual expressions of masculinity, in the form of the type of play I have described, were directly connected with the operation of racist images.

Incident D. The disco

This incident took place during a disco held in the club (also referred to in Ch. 3). It was an extraordinary night, and during the course of the evening I am about to describe, an explosion of race consciousness manifested itself. The disco was full of incident but, with regard to the concerns of this chapter, two events are particularly apposite. It must also be added that the youth worker team was particularly concerned with heavy drinking amongst the user population. Drinking had been prohibited in the club but there had been a running battle between youth workers and users concerning enforcement of this rule.

The first incident involved the following people: Lisa, a 30-year-old white English youth worker who had lived on the estate for 20 years; her sister Karen, who was 15 and one of the youth club users; Alice, Lisa's and Karen's mother, who has lived on the estate for as long as it has been open; and Christine, a 33-year-old, Afro-Caribbean youth worker, who lives in a neighbouring part of the same borough. In the following extract I reproduce the account of this incident as it is written in my field notebook. This account is the composite product of a number of versions of this event by people who were present.

The disco started and as the kids came in it became apparent that some of them had been drinking. Around this time Thunderbird wine was a popular drink and it had been banned in the youth club. As the evening progressed it was rumoured that "puff", or marijuana, was also being smoked on the site.

The following incident occurred while I was on door duty. Christine caught Karen coming out of the girls' toilet and noticed the smell of marijuana. Christine reported this to the leader of the club and he called Karen into the office and told her that she had to leave because she had been caught smoking "puff". It was never ascertained whether Karen had been "smoking" or not.

On her way out Karen confronted Christine and said that she had "grassed her up". Karen was pointing and swearing, then lashed out at Christine (one account of this exchange reported that Karen was "cussing" Christine's colour). Christine struck her back. A knife (belonging to Karen) was either pulled out or fell out (this has been reported differently from informant to informant). The knife was then picked up by Scott and thrown out of the window. Karen stormed out of the club. On passing, her sister Lisa and I heard her call Lisa a "slag". Karen ran down the stairs past me and out of the club.

Ten minutes later Karen returned with her mother, Alice, and was accompanied by another woman whom I recognized, Pauline. Pauline hesitated in the entrance of the club. Alice turned around in the doorway and said to her, "What are you waiting for – whose side are you on? The bloody social workers?" Both women then entered the club. Alice asked me if I was the leader of the club. I said, "No". She demanded to see him. They both went upstairs with Karen. According to one account Alice demanded to see "the nigger who had clouted my Karen" as she walked up the stairs.

After another five minutes I was replaced on the door and went upstairs. As I reached the top of the stairs I saw Lisa crying and leaning over the banister looking down. I asked her what was wrong and she said: "My mother has disowned me! She told me never to call on her again. That's it, I've had enough, I'm getting away from this place." The disco had stopped, although the lights were still off.

Karen and Alice were talking to the leader of the centre and Christine. I stood next to Lisa. The young people in the centre were standing talking. I heard groups of friends recounting the incident. Karen and Alice left the club together.

The disco continued playing a combination of reggae, soul and hip hop.

Alice and her family are long-established residents of the estate. In addition to her two children – Karen and Lisa – involved in this incident she has three sons (one still living at home). Alice is renowned within the area for being hostile to "outsiders" and she voices her contempt for "social workers" on entering the youth club. This comment typifies the wider notion – collected in other accounts – that community and youth workers are those who "work on" rather than "work with" residents. Alice brings into play a notion of "sides" and boundaries. Significantly, the figure who is subjected to Alice's racism is both black and a youth worker. For Alice, Christine is an "outsider" not simply because she is "black" but also because she is a community professional. In this comment there are traces of a common claim that "liberal ideology" (the logic of the "red-rimmed glasses and woolly jumper brigade" – as one local woman put it) has one law for "them" (the "others", the "foreigners", the "darkies") and another for "us" (the "English", the "whites"). So, here we have an example where racism is in operation against a black professional. Its meaning therefore has to be located in the exchanges, attitudes and resentments that this working-class woman has for "caring professionals". It is not simply anti-black but also contra the "superior logic" (Cohen 1988a) of multiculturalism that in this case is given expression in the club. I am not suggesting that somehow racist constructions are justified because of the nature of class oppression. I am seeking to show that, as in this example, racism is not necessarily intra-class antagonism: rather, it is brandished as a weapon to counter the professional authority of youth workers.

A further point I want to make about this extract is the effect that family dynamics have on the reproduction of racism. Significantly, Karen seemed to be assuming the voice of her mother in this conflict, by leaving the club to collect her. Alice, on arrival, then adopts racist rhetoric in the process of acting as the representative of her daughter. The congruence between Karen's and Alice's utilization of such a rhetoric suggests that in this case racist ideology has been transported from one generation to another. However, this process is neither simple nor uncontested within the family.

Whereas Karen calls into play her mother's "voice", Lisa on the other hand challenges racism, for which she is subsequently ostracized. Within the relationships between these three women, boundaries are being drawn to the point where Lisa's refusal to rally behind her sister prompts her mother to disown her. This is not simply indicative of Lisa's occupational status in the youth club. On a subsequent occasion during an interview, Lisa told me about the "battles" she had in her family:

> Well, it always been like a running battle with my mum and dad. I've always had black friends and – like when we was kids we all mucked in together. I used to – and still go to my black friends' reggae parties and they come to my house. But it's like everybody looks on to everybody else in this place [meaning the estate]. And I've – I mean last week my oldest daughter Nicola [who is 11] has got her first pretend boyfriend – you know little Anthony [who is a black child]. She came to me crying last week saying that one of the kids had called her [she lowers the volume of her voice] a "nigger lover". I mean where do kids hear that stuff from – you know what I mean? I don't mind who she brings home but I don't want her to have to face that all her life. I just want to get out of here and get my kids away. Like my mum said that she would disown me, and my sister still doesn't speak to me. But it's like this job and the courses I've been going on have opened my eyes to things. Not just the way I think about things but also what I can do. It's like all you see on this estate is women and babies. I don't want to be like my mother.

Here Lisa is obviously voicing her discontent with the "inherited wisdom" of her family. It is hard to deduce the formative experiences that have facilitated the interruption of racist ideas. She mentions the significance of close friends and maintains that she does not want to be like her mother. Even so, she accepts the existence of racism but wants to escape it. In the account she gives of her child who is berated for being a "nigger lover", her solution is to get away from the situation (Riverview context) and the possibility of this recurring (the likelihood of Nicola having a black boyfriend). Her answer to the experience of racism and the personal pain it has caused within her family is to "get away", to go to a place where she will not have to deal with those "things".

An important issue is raised when running through the logic of Lisa's desire to "escape". Is it simply that Lisa wants to get away from a situation that is racist, or does she want to move to a place where the manifestation of racism is made problematic by the resistance of black people? Although the answer to the question in Lisa's individual case is of limited importance, the broader issue highlighted here is that, while racism threatens the black presence in Britain (CCCS 1982), black people's resistance to it questions the very logic that seeks to circumscribe their existence. The nature of inter-racial contact – in Lisa's case her friends and colleagues – prohibits a simple reproduction of racism. Thus, the interactional politics of contact, although unable to forge a programme of its own, interrogates the meaning of racism through the experiences whites are forced to go through (Jones 1988).

Clearly, this abstract shows that racist ideas are not reproduced and passed on from parents to children in any simple way. In Lisa's case black friendship networks and alternative ideologies on "race" made available through her training as a youth worker have pulled her away from the views circulated within her family. She does not confine her comment only to racism, but also refers to gender and class and professes the desire to do more than what is expected of a working-class woman. She says, pointedly, "I don't want to be like my mother".

Incident E. The sound system incident

As the evening at the disco drew to a close another incident occurred, this time around the sound system. The four youngsters involved this time were the three boys running the sound system – John, 15, who has a white English mother and a Jamaican father (and who was the DJ); Tony, 19, who is black British of Jamaican parents and lives on a neighbouring estate; and Scott, 15, who is white English and lives in Riverview – and Pigsie, a 15-year-old, white English boy who lives on the estate.

John was having problems with the turntables. Scott and John were trying to fix the hi-fi and Tony was standing behind them. Pigsie walked up to the sound system.

Pigsie: Hurry up and turn the record over you black bastard
[laughing, expecting John and Scott to join in].

[All four boys stop. There is a pause]

Tony [in marked Creole]: Gwaan likkle yout [Go away little boy]!
[Stares at Pigsie]

Scott: I think you'd better go Pigsie!

[Pigsie turned around and walked away from the sound system]

The disco ended about half an hour after this incident.

Scott and John recounted the incident to me in the office while
packing the sound system equipment away. Scott said repeatedly that
"Pigsie was out of order. It's out of order saying anything about someone's colour." John repeated this statement. In the post-session staff
meeting, Brian – a black youth worker – reported that he had spoken
to Pigsie after the meeting and that Pigsie had said: "I'm sorry I said
that. I didn't mean anything by it. I've known John all my life, for
years – it didn't make no difference. I don't know why I said that."

Pigsie used a racist insult in what he regards as a play context. At
the very end of the evening he protested this to Brian. So, for Pigsie,
the insult did not denote what it stands for in usual usage. On many
other occasions John, Pigsie and Scott have "played with" race concepts during cussing and wind-up exchanges. On one occasion the
three boys took on inverted racial roles, i.e. John articulated crude
white racist rhetoric while Pigsie and Scott accused him of being a
member of the National Front. This phenomenon has also been reported by Roger Hewitt (1986) in his analysis of inter-racial friendship within this area. Hewitt maintains that spectacular inversions of
this kind "seek to acknowledge and deal with its [racism's] undeniable presence whilst acting out the negation of its effects" (Hewitt
1986: 238).

Pigsie claims that "race" is irrelevant to him, but this attempt to
subvert racist meanings by making them the subject of "play" is con-
founded partly by the sheer prevalence of racist incidents during the
disco and, secondly, by the fact that the role Pigsie takes on is
uninverted. Pigsie is white, and by using racist language he adopts a
racist position and in doing so acknowledges the presence of racist
abuse within their social world. He attempts to deny the applicability
of racism in his friendship by placing it outside of his immediate circle
of friends. However, the degree of "fit" between Pigsie's whiteness

and his use of racist language makes the altered "play" meaning impossible to sustain.

This instance shows the crucial element of agreement within the process of defining "play" meanings. Although Pigsie was a good friend of John's, he was unknown to Tony. Tony uses Creole not only to check Pigsie's racist posturing but also symbolically to counter Pigsie's "race talk" via the language of resistance. There is no agreement to banish "race" as a meaningful register, for the racism that such comments "stand for" cannot be successfully subverted in this context. Significantly, John and Scott condemn Pigsie's actions as being "out of order" when reflecting on the incident. In doing so they define the terms of their friendship but also repair the volatile cultural space in which their friendship exists.

Conclusion

The racist episodes that I have described here have to be understood in the particular context of white working-class life in South London. Although the discourses that young white people use are connected to the racist formulae that are circulated within the parent culture, they cannot be simply reduced to them. The racism that developed in relation to the material conditions of working-class London during the 1970s and early 1980s (Phizacklea & Miles 1980) has not been uniformly transmitted to young whites growing up in this area. Important dialogues take place within this adolescent community, creating conditions where a limited form of de-racialization is achieved. Even so, outbreaks of racial abuse continued to occur.

In all of these incidents racist names are used by young whites, despite the proscriptive rules of the centre and the de-racialized common sense of the young people themselves. There are two important points to emphasize. First, racist constructs are used as strategic resources. Young whites do not utilize racist notions in total or unitary ways. In this sense the racial consciousness of white young people is highly fractured and ambiguous. The relationships that young whites share with their black peers are in direct opposition to the use of racist rhetoric because of the divisive potential of "race" as a social parameter. It is in "cussing" and "wind-up" situations that the relationship between black and white youth is most vulnerable. Any attempt to interrupt racism must be informed by an understanding of the dynamics of these rituals. Secondly, the racial common sense of young whites exhibits a multiplicity of race symbolisms that permits positive evaluations of black people to coexist alongside crude racist imagery (Billig et al. 1988). In the context of name-calling this leads to the use of racist language followed by a denial that these words mean what they stand for, i.e. "But it don't mean nothin'."

It is not enough to label duelling play as "bad behaviour" and prohibit it in the hope that this will stop racist abuse. The wider functions that this play performs are important and central to the experience of young people in this area. The goal should be to articulate these rituals with alternative forms of representation (Cohen 1988a). This does not mean replacing negative stereotypes of black people with positive ones, but rather leading young whites to "resist the captivation of any medium or message which tells them that they can become only what they already are" (Cohen 1989: 14). I am not suggesting a kind of "psychic surgery" where racist ideas are removed by ideological incision. As I have already shown, there are elements within the experience of white young people that oppose, or are at least in conflict with, the use of racist language. Anti-racist strategies must make use of progressive "folk" practices that are already in place – like the existence of a partially de-racialized common sense – in order to develop a grounded programme for intervention (Macdonald et al. 1989, Back 1990).

Before moving on to discuss the second neighbourhood within this study I want to pull together some of the major findings I have referred to in this section. In Riverview, the expression of racism is closely connected with the management of this housing estate as an urban resource. A relatively affluent working-class population was allocated this unit of housing through discriminatory housing procedures. With the change in allocation criteria and the shift in management of the estate to the local borough, new populations were settled in this area, some of which included black people and Vietnamese refugees. Thus racist reactions identified in the adult population have to be viewed in terms of how working-class people react to and make meaningful their economic and social position. Racism became a way of explaining the declining housing conditions by correlating these changes with the presence of "black" and "yellow" people. Here discourses on community provide the terms in which racism is articulated. The nature of "the community" was invested with racial meanings. In the "golden age", the community was almost exclusively white, while the "death of the community" is signalled by the settlement of black people and refugees from Vietnam. The local housing economy provides a basis for local racism.

Despite the prevalence of racist explanations in the locality, young people do not passively reproduce the ideologies of their parents. In the adolescent community, an inclusive localism is formulated where it is wrong to exclude people on the basis of colour. Here a syncretic working-class youth culture develops that is neither black nor white but somehow a celebration of shared experiences. This constitutes a volatile working-class ethnicity that draws on a rich mixture of South London, African American and Caribbean cultural symbols.

The culture that black and white young people share in Riverview has not led to the complete rejection of racism. Incidents of racist name-calling recur, where racism is used as a strategic resource by white young people against black peers. Also, the construction of black insiders as locals does not prohibit the racist identification of black young people from other areas. In addition, young people of Vietnamese origin are excluded from the cultural dialogues going on between black and white youth.

The three chapters viewed together outline the ambiguous social ground inhabited by young people in this area. It is characterized by contingent forms of inclusion and harmony juxtaposed with differentiation, exclusion and racism. The reality of ethnic relations in this area is extremely complicated and presents at one moment a glimpse of racial harmony, and, in the next, the most crass and brutal expressions of popular racism.

PART II

Transculturalism and the politics of dialogue

CHAPTER 5

"Our area": community, resistance and multiculture

Introduction

In this chapter I introduce the discussion of adolescent interrelations in Southgate by describing the social composition of the area and the contexts in which "community" is defined. Although Southgate is only a short distance from the area I have already discussed, there are some striking contrasts between the two districts, for, unlike Riverview, there is a strong and established black cultural presence. This manifests itself at all levels, including the stocking of Caribbean food in the shops, black churches, and the rhythms of black music that drift out from the pubs and youth clubs. The relative strength of the black presence has meant that important negotiations have taken place here, and in many respects the expression of openly racist behaviour from fellow residents has been muted. However, the area is subjected to a racist construction from outside, to surveillance from the police and to dubious housing allocation procedures.

It is important to comprehend analytically the contours of the "urban imagination" in order to allow the discussion of the ways in which the residents of cities socially construct their world. It is to this project that Manuel Castells has devoted his later work, in recognition of the shortcomings of his earlier critique of urban sociology:

> As a result [of the separation of "grand theory"] we are left with urban systems separated from personal experiences; with structures without actors, and actors without structures; with cities without citizens, and citizens without cities. (Castells 1983: xvi)

Hijacking Castells' phrase, there is no *one* field of reality that can be termed urban (Castells 1977: 6), but urban communities are actively created, imagined and projected on to the cityscape. In short, urban space constitutes a signifying system. I employed this approach in the discussion of the symbolic nature of "community" in Riverview. It is to the quality of this system within Southgate that I now turn.

"Creating the ghetto": mass housing and the Southgate development

The 1981 census material shows that 23 per cent of the people living in Southgate were born in the New Commonwealth (Appendix 2). Of this figure, 70 per cent were from the Caribbean and a further 16 per cent from Africa. The proportion of black people recorded living here is nearly three times the figure for Riverview (8.6 per cent) and shows clearly the contrasting character of the two areas. It is important to realize that this figure does not include British-born black people. Taking into consideration the pattern of housing of young black people in this area, the black population for this district is probably somewhere between 30 per cent and 50 per cent. The ethnic breakdown found in the 1981 census material also shows a significant population of Mediterranean origin (Turkish and Greek Cypriots) and relatively small numbers of people of Indian origin. An important development during the 1980s was the settlement of Vietnamese refugees in the area and I have already mentioned this in relation to Riverview. However, my impression is that fewer refugees were housed in the Southgate area. Certainly their presence was not nearly as visible as in Riverview at the time the research was conducted.

In contrast to the Riverview development, Southgate was not invested with the community aesthetics I described earlier (see Ch. 2). Southgate was built to house as many people as cheaply as possible.[1] The estate was completed in the 1970s, but as early as April 1969, when the first blocks were opened, inadequacies in design and provision were already clear. The local newspaper reported:

> The first stage of Southgate's new showpiece estate was ceremoniously handed over to the Council on Saturday . . . together with a petition from 30 worried tenants . . . The parents, who were moved into the first blocks only a month

ago, are demanding a fence to stop their children from dashing across the road.

Unlike Riverview, the estate was owned by the borough council and the rents for flats on this estate were considerably lower. There was also an open commitment to re-house people who had lived in the area during the pre-war period. It was hoped that resettlement of former residents would foster the community spirit thought to have existed previously in working-class districts in the borough. The first residents were predominantly white and working class, but a significant population of black people was housed here from the very beginning. Erwin, a black British man, whose parents are of Jamaican origin, remembers being a child on the estate:

> At the time when me and my mum and dad first lived on the estate it was still being developed, we got moved into one of the low-rise blocks. It was a mixture of black and white but even so as it being a mixture it was working-class low life white people and working-class low life black people.

In Southgate there was an ease of access to housing and, unlike Riverview, no process of selection was operated: people were simply housed according to need.

In addition to ease of access, it was relatively easy to move around within the estate because of an exchange scheme that was in operation from the mid-1970s onwards. Debbie, a resident on the estate from 1978, explains:

> In the beginning they wasn't putting families into the tower blocks. It was quite easy in those days to get out, especially if you had a child. There was quite a lot of choice because we had a transfer scheme actually on the estate.

A tenants' organization was established during the 1970s but it was poorly patronized by the residents. It was re-formed in 1978 and its work was principally around campaigns relating to conditions on the estate. The borough housing stock was rife with design problems. The Tenants' Association campaigned on a whole range of issues, from asbestos found within the flats to infestations of cockroaches. Debbie, a 35-year-old white woman who was chairperson of the Tenants' Association at the time of this interview, described the campaigns:

> We had infestations of bed bugs just before I moved in and then all the towers had cockroaches. And we had to have a big campaign; it was the first thing that the Tenants' Association did, was to have a big campaign against the cockroaches. Some blocks had Pharaoh's Ants. There had been a Tenants' Association on the estate from when it was first built but it sort of declined. The new Tenants' Association was formed largely due to the impetus of community workers that were coming onto the estate. I was involved with that from the beginning.

Community workers instigated the Tenants' Association but the condition of the housing stock and the growing poverty in the area meant that there were ample issues to campaign on. Debbie again:

> Well, we threatened the council with legal action. We took a load of tenants along to the District Housing Committee meeting, and we emptied the cockroaches onto the table, which didn't please the councillor very much.

The Tenants' Association achieved some major successes but it was weakened by unsustained participation generally, and the lack of black involvement in particular. In the following extract Erwin talks about his reservations:

> The community spirit on the estate is very poor because nobody wants to talk to anybody. I mean a few tenants will talk to other tenants and that's about it, they won't go any further. They'll have the Tenants' Association meetings and you'll get, I don't know, maybe ten tenants. I am actually not on the Tenants' Association. I've been asked to join it but I would be a token because basically the Tenants' Association is a white association.

During the research period the tenants' organization was operational, yet despite the undoubted need Southgate was conspicuously short of resources.[2]

Southgate became a "hard to let" estate open to those who were willing to live there, as Debbie comments:

This estate has been a "dumping ground" for a long time. I mean eight, nine years ago when I got offered a place, they [the council] said to me, "Well if you want a place immediately you can have Southgate, otherwise you will have to wait a couple of years."

In the 1980s those in greatest need were being allocated premises on the estate. In particular, young black people whose parents had once lived in the area and moved away were being housed back in the environment of their youth. Cynthia, a 27-year-old youth worker of Jamaican origin, explained how the pattern of housing allocation was informed by stereotyped ideas about the "black community":

You see the council put all black people down Southgate because they assume we want to get a community spirit going – they assume that Jamaica is like that, they don't understand that there is as much diversity within the black community as there is within the whites . . . the only advantage that I can see coming out of their ignorance is that there could be a move for unity, awareness . . . the unification of black people. The funny thing that they [the authorities] forget that it is not a question of "Oh well, let's go and move to Southgate because everybody down there is black" . . . or anything like that. It is nothing to do with freedom of choice. The choice is between being in poor housing where you know there are only a few black people and there is a reputation of racial harassment or poor housing where at least you know it's safe to walk the streets.

Erwin, quoted earlier, explains his motivation for accepting a flat on Southgate:

Racial problems are not so much on Southgate. When I was livin' on the other side of the borough then there was racial arguments . . . My brother lived in that area and he had to be moved out because we had National Front sprayed on our door. I mean we had a fear, we were literally frightened to go home because we didn't know what was happening, we didn't know if there was going to be somebody waiting for us. We were burgled by the NF, they poured ink all over the carpet – it was a cream carpet and they poured red ink all over the house sort a thing. I mean that is basically why we moved out. I don't find much of the racial problems now because I think the area is too dominantly black. I mean out of the 74 houses in my block, 15 to 20 people are white, the rest are all black. I think I know of two Asian families living in the block. The Asian families, they don't come out of their house.[3]

The area has been a site where black people feel that because of their numerical preponderance there is only a limited threat of racism and racial attack. In a study commissioned by the borough on racial harassment it was shown that the Afro-Caribbean residents surveyed had positive views on the nature of the area and race relations generally: "The Afro-Caribbean sample [were] the most sanguine about race relations, the least likely to accept that racial harassment occurred on their estates and the most likely to say that, if it happened at all, its incidence was decreasing."[4]

Although it is tempting to become over-enthusiastic about the apparent confidence that black people had in the area with regard to overt racism, it must be kept in mind that the poverty that sections of the population experience and their poor housing conditions meant that Southgate was far from being an "inner-city Eden". In the 1980s the area was an ethnically heterogeneous space, where mainly young people lived and suffered considerable hardship.[5]

"A no-go area": the criminalization of Southgate

Southgate is characterized in adjacent council estates, and specifically in Riverview, as a "no-go area" where crime is prevalent. There exists in fact a process of reciprocal folk classification in these areas: Riverview is viewed by black and white people alike to be an area where black people should not go because of the intensity of street racism; Southgate is seen as being "off limits" to white people because of the prevalence of mugging and drug-related crimes. The result is a local taxonomy that divides the South London landscape into safe and unsafe areas for black and white people respectively.

There are important semantic connections in the discourse on race, crime and community in which the mention of crime can sometimes allude to "race" without directly mentioning black people. For example, during my fieldwork period I was also employed as a youth worker. In the course of this work I developed a video project that used equipment from a neighbouring college. On one occasion I went to pick up the equipment from the Audio Visual Department and the white male technician, who lived in a neighbouring district, asked me where I was going that night. I told him that I was heading down to Southgate to work with some young people in the youth club. He knew the name of the youth club and he said, "Oh you should have some fun down there!" I asked him how he knew the club. He replied, " . . . drugs!" He did not have to mention that this was a "black" youth club to signify the connection between black people and drugs. Thus the notion of drugs and deviancy is invested with racial meanings. A similar process is in operation when it comes to street crime.

During the course of the fieldwork I had a tax disc stolen from the small motorcycle I rode at the time. The theft took place in Southgate. I reported the incident to the neighbourhood security patrol and, before I had a chance to tell them all the information I had, they replied, "Black guys!" even though a white young man with dark hair had been seen tampering with my bike 25 minutes before I found that the disc was missing. In this situation the interconnections between crime, race and community operate in such a way that invoking one element connotes the other two. As a result, within this local racialized discourse the mention of crime evokes a geographical area (Southgate) and a group of actors (black people, principally young men).[6]

The local criminalization of the district and the black citizens of the area is also reinforced by the way in which the area is reported in the local and national media. This process is consistent with the criminalization of black people in a national context (Hall et al. 1978, Gilroy 1982a, 1987, Gilroy & Sim 1985). Such ideological work results in the definition of a "located and situated black crime, geographically and ethnically, as particular to black youth in the inner city ghettos" (Hall et al. 1978: 329). Gilroy shows that the racialization of "black crime" has wider consequences (Gilroy 1987: 76). Black criminality is constructed to "prove" that black communities are incompatible with civilization, where civilization is viewed as intrinsic to the "British way of life". Thus, what I am reporting from this particular locality is consistent with the wider ideological construction of crime at a political level.

There are at least two sites for the criminalization of black people within the borough, namely the local criminalization of the area and the wider context of national political discourses on race. Although there exists no linear relationship of cause and effect, the two systems of meaning and communication seem to feed off one another, sometimes overlapping to such a degree that it is impossible to separate what is a local construct and what is a media formulation.[7]

Whether constructed locally or by the national press, Southgate is defined from outside as an area of typical urban malaise, high levels of unemployment, racial conflicts, street crime and drug abuse. Its tower blocks and mass housing form a perfect backdrop for these constructions and meanings. The power of these discourses is that they make almost any story of "social degradation" within the area believable.[8] As one young black person put it: "You could say almost anything about The Ghetto and people would believe you." It is the question of what is believable and believed that I want to discuss in this chapter.

The image of the estate as a dangerous focus of criminality is rejected by the residents of the estate. Debbie, quoted earlier, comments:

> Well, everybody says that [street crime and mugging is prevalent], and I've got a friend who has been mugged three times, but I've walked through the estate and I've been coming home late at night and nothing ever happened to me ... I think that certain sections of the community talk about it as being a big problem – that is mostly middle-aged white people who read the Daily Mail, you know.

The construction of the estate from outside as a criminal area is embraced by some of the residents I have interviewed, and I will return to this, but, for Debbie, the idea of her son having black friends and growing up within this area is seen to be an advantage:

> I think it is a positive advantage to have him mix with people from a lot of different cultural backgrounds and races and things, and I think he'll get a lot out of it. He's certainly a lot

more tolerant of people than I was at his age . . . I mean when I look around at other estates I am glad that he will have a lot of black friends. Look at the hard drugs and "scag" in the white areas and the house-breaking and crime they get into.

Debbie herself had had close friendships with black young people in her youth and her experience is important because it belies the assumption that whites in districts such as Southgate are inevitably antagonistic towards black people in general. Clearly, physical proximity and the sharing of experience are a powerful influence on the kinds of ideas held on "race".

In the following quote, Debbie describes the limited degree of racial antagonism within the area and shows her experience of witnessing the way the police treat young black people:

The only trouble that does happen on the estate is between rival black factions and that isn't much . . . I mean there are several families of white crooks, I think most of them are locked up now, but people don't think about that – they think, "Ooh, a black area, there must be a lot of muggings." But there has been very little aggression in the pub between whites and blacks and certainly the few times there have been police raids [on the pub] white people have been just as angry about it as black people, who were largely the people being arrested and put up against the wall. There were black and white people saying "What the bloody 'ell do you think you are doing?"

Experiences such as this are important when attempting to understand the way in which communities are defined within the area. For Debbie, the collective rejection of racism and police harassment is integral to what she sees as attacks on *her* community. As I will show in what follows, important notions of "community" are formulated around a collective rejection of racism. This is also clear in this next extract, which documents her reaction to, and memory of, the New Cross fire, in which a number of young people from Southgate were killed.

I remember the New Cross fire because I was quite friendly with the people who lost kids in that fire and I knew quite a few of the kids . . . I felt that quite personally, I was really upset by that. I went on the march and things. I remember it rained. I got soaked to the skin . . . that actually did a lot, I think, to bring the "community" around here together. There was a terrific feeling in the pub and on the estate, where a lot of the bereaved families drank, and people were coming up and saying "I've heard about your loss". That [event] really sort of brought people together quite a lot. Both white and black people think a lot of the kids who died.

The issue of the effects of white knowledge of the black experience of racism is something that I will address in the next chapter. It is sufficient here to make the point that these examples show quite clearly that the proximity of white people to these events is formative and results in an understanding of the meanings and forms of racial injustice. This was also recognized by black people who live in the area.

However, for black people living in the area it was also clear that whites had a choice not to associate with black people and thereby avoid police harassment. Erwin, whom I mentioned earlier, states this clearly in the following extract:

It's like there is a guy who lives downstairs from me. He's basically just the same as all of his friends and all of his friends are black. His mum gets on with black people in the area. I mean he is just the same as the black guys he goes around with. In fact he gets in trouble with the police more than his black friends. The police can actually look at him and the police in Southgate police station actually know his name, you know what I mean, they walk down the road and . . . they say "Alright Barry?" Whereas the police aren't intelligent enough to be able to recognize one black person from another. I mean where he stands out is because he is with the black people and he does what they do. When his mates get arrested for being black he gets arrested with them. There are not many white people living round there that are oppressed in the way black people are oppressed. I mean if Barry wanted to he could bring himself up from there because he is white and his black friends would find it harder to bring himself up from that position.

The important point to stress here is that the shared experience of police racism is acknowledged at the same time as the prevalence of racism in determining different life chances for black and white young people is recognized.

"The area": discourses on locality

In this section I want to look in more detail at the ways in which social relationships and notions of community are talked about in this area. No single discourse monopolizes the meaning of community in this district. The most important point that I want to make is that discourses on community have an attendant "racial" agenda. In this sense people talk about race and racism *through* the language of community. In the following discussion I outline the spectrum of community discourses that were articulated in qualitative interviews with adults from the area.

The "our area" semantic system

I am going to identify two contrasting ways in which "community" is made meaningful within Southgate. Here "community" consists of a semantic system that is composed of identifiable discourses. The first I call "our area" system, which is composed of two discursive elements, the first of which I refer to as the "harmony discourse".

The harmony discourse
In accounts of living in the area offered by black and white people a common claim is that the local "community" is free of racial tension and that harmonious relations exist between its various parts. These assertions are made by black and white people with striking regularity. This notion is utilized most often within Southgate but it has also appeared to a limited extent within Riverview (see Ch. 2). In the following account a black young man describes this multiculturalist ethos:

> Funnily enough over the years it has grown into a family thing, white, black, all races. I see myself as Southgate to tell you the truth. And I know so many things, well I know things I shouldn't know. It just doesn't seem to matter any more

> down here, maybe in a different area, but down here every-
> one is integrated and mixed. I don't even think of colour, the
> way we integrate and mix and I know everyone. I could talk
> the most cockney you'd think that I was a white man standing
> the other side, or I could talk Jamaican and you wouldn't un-
> derstand a word that I said, you know what I mean, so I fit in
> both worlds. I fit in perfect. There is no racist stuff, I want no-
> thing to do with colour. (Michael, 24, Jamaican parentage)

Michael characterizes Southgate as an area where everyone gets
along regardless of colour. He offers himself as a personification of
this area, "I am Southgate", a place where people can move in and out
of different kinds of self-presentation. One gets the impression that
Michael views the kinds of cultural differences that are found in
Southgate as languages that he speaks and can slip in and out of at
will. In short, he views them as part of his "self" or "selves". This
kind of account is often repeated by white informants who feel that
they can cross the same cultural planes.

It is important to keep in mind that this account has been offered
to a white audience – the interviewer – and it is hard to monitor the
extent to which this influences the account. However, I am sure that
Michael would offer the same version to a white peer in the area, and
that is exactly the point, i.e. this discourse offers a common ground
that opens and crosses lines of social differentiation (in Michael's
terms between black and white) within this particular context.

The harmony discourse thus acts as a resource that banishes "racial things" from everyday experience, allowing the kinds of inter-
racial friendship that are prevalent in Southgate. Consider this
comment by a 13-year-old black young woman:

> Well it doesn't matter what colour you are. I mean I've got
> white friends and black friends, and Chinese friends – we all
> listen to the same music and do the same things and we all live
> in this area, we don't deal with them things. All the people in
> the area feel the same and we're safe – you know what I mean.

In many ways it does not matter if the assertion that is being made in
this discourse is true or not, because within it is an expression of the
ways in which difference, or the lack of it, is understood and talked
about.

112

Integral to this discourse is the rejection of racism as defined within this district. In particular, racial chauvinism is pushed back through a black and white consensus. There is a question here of how racism is being defined. Michael identifies the possibility of black and white racism: "I do know people obviously – black and white – who are racist. I just stay away from them." It is important to be clear that Michael is talking about prejudice. In other words, comparable racialized discourses do not exist for white people, and thus racialized meanings are not symmetrical. However, it is important to acknowledge that definitions of racism as "symmetrical" (i.e. black and white prejudice) have currency within the area.

The important point to grasp is that, within the notion of harmony discourse, locality is invested with meanings that starkly contrast with those projected at it from outside. Debbie comments:

> There are some [inter-racial conflicts], but it is not as bad as you'd expect. By and large people tend to get on quite well. I think it is surprising how well people get on on this estate. I mean you hear about riots on Broadwater Farm and my mum says [shrill voice], "I don't know how you can bear to live on that estate – you're going to be another Broadwater Farm," and I am reasonably certain that it won't happen down here because things really do seem to tick along quite smoothly and there hasn't been a lot of conflict.

The black community discourse
In other contexts, and sometimes alongside harmony discourse, an additional formula is utilized that marks the borough as a "black area", an account that sees the area as the site of black struggles and institutions, a place where black people have fought to make something of their own. This construct is also invested with a notion of black political agency[9] and locates black resistance to racism and self-affirmation in this particular area. Within the discourse, black people lay claim to the area vis-à-vis other discursively constructed social spaces. As Hall says about young black people in London, "They look as if they own the territory. Somehow, they too, in spite of everything, are centred in place" (Hall 1987: 44). This notion of centring is expressed in what I call black community discourse.

Black community discourse is utilized not as an alternative to harmony discourse, but as a way to particularize black experiences. In this next extract, Louise, 19 years old and of Jamaican parentage, shows how these images of the area are operated. She starts off by describing the nature of inter-racial relations in Southgate:

> People get on pretty well in this area and in a way it is like a family but you always get the ones who lock themselves in-doors case they get [with emphasis] mugged by the demons who wander round outside. But this area is really known as a black area, you know what I mean? In many ways it is be-cause you couldn't buy mango and plantain and Caribbean foods in other areas. I suppose black people have made their own way and this happened to be the place they did it.

In this extract Louise starts by introducing the harmony discourse and then refines that particular notion to a set of ideas that locate black struggles in this area. The importance of this discourse is that it can be operated as a way of defining a social constituency and thereby stimulating political action. The cultural institutions of black London operate as what Paul Gilroy has called an "alternative public sphere" (Gilroy 1987: 223) where this discourse can be generated and repro-duced (see Ch. 8).

The discourse sets black experiences in geographic space. Erwin describes this metonomic process of claiming:

> I mean there are areas that you can mention and you just place them out to be black areas. I mean Lambeth, when somebody mentions Lambeth, Lambeth is a black area. If somebody mentions Southgate, Southgate is a black area.

This is completely distinct from the process of labelling and the racist criminalization imposed on the area discussed earlier. The contrast is simply that they emerge from different sites. Black community dis-course is produced within the institutions of black London, and the process of criminalization of black people is directed at this commu-nity from outside.[10]

Harmony and black community discourses are mutually reinforc-ing. This relationship generates what I refer to as an "our area" se-mantic system. I have represented these relationships in Figure 5.1.

This diagram depicts the mutually reinforcing elements in this sys-tem. The acknowledgement and rejection of racism found within

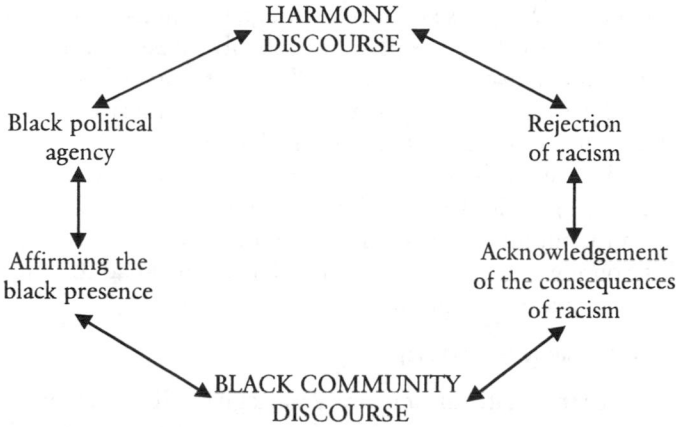

Figure 5.1 The "our area" semantic system

harmony discourse allow the expression of black community discourse outside any notion of racial conflict and exclusion. White people can utilize this discourse, which simultaneously allows the rejection of racism and alliances with black people *and* the legitimacy of black people's claim to the area and their cultural institutions. For black people, harmony discourse allows the area to be defined as free of racial antagonisms. Also "blackness" is recognized as a legitimate identity. In short, this system allows the rejection of "race" as a product of racist discourse, and at the same time allows the construction of a community based on racial metaphors (i.e. blackness) free of racism.

The "white flight" semantic system

Yet the black presence is not universally accepted in accounts of white people who live in this area. I encountered what I have previously referred to as the "white flight" semantic system less often in this area than in Riverview, but the presence of these formulations should still be acknowledged. In this system the area is characterized as a growing black space and defines a set of consequences for white people.

Intrinsic to this discourse is an attempt to pathologize the black presence. We see this in operation in the following account from a 25-year-old white man of French and English parentage called Phillip:

Southgate? Well, it is no more than a ghetto. In fact, they call it The Ghetto. Now the place is probably 60 per cent black, but in about five or ten years it'll end up somewhere near 80–90 per cent. Everybody who lives there wants to get out. People are getting up to their eyes in debt to get off the estate. I lived there for three years. The bloke next door was a complete animal. He had dreadlocks and everything. I am not racialist, but the man lived like an animal. I am not kidding – his house was full of cockroaches. The council had to fumigate the place several times.

[Later in the same interview]

I can see the estate turning into a black ghetto. Didn't you see it on the telly the other night? Postmen getting mugged. They are mugging the postmen to get at the giros, do you believe that? How low can you get? I am not racist, but mugging is a black problem. You look at the amount of muggings and most of them are black. I am not saying that whites don't get involved in crime, but that's mainly break-ins. What riles me is that people just won't do anything. I know it sounds racist but it ain't right.

Here we see "race" being brought into play as a significant marker, with the result that black people are blamed for bringing the area down.[11] Also, mugging is referred to as a "black problem", reproducing a common strategy that criminalizes young black people. Equally, break-ins are also racialized and attributed to white young people. Phillip is characterizing the growing presence of black people as the prime reason for his motivation to move out of the area. There exists a process of elision between individual and collective racialized characteristics. If, for example, I had accused Phillip of suggesting that all black people "live like animals", he would have denied it, protesting that he has close black friends, and said there is "good and bad in all races".[12] However, what happens continually in accounts like the one quoted here is that individual cases are conflated to represent overall trends (van Dijk 1987). In Phillip's anecdote, regardless of the truth or falsehood about his neighbour's behaviour, a single person is personified as symbolizing future trends.

As in Riverview, the working-class community is seen to have disappeared or to be in decline. Here a connection is made between ideas about "race" and racism and the death of working-class community. This is clearly stated in the following quote by George, who is 66 and has lived in the borough all his life. He begins by stating that in his recollection there have always been black people in the borough, but what has changed is their numbers.

Well let me say this – a coloured fellah lived in Empire Street where I lived. I used to play with a coloured fellah when I was a boy. There were quite a few coloured people in the area, and I mean a few. There was a family called Martin, a quite well-known family in the area. One of them became a professional boxer. The chap I knew, his name was Johnson. He was a coloured bloke – but no one worried if he was black, white or yellow then. You were just like all the other people. The community was such that you didn't care whether you was Irish or what you were – it just didn't matter. But what really mattered was that, first, you had to get a living, and second, that you had to go without. We all had to suffer at the same time.

Unlike harmony discourse, this construction of community actively denies that "race" or colour should be a legitimate frame of reference. Harmony discourse as part of the "our area" system recognizes the legitimacy of the black presence and accepts ethnic pluralism. What is communicated in this extract is an assimilationist position that excludes blackness in favour of a colour-blind notion of working-class community. Denying the relevance of race is not the same as rejecting racism. In the former, "race" is seen not to matter, whereas in the latter, racism is actively rejected. This I feel is important because it contrasts suppression (a colour-blind ethos) with a pro-active rejection of racism.

George again shows that in this discourse "race" is seen to be an "interfering influence" that deserves little attention. What is important is the shared notion of working-classness and the rigours and discipline of work:

When I was working in the docks I worked with quite a few Caribbeans – um West Indians. I got on with them. Well, I thought they were quite decent people. This was just after the war. There must have been at least a half a dozen there

117

out of a workforce of about thirty something. I found 'em exactly the same as I am – not different. They all wanted to work, they were good workers and I only found one that didn't, and of course, you always get one in all walks of life, but the majority were happy-go-lucky. I think over the years it has changed a bit because I think people are more racially aware these days, I don't know why but they appear to me, on both sides, I mean racism works both ways. You always get someone with a chip on their shoulder, be they white or black, you always meet them don't you? I think some people pick it up in conversations with people – you always get someone stirring it up. I've seen that in the docks. I think this is what's happening to some coloured people today – their minds are being made up for them.

In this sense George sees "racial awareness" as a lamentable consequence of the contemporary situation. Black and white consciousness are seen to be equivalent and within this discourse the struggle against racism is reduced to "trouble makers" stirring things up "on both sides". Racism defined in this way can thus be rejected:

As for racialism I don't believe in racialism. I don't think there is any need for that – you get the agitators whipping it up. I mean I've seen all these clashes before. I went up Mill Pond Bridge, Southwark Park Road, this was pre-war, and I saw the clashes between Mosley and the communists.

Yet alongside this rejection of "racialism", black young people can be criminalized as a group, the community can be characterized as being on the decline and objections can be made to the "over-representation" of black people in the area.

In the following extract George talks about a situation in which he thought he was going to be "mugged" by a group of young black people. The incident took place in the early 1970s. What we see here is a scenario being invested with racist assumptions, i.e. black young people associating with each other constitute a group of potential muggers.

Another thing is, where I live in Southgate there is a lot of muggings goes on. Well I've seen mugging go on where I live out the window. But I can honestly say that, in all the years I have been there, only once did I ever think I was going to be mugged. I'd been warned. I used to go out at half past five in the morning and I'd been warned that there was people being mugged early in the morning.

This particular morning I was walking to the station and I could see this crowd – all coloureds. I don't know if they had been out all night or if they'd just come off the train out of the West End or what, I don't know. They saw me and called out, and they was only a matter of twenty yards away, so I didn't take notice. I thought to myself "oh that's it". I shot across the road and they still came. I thought my best refuge would be the police station that was on the way, if there's going to be any bovver. So I shot into that road and they went by the top still hollering out and that was it and I carried on to the station.

Whether I was doomed to be mugged or not I don't know. I did feel a bit of a flutter, put it that way.

The fact that there was no attack and that the young people obviously were not interested in George is not used to demonstrate the inappropriate nature of his assumptions. The notion that a group of young black people are bound to be muggers is left unexamined and what is offered instead is the assertion that on this occasion he was lucky. Although George rejects "racialism", he operates a whole host of racialized stereotypes. These ideas are not unrelated to one another.

A series of interrelationships operate within the accounts I have referred to here. These connections result in a system of meaning that I have called (in Ch. 2) "white flight". The constitutive elements of this discursive system are:
  (a) that the area is being *"swamped" by black people*.
  (b) that the sense of *community* in the area has *died*.
  (c) that white people are being *forced out*.
A metonymic relationship exists between the three elements of this discursive system, and reference to any one element connotes meanings associated with the other two (Keith 1993). The result is that people do not have to speak directly about black people in the area to convey messages about their presence. In this situation it is enough merely to say "there isn't any sense of community now" in order to suggest that (a) the causes for this situation are the *over-representation*

of black people in the area, and (b) a consequence of this situation is *a desire to leave.* The interconnections of this system may not always strictly conform to the triggering of other meanings suggested here. For individuals, especially the elderly, who have a long-term commitment to the borough, the identification of black people as the "root of the problem" may not necessarily propel them towards a desire to leave the area. It may merely result in them lamenting the passage of a bygone age of sociability that pre-dated the presence of significant numbers of black people in the borough.

In this section I have described two semantic systems that construct "the community" and in so doing projected two very different images of inter-racial relations in the area. In the final section of this chapter I want to discuss the relative prevalence of these two systems within this district.

Conclusion

Throughout this discussion I have maintained that "community" is constructed and projected onto this area and is not a self-evident product of the local social system. Also I have argued that, despite its criminalization in the local media and adjacent areas, there exists a low level of perceived inter-racial conflict within this area. The discovery of low levels of racial antagonism in urban districts in Britain has been noted in other studies (Ward 1979, Wallman et al. 1982, Hewitt 1986, Jones 1988). Sandra Wallman documented similar claims in the South London district of Lambeth (Wallman 1975–6). However, beneath the claims of racial harmony there exists a complex process whereby the imagined politics of community is manufactured.

The claim that the local community is free of racial tension is not to be taken lightly, and, as I have shown, these claims are made by both black and white people. In other contexts, and sometimes alongside harmony discourse, an additional formula is utilized that marks Southgate as a "black area" and a site of black struggles and institutions. Further, the "white flight" semantic system projects yet another claim on the character of "the community". Here a xenophobic vision is offered of a declining white community in the face of "foreign invaders" and concerned with the passage of a bygone age when there were few problems, less crime, fewer blacks, and white working-class communities. In many ways the discourse laments the demise, or more correctly the transformation, of white working-class culture as a whole. I must emphasize that this account is not just used by adults as a way of harking back to the "rosy past", rather, it is also called into play by some adolescents when authoritative accounts are asked for (see Ch. 3).

These discourses have different organizing themes and they project contrasting images of the area and the people who live there. Such ideas give meaning to the flow of everyday life and reflect how social differentiation is talked about at a micro level. They provide a number of resources that may be strategically mobilized. In the case of the harmony discourse, it may provide a black person with a notion of community that is free from the gaze of racism; for the white user it provides a space in which dialogue is free from cultural absolutes. However, the imaginary politics of community is not free from conflict. Within the terrain of these discourses, "community claims" are fought over.

In contrast to the Riverview situation, the ascendant definition is what I have characterized as the "our area" semantic system. The result is that expressions of racism identified in Riverview are muted, even silenced, within Southgate. The point is that this local anti-racist ethos must be seen as contingent upon its ability to counter other definitions projected at it from outside and racist reactions from within. Thus, symbolically constructed communities have histories and are subjected to development and transformation.

We are left with the two images of Southgate offered here by Tony and Debbie.

> Well, it just doesn't seem to matter what colour you are any more. People have learned to live together – maybe there are a few of the older ones – but this is a community area right now, it doesn't matter where you come from. (Tony, 18, black, Jamaican parents)

> It's very prejudiced – here it is unbelievable right, but the point is that it is undercover now . . . like when I was younger it was out in the open, you knew who was racist and I liked it better then. Yes, because people don't want to be called racist now because it is something to be ashamed of. (Debbie, 19, white, German and Italian parents)

For Tony, in Southgate there exists a seamless harmony of all "races", whereas Debbie views this as if it were a veneer hiding insidious under-cover racism. In a sense both statements are true, and that is precisely the point. The "our area" definition of community used by Tony provides a powerful means of producing inter-racial solidarity. This does not mean, however, that racism is completely banished from this area. The point I am making here is that this discourse facilitates inter-racial contact. In short, "our area" notions of community are winning out against other definitions of belonging. But, as Debbie reminds us, the hegemony of this discourse is contingent and never uniformly dominant.

In comparing the situation I have described in this chapter with the account given of Riverview, it is clear that there are some important similarities. In both areas the language of community is invested with a racial agenda. Also common to both areas is a construction of a past era when a white working-class community flourished. What is interesting is that this is dated to different periods in the accounts that are given by residents. In Riverview, the "golden age" survives into the post-war era, whereas in Southgate it is clearly dated as being a pre-war phenomenon. The difference between the two districts is that the dominant construction of community in Riverview is what I call the "white flight" semantic system, but in Southgate the "our area" construct predominates. Yet, at the same time, these dominant definitions never completely exclude alternative images of the area. The most important feature that distinguishes Southgate is the existence of a powerful and racially inclusive localism.

In the next chapter I extend this perspective and address the ways in which the social identities of young people growing up in this area are being affected by, and transforming, the situation I have described.

"Not something we're new to, it's something we grew to . . .": youth, identification and alliance

Introduction

This chapter discusses the nature of adolescent identities in the ethnically mixed neighbourhood of Southgate. I argue that young people are involved in interesting and innovative dialogues within the school playgrounds, youth clubs and street corners where they come to know themselves and each other. I challenge van Dijk's (1987: 383) assertion that, within multiracial contexts, people learn about "others" via mediating texts and stereotypes and I suggest that, although stereotypes are available to young people, they are not used in any crude sense.

The picture that I will present shows that the dialogues occurring between black and white people in Southgate produce a more rigorously syncretic youth culture than the situation I described for Riverview in Chapter 3. I argue that this results in a form of ethnicity that is born out of negotiation. This negotiation occurs at two levels. One relates to the interactions and cultural exchanges occurring between the young people themselves at the individual level. The other refers to negotiations with the wider meanings associated with race and nationhood. I suggest that these negotiations are resulting in new forms of working-class Englishness. To use Roger Hewitt's phrase, the "apprenticeship in social semiosis" that young people pass through in Southgate produces a new ethnicity that contains a high degree of egalitarianism and anti-racism. In the following analysis I want to discuss the implications these developments have for the analysis of racism and the politics of "mixed" ethnicity.

Inhabiting and vacating identity

In Southgate, a spectrum of social identities is available to young people, including racial classifications. During the course of fieldwork I noted the descriptive names young people used to classify others. In total I collected 50 events where young people between the ages of 15 and 19 described an anonymous other of the same age as themselves.

"Race" categorizations were found in 82 per cent of the descriptions offered by young people. The audience to which the description was offered affected the terms and content of the "race" aetiology. There was a variation in the ways in which people of mixed parentage were described, i.e. "half caste", "mixed race" and "light skinned". Where black on black descriptions were offered, "race" was not referred to unless related to non-blacks, but, where the audience was "white", "race" classifications were included. Additionally, there existed a significant difference between accounts offered to young people and to adults. Where descriptions were offered to young people, terms such as "black" and "white" were used, but where young people (both black and white) offered descriptions to white adults, "coloured" and "white" were adopted. Having said this, it is important to state that black young people used "coloured" in fewer instances. Young people thus recognize a number of "race" vernaculars and, where a black questioner uses the term "coloured" when speaking to a white audience, she/he is speaking within the race aetiology of the respondent.

Although identity is usually associated with how people answer the question "Who am I?", it is by implication also related to the statement of who I am not. For political movements in Britain the idea of "difference" has been central to the way post-war social movements such as feminism(s), black struggles, and anti-nuclear and ecological movements have defined their identity (Mercer 1990a, Weeks 1990). In the context of youth identities in South London, claiming "difference" makes new formulations of identity possible. In the South London situation, identities, or combinations of social selves, are being inhabited where other public notions of identity are being vacated. Here I am discussing something close to Tajfel's (Tajfel & Turner 1979) notion of "feeling" associated with group identification. However, the notion of "vacating" is broader than this because it refers to the feelings of an individual towards the potential points of identification. It is my contention that the process I call "vacating" (i.e. the process whereby individuals distance themselves from a particular social definition) is as important as the kinds of identities that are taken on board. The process of inhabiting and vacating social identities manifests itself daily in adolescent peer relationships.

In the following interaction this process is in operation. The exchange involves three youngsters, all of whom are 13 years old – Chris, Bertie and Cyril. They are friends and this interview was conducted in the youth club where they were attending a lunch club. I asked Chris if he would let me interview him and he said that he would agree as long as he could pick some friends to come with him. The following exchange occurred during the interview:

Les [looks at Chris]: How would you describe yourself?

Chris: I'm alright. What do you mean, in terms of colour?

Les: Yes.

Bertie: Half caste!

Les: What do you mean?

Bertie: Someone who is half white and half black.

Chris: No! I ain't half caste. My dad is black and my mum is white. [Stands up] I am a "white nigger".

[All three boys laugh]

Bertie: Half caste!

Les [looking at Cyril and Bertie]: So, would you describe yourself as white?

Cyril: Well what would you describe yourself as – green? [Looks at Bertie and laughs]

Chris: He's an Englishman – an Englishman.

[Cyril looks down and says nothing]

Les [looks at Bertie]: Would you describe yourself as English?

Bertie: Na not me, I'm Polish.

Les: Are your parents Polish?

Bertie: My grandfather.

Chris: So your mum and dad are English.

[Bertie looks down and says nothing]

In these exchanges two notions of identity are being vacated, i.e. "half caste" and "English". Bertie lays claim to a "race" classification and applies it to Chris, who then refuses to inhabit that definition. Equally, Chris then invokes a notion of "Englishness" and applies it to the other boys, who in turn resist identifying with this concept. There are two antagonistic sets of processes going on here. First is the attempt to introduce sets of social classification in order to hurt or accumulate status and power. Bertie attempts to define Chris, thus conferring defining power on himself, and Chris attempts to do like-wise, thus combating Bertie's accusation and elevating his own status. Second, in the process of introducing these classifications, the friend-ship group threatens to endorse a set of terms that allow conflict and status-ranking. As I will argue later, the validity of these externally de-fined frames of reference is frequently challenged within multiracial peer groups to such an extent that status-ranking is suspended, albeit temporarily.

The accounts given in these exchanges are to some degree con-fined to this particular context. I followed up this group interview with a series of individual interviews. In the account that was offered in this context, Chris identified himself as "half caste", "mixed" and "English". Bertie and Cyril also identified themselves as "English" and "white" but qualified this identification with "but it doesn't mat-ter". However, what we see in this extract is a process where the meaning and desirability of social classifications are adopted and re-jected by young people, providing a glimpse into the status of these concepts within peer groups.

This kind of peer interaction does not always result in the kind of avoidance cited above. The following extract involved three young people: Cinta (mother white, father black, 13 years old), Joel (black, 14 years old) and Errol (black, 14 years old). This extract was re-corded during a summer play scheme in which an incident arose around a dispute over access to a football.

Joel: Cinta – come on give me the ball, we want to take it now.

Errol: Come on Cinta, you can go over wid dem, let us have this one and you can . . .

Cinta: Na, I'm using it!

Joel: Give it to me [getting annoyed].

Cinta: No [raised voice].

Joel: Half-caste bitch!

Cinta [turns, faces the two boys and says with anger]: Black bitch!
[She turns away from the boys]

Errol: Leave her.

[Both boys turn and walk away]

The dispute results in Joel directing an insult at Cinta. The purpose of the abuse is to hurt her. The content of the name-calling has both a race and a gender component and in both cases the names are intended to be derogatory. However, Cinta resists these definitions and modifies the "race" characterization "half caste" in favour of the term "black".

Cinta identifies closely with black cultural symbols and this is encouraged by her mother and father. Her hair is cane-rowed, which is a black style, and she listens to "black" forms of music, identifies herself closely with the black style and has an appreciation of black history. Cinta is identifying with the wider processes of self-affirmation and political organization being conducted around black identity within urban communities (Hall 1982, Gilroy 1987). She is, with the encouragement of her parents, placing herself outside of a "racial fraction" (i.e. half caste or mixed blood), which is itself a fixed notion of identity, and inside the cultural politics of blackness. Cinta's comment would be meaningless if there were not a movement for black self-affirmation occurring in South London. Cinta is placing herself within an inclusive notion of blackness.

The purpose of these two extracts is to give an idea of how young people engage with socially available classifications. In the process some identities are inhabited, but, equally, others are vacated. In the next three sections I want to focus on the content and meaning of the identities that are being adopted. This will include a discussion of the meaning of whiteness, an analysis of black identities, and a short discussion on the position of "mixed race" youth. First I focus on the way that notions of "race" and ethnicity are articulated by young white people.

"White identities" and refusing dominant definitions

I think for black people who live in Britain this question of finding some way in which the white British can learn to live with us and the rest of the world is almost as important as discovering our own identity. I think they are in more trouble than we are. So we, in a curious way, have to rescue them from themselves – from their own past. We have to allow them to see that England is a quite interesting place with quite an interesting history that has bossed us around for 300 years [but] that is finished. Who are they now? (Stuart Hall, taken from "After dread and anger", BBC Radio 4, 1989)

This provocative quote from Stuart Hall sums up the position that I have adopted throughout this study. In many ways, it turns the tables on the discussion of race and identity offered by British race relations sociology and referred to in Chapter 1. What I showed in Chapter 3 was that whites experience their "race" in contradictory ways. In this section I want to examine how young whites identify with their black friends in an attempt to resolve their position.

"Colour don't come into it!": youth egalitarianism and white use of black cultural codes

Evident in many accounts recorded with young white people in this area is a constant denial that "racial" differentiation is relevant or meaningful to them. Yet "race" vernaculars abound in Southgate. Although white youths recognize the existence of these categorizations, they almost unanimously deny their salience. Comments such as "It does not matter what colour you are", "It doesn't make any difference", "I don't believe in racial things" are common. Encoded in these statements is the desire to banish "racial things" because of their potentially divisive nature. There are clear similarities with the situation I described in Riverview, but in Southgate the denial of racial difference leads young whites to adopt black cultural practices in a more spectacular and profound way.

The degree to which "black" cultural forms are adopted by white peers can vary and depends on numerous factors, including whether black friends censure or challenge these appropriations. Where young people distance themselves and avoid "race" and Englishness as salient identities, a cultural vacuum results. This process is most prevalent in early to mid adolescence. It is during this time that white young people are most free to adopt cultural and linguistic materials outside of the ideological inheritance of the adult world. This is what Gerald Suttles (1968: 26) has referred to as the development of a cultural space that is based on "private understanding rather than public rulings". Young whites are able to fill this cultural space with black symbols precisely because the significance of colour is denied. English racism that characterizes black and white cultures as mutually impermeable phenomena is ridiculed by the development of a style, language and culture that cannot be defined as being black or white but is somehow a synthesis of both. This hybrid culture is composed of items that are equally valued, relating to one another in what Bastide (1978: 283) refers to as a "system of equivalences".

One of the results of this process is linguistic sharing[1] and the incorporation of black linguistic items into white speech. This operates at three levels, ranging from Creole language of Caribbean origin, to urban black American vernacular and lastly to black London speech. I refer to these linguistic forms as black codes. Code is defined as grammatical rules, pronunciation and lexical items that are associated with a socially defined group of speakers. Thus I am examining the way that codes that are associated with black speech are appropriated by white speakers.

The most spectacular manifestation of this process is white Creole use,[2] which varies from just a few words to ethnically marked pronunciation and a high degree of proficiency in Creole (Hewitt 1986: 128–33). In Southgate, the presence of Creole words was much higher than the situation described in Chapter 3. For example, within Jamaican speech, adverbial tags or particles are often connected to verbs, the most common of which are "off" and "up". In the following extract, Mark, a white boy aged 15, uses this form. He is talking about a local reggae sound system called Saxon Studio:

> Saxon is the baddest [best] sound, [switches to Creole] *pure murderation them jus nice-up deh dance and dem bass jus lick off your head*, [switch back] you know what I mean.

Mark also uses inversion (i.e. "bad" meaning "good"), which has its origins in black American speech (Sims Holt 1972). Black American forms are particularly important because their presence runs parallel with the emergence of black American youth culture.[3] However, the influence of Caribbean Creoles persists. The use of Creole by whites may be checked, particularly in the presence of black strangers. In this sense, white Creole use is dependent on peer consent.

The third level at which black speech enters into white usage is from black South London vernacular. This black code is completely accessible to whites. It is created by incorporating standard English words that, when used by black young people, take on an altered meaning. Thus dominant forms of communication are appropriated and subverted. Some linguists have referred to this as "Black London English" (Sebba 1983a). For example, a word such as "safe" (meaning free from danger) is appropriated as a prestigious term to mean excellent, sound and certain (this word has been re-translated into Creole and pronounced "seafe"). These altered meanings were then re-circulated to white Londoners, who operated these words, complete with their black inflections and connotations.[4] These codes take their place alongside words of various origins, including Yiddish – e.g. *nosh* (verb: to eat), *schlepp* (verb: to drag or travel), *schtum* (noun: secret) – and Irish lexis – e.g. *crack* (noun: a happening or atmosphere), *ninety* (adjective: brilliant), *poladic* (adjective: intoxicated) – which all contribute to South London speech. This form has been referred to as a de-ethnicized, racially mixed "Community English" that is open to all young people regardless of origin (Hewitt 1988b).[5]

Thus the language of white young people in this area has a rich syncretic quality. Where there are strong relationships of trust, whites can gain access to all three black codes. Greetings such as *"whaapen"* and other ethnically marked forms of speech are important because they mark both the boundaries of adolescent peer networks and the cultural frames of reference in which multiracial friendship exists. Being around young people in this area, one can see that ritual greetings mark the boundaries of an alternative public sphere (Gilroy 1987). Within these spaces whites can take on black codes as their own. These appropriations are recognized as legitimate in this context, resulting in what one white young woman called "nicing up" her language.

Cultural exchanges are not just confined to language. Black youth cultural styles are also viewed positively by whites (Gilroy 1987: 231). In the following extract, an 11-year-old white girl discusses her affiliation to black music and style. She shows how the rejection of "race" and racism facilitates her use of black symbols.

> All sorts of people like reggae, black, white, um Chinese . . .
> Yes, because I don't think people should be racist, just

because, like say I was black right and I was singing it, white people might not like that, but I've been brought up not to be racist.

When asked how she would define herself, Corina replied that she is a "ragamuffin". This is a style associated with dance-hall reggae and sound system culture (see Ch. 8). Corina speaks Creole with a high degree of proficiency and has a network of black peers. Her friends refer to her as "Ragga". These nicknames are the most positive classifications that black young people apply to white peers. Whites are placed on a continuum ranging from racists (common names were "satan" or "devil", "porkhead") to white insiders who are given black style names or personalized Creole names.[6]

When asked about her friends Corina launched into a tirade denouncing racism:

Corina: They [my friends] are nice people, not racist, because our mums have brought us up not to be racist. The people that are racist are stupid.

Les: What kind of people are racist then?

Corina: People just say like "white honky", and to black people say – this is a bit racist – "black niggers", but if my mum heard me say that, I wouldn't live to say that again. My mum says that I'm not to be racist to other people.

Les: Do you know any racist people?

Corina: Yes. My mate. She was racialist and she called my mate a black bitch. So I said if you want to cuss someone's colour, or any religion you can just go away from me and I won't play with you any more. And she goes, "I can cuss them if I want." And I goes, "If you want to cuss them you can cuss them, but if you are walking around with me then I will hit you." Which I would because I don't like people who are racist. I've never been brought up to be racist.

Corina does not accept that "whiteness" is an appropriate social classification. Here rejection of "race" is closely bound up with a rejection of racism. This is astonishing given that she is just 11 years old and it indicates how threatening racism is to young whites in this area. Corina explains her anti-racism in terms of her mother, who condemns racism, and her friendships with black peers. There is a connection here with the neighbourhood discourses mentioned in Chapter 5. Corina's mother is strongly committed to the notions I referred to as "harmony discourse". Corina herself articulates this formula when reflecting on the neighbourhood:

> 'Cos we are all the same, we've got all – underneath our skin we've all got blood and things. You can't pick and choose who lives in your estate, white or black. Whoever lives on your estate, lives on your estate. It's not your business what colour they are.

The rejection of racism and the denial of the importance of race opens black cultural symbols to white appropriation. What results is an identification with black people and black symbols. This is located within the specific context of the Southgate adolescent community that is situated in the area's neighbourhood philosophy and the "our area" semantic system. In this context black language is claimed by white young people as a legitimate cultural resource.

Limits on the white appropriation of black forms

When I met Tony he was 17 years old. He was intimately involved with black cultural practices and in friendships with black peers. He maintained that his use of black talk was legitimate because he shares the same social locations as his black friends:

> I mean people often say I sound like a black man – that is to say I sound black. But you see when I learned to speak English, I suppose it ain't really English, I learned to speak it the way people around me spoke – na mean? I mean when Michael [a black friend] comes up to me and says to me [switches to Creole] "Whappen Tony cool", I don't answer him with [fakes a public school accent] "Oh yes Michael, I am quite cool thank you". I say "Yeah man – safe!" I might not use the talk as hard or exaggerated as him, but I'm talking the language I learned to speak, it's – it's my natural language.

Tony is talking here about a social and linguistic space where emergent identities between young people, regardless of background, are formed. However, the boundaries of this process are subject to close scrutiny, as we see in the following extract. It involves Tony and Michael (the boys mentioned above) and Brian. All three boys were 17 at the time of this incident. Michael and Brian are of Afro-Caribbean origin and Tony is white. The incident took place outside a kebab shop in Southgate. The three boys had just walked out of the shop with some food. There had been some banter between the person serving and Tony, and all three boys were laughing.

Michael: What did he say to you? Something about . . .

Brian: He said next time he is going to run you out of the shop if you don't give him the money straight away [laugh].

Tony: You know what I mean, [switches to Creole] the *man chat nuff lyric.*

Michael [in Creole]: *The man was bad rasta.*

Brian: I tell you, I think Tony gets blacker everyday [laugh]!

Tony: Yeah sometimes I wish I was black you know [laugh].

Brian [turns and his mood changes]: No you don't!

[All three boys stop talking, an air of seriousness descends on the group]

Tony: Anyway I ain't going back in there again in a hurry.

[All three boys start laughing]

Tony uses black forms of language in this situation. His use of these symbols is legitimized by his two black peers, who both allow him access to these cultural forms but also encourage him to be involved in black music and black styles. However, this incident marks the limits of Tony's participation. Simply, Tony's claim to "want to be black" is too much for Brian, who checks Tony's over-zealous claim. Being close to this interaction, I felt that the boundaries of Tony's relationship to blackness were being defined. In the private context, the presence of racism can be exorcised. But Tony's lack of appreciation of the public prevalence of racism is not reckoned with in his playful desire to be black. This is what offended Brian. When I asked Tony about this incident he said:

Well, I realized that I had gone too far – you know what I mean. I know I can't ever be black or nothing and I realized that what he was coming off with was right. I mean they go through a harder time and all that – that is to say there are things I don't have to deal with when I am on my own because I am white, but because I am with them, I see what goes on and how people act the same towards me when I'm with them.

Tony's account is interesting because he realizes that he overstretched his relationship with his black peers. Clearly, he understood that there is more to being black than ebullient street styles and prestigious linguistic codes. By adopting and articulating black forms of style and speech Tony was encoding his identification with blackness. However, the contradictory nature of this identification becomes impossible to sustain when it is made explicit. Tony identifies with "black" symbols but knows he can never feel the consequences of racism and the experiential foundations of blackness.

Accounts of young white people wanting to be black during the period of mid-adolescence are not uncommon in Southgate. In a sense, these constitute extreme moments of identification but they are continuous with the operation of black cultural forms by white young people. This phenomenon is a curious inversion of academic treatments of race misidentification (Clark & Clark 1947, Weinreich 1979, Davey & Norburn 1980). Through these engagements with blackness, young whites are forced to interrogate the meanings of their whiteness. They move from the youthful assertion of "it doesn't matter what colour you are" to a more profound and lived knowledge of how racism structures their lives and relationships.

These identifications with blackness often go hand in hand with the rejection of Englishness. Although many of the young people locate themselves within this notion of national identity, others either distance themselves from the concept or qualify its meaning. In the following quotation, Paul (17 years old) accepts the descriptive notion of English but then unpacks and disposes of some of the ideological baggage associated with the concept:

Yeah, I am English. I was born in England but there are things about it that I don't agree with – like when I was younger I remember seeing the Union Jack on NF stickers. If that is being English, I am not English. Like skinhead and all that. They were proud to be English, like I'm English and I'm going to kick your head in. They are things that I don't want to be associated with – I mean I've grown up with black people.

Accounts such as this associate "Englishness", "whiteness" and racism in an interrelated ideological triangle. In this sense, racism is coupled with a particular construction of nationhood that is unattractive to many white young people who have close black friends (Hewitt 1986: 93). To accept this identity would in turn make close relationships with black friends untenable or less feasible. Paul has had close "black" friends all of his life. At school he was best friends with a black young man. Thus the lived experience of whites and their social knowledge of black youngsters is directly at odds with new racism and its attendant definition of English nationalism. In this sense the aesthetic of Englishness is totally unattractive to young whites in Southgate. For them the Union Flag is not associated with national unity and pride; rather it connotes neo-fascist politics and an image of skinhead youth who champion the bigotries of racism and national chauvinism. In this way young whites vacate whiteness and Englishness as appropriate identities in favour of an encoded identification with blackness and black people.

Debbie is a white young woman who was 19 when I interviewed her. She is of Italian and German parentage and has lived in South London all of her life. She was part of multiracial peer groups throughout her youth and had a black boyfriend with whom she had a son. Her story is about coming to terms with racism and whiteness and the meanings placed on her own difference. In her mid-adolescence Debbie was closely involved in black youth culture and peer networks. She comments:

I mean I went through a stage when I was fourteen or fifteen when I wanted to be black. I mean I wasn't really accepted by the English people and I wasn't really accepted by the black people because I was white. So I thought if I could change my skin colour then I would be alright.

Debbie's speech is rich with black codes. Often she is mistaken in telephone conversations for a black person. She is a Creole speaker and can switch from black London argot to fully marked Creole. She commented that she used to "carry herself" like a black person: "I used to walk with a slight limp, you know, like black people do."

Throughout her mid-adolescence, from about 12 to 15, she passionately vacated any notion of whiteness or Englishness. Her accounts of this time are strikingly similar to those of the young woman I called Corina in an early part of this discussion. This distancing herself from white or English identity went as far as:

> I used to cuss off white people. It didn't matter where they were from. It didn't matter if they were English or whatever – "look at that white person". And a lot of my black friends used to call me, what did they used to call me now, they used to call me "Ragga".

Debbie gained complete access to the culture and sensibilities of her black friends.[7] This developed to such a degree that Debbie became more hostile to whites who lived outside of Southgate than her black friends were. During this time she also became totally submerged in the rituals of black culture. She wore her hair in black styles:

> I used to cane-row [parallel plaiting] my hair, always plaiting my hair, my black friends would do it for me. I made sure that the beads were always red, gold and green. Also I used to have my little, what was it, I had a cap and it had Africa on it and all the colours and I used to wear all African, all Rastafarian badges. I had Gucci shirts and you had suede collars, that's what black people wore.

Debbie's adoption of black styles went hand in hand with her complete rejection of racism. Her identification with blackness operated as an alternative to both her Italian and German parentage and white Englishness. Her absorption within black culture during this period was developed to an extraordinary degree. Blackness was registered in her language and style of self-presentation, her clothes and style preferences and even went as far as the kinds of make-up she wore. She remembers:

> I even used to wear black women's make-up. I used to think that my black friends would be impressed by this, right. I had all these dark ruby, reds and dark browns and really dark colours, you know that would show up on black skin but would

look too strong on white skin. When I look back I must have looked like some freak.

Debbie fully participated in the culture of black London. She attended sound system dances (see Ch. 8), she wore black styles and she articulated black sensibilities. Through the critical tools contained in black youth culture Debbie learned about the racial inequalities experienced by black young people in the "second Babylon" of Britain. She moved from the youthful rejection of "race" ("it doesn't matter what colour you are") towards a profound appreciation of the structural inequalities that follow from racism in British society.

However, she found that her identification with blackness could not be sustained at the level achieved in her mid-adolescence. She came to realize that within a racist society she could never legitimately "be black" in cultural terms because racism defines black and white culture as separate entities (Lawrence 1982, Gilroy 1987). Within the logic of racism, people such as Debbie cannot exist, and, as a result, racism constantly undermines the cultural legitimacy of the white use of black codes. Additionally, her identification with blackness was checked by black people who were not friends because she was perceived as "stealing their culture". Thus she was brought back to the meaning of "whiteness" and the need to resolve her own sense of self.

It was like waking up one morning and saying "Come on, grow up". You know because I think my mates started to notice it in the sense of, I was becoming a different person to what I was before, you know, and they was saying to me, "We know that you are white, we can't mistake that you are white. We know you are white, okay, but we love you, we don't care and you are original for who you are." I was changing too much into becoming more black, black awareness, that I was forgetting that I was white.

It is at this point that Debbie is propelled towards a critical evaluation of what whiteness means. Throughout her earlier discussion she used whiteness and Englishness as synonymous terms. What is being evoked here is what I referred to earlier as the ideological triangle that places whiteness, Englishness and racism in an interdependent relationship. What she then does in her account is disconnect whiteness from the attendant connotations of racism and Englishness. This is coupled with her realization that her "originality" was acknowledged and respected by her black friends.

> Look, I know that not all black people are good – I mean I went through that phase a long time ago – but they taught me to value who I am – my Germanness, my Italianness. It's important, you have to have an identity, right. I mean it's hard for me, right, because English people say I'm not white. Now I don't think you get any whiter than that (pointing at her skin). But I feel I'm white and I get confused sometimes. What am I supposed to be? Because it is important to have a colour. That's the only – unless you accept what you are and your colour, then you don't get anywhere right? I am proud of being white, but I don't want to be accepted as English, not on those sides.

Here the disconnection of whiteness from Englishness allows her to inhabit a notion of race free from racism.[8] Her solution is to separate the notion of colour from that of nation. As a result she utilizes a version of race identity in a re-worked form while vacating the concept of Englishness. Debbie's case shows that the social and cultural spaces that act as the site of white identifications with blackness cannot remain fully autonomous from the adult world. Ultimately, white young people are brought back to the cultural equation of "race" and nation and forced to locate themselves within it. As Debbie trenchantly points out, "You've got to have a colour". However, Debbie shows us that having a colour does not automatically result in succumbing to racism and nationalism. In this situation Debbie espouses a notion of "white difference", and this is supported by identification with her Italianness and Germanness. This enables her to maintain a healthy distance from Englishness and racism.

In all the examples I have mentioned in this section, white people have espoused a notion of identity that rejects Englishness that is defined in racially exclusive ways. Like Debbie, they are all searching for some sense of identification that places them outside the dominant categorizations of race and nation so prevalent in the late 1980s. White young people are in an ambiguous position, which can be summed up as a search for notions of identity that are not laced with racism.

Black rejection and white racism

Close associations between black and white young people do not uniformly produce the kinds of anti-racist outcomes I have mentioned. In two cases that I documented during the fieldwork period, white young people who were rejected by their black friends were propelled into racist explanations of their plight. Mark, a 15-year-old young man, went from close relationships with black peers to developing a friendship with Joe, who lived in Riverview. I knew both youngsters very well and over a three-year period I spent a lot of time with them in informal leisure spaces in and around Riverview and Southgate.

One particular day we were having breakfast in a cafe close to Riverview. During the course of the discussion, the issue of why this area of London had become so run down was raised. Mark replied in a quiet, almost embarrassed tone, "Well it's all the blacks isn't it?" I challenged Mark and said that the area would be exactly the same if all the black people decided to move out. Mark replied and then was supported by Joe:

Mark: Well tell me this, was there any muggings and the level of crime there is now before the blacks came here!

Les: But . . .

Joe: And the drugs – it's the niggers that are dealing the drugs.

Les: You know as well as I do that it is not only black people who deal drugs. How many people do you know on Riverside who are white and deal?

These two young men are using the local racist discourse I referred to in the previous chapter as the "white flight" meaning system. Here the economic decay of the area is blamed on the presence of black people. Equally, the black presence is characterized as generating criminal activity and explaining the emergence of drug misuse. Joe goes on to take these discourses to their conclusion:

But they are taking over; you've seen all the "boatys" [Vietnamese] on our estate [Riverview]. Yeah, I walked in the youth club the other night and it was all chinks. And any time something new is built it is built for the "effnics minority".

This characterization is closely linked with the "white flight" discourses. It maintains that white working-class people are being left out and it is the "immigrants" who are getting special treatment. This theme is very common in white working-class racism.

Throughout the discussion I countered the assertions being made by both Joe and Mark in an attempt to puncture the logic of their racism with "facts". For example, I pointed out to Joe that there were only just over 50 Vietnamese families living on Riverview. The two boys would counter these "facts" with more racist explanation. At one point they "wound me up" by telling racist jokes. It was at this point that Mark referred to his experience of being involved in black peer groups as a way of justifying the validity of his remarks. He comments:

> You see Les, you don't want to know. I know what they are like – the "butt butts" [racist characterization of Asians] the same as the "jiggs" [abbreviation of racist construct "jiggerboo"]. See, I used to go around with the black kids, I used to hang around with them and I know what they are like. I am not racialist but the jiggs are taking over. It's the English people who are in the minority now. Whatever happened to us?

In this instance Mark uses his knowledge of young black people to legitimize his use of racist constructions. He ends his statement with a rhetorical question – "What about the English people?" He implies here that only white people are English. Mark and Joe use a whole armoury of racist terms (niggers, jiggs, butt butts, boatys, chinks) but they maintain that racism is not their problem; the real issue, for them, is that black people are taking over. In this case these boys do not attempt to develop a notion of "white difference" free of racism; they place themselves squarely within a notion of Englishness that is defined in a racially exclusive way.

Joe's position is more complex, because although he was born in South London his parents are from Northern Ireland. However, Joe totally rejects any notion of Irishness and he often talks with contempt about "thick Paddies". Joe fully inhabits an identity of Englishness to the exclusion of any identification with his parents. The identities of both youngsters are cast by the logic of local racism and the new racism being circulated at a national level.

Although both boys have black friends, these friends are seen as exceptional individuals. They move within predominantly white peer groups and view "others" from an insulated group of family and peers. Black people in their peer group are viewed as insiders despite their blackness. Joe in particular had a very close black friend. In a disagreement between Joe's black friend and a white young man in a local disco, Joe got involved in a serious fight defending this person. Joe defined this relationship as one that "was worth fighting for" and not a casual friendship. The same processes I identified in Chapter 3 that define black insiders as "special individuals" are in operation here, but this case stands in stark contrast to the multiracial friendship networks I described earlier.

Although the dialogues occurring between black and white people described earlier in this chapter may be predominant in Southgate, they are not universally applicable to white young people in this area. Local racist discourses are available to them. In Mark's case, his rejection by a black friendship network triggered a reappraisal of his situation and resulted in his turning to local racism.

Summary

In summary, notions of white identity are far from simple or straightforward. Young people engage with the dominant definitions of "race" and nation in creative and critical ways. Clearly, their friendships and identification with black peers provide fertile alternatives to racial or national chauvinism. Vron Ware has argued in her discussion of feminism and anti-slavery that it is important to appreciate such transcultural identification without idealizing the political potential of such gestures: "This kind of political empathy or affinity may be a preliminary stage towards but is not a substitute for making actual alliances" (Ware 1992: 239). Similarly, the white identification with blackness discussed here demonstrates a comparable pre-political potential. There exists a significant cultural space that young white people share with their black associates. However, claims over the terms and cultural and linguistic content of these common links are not without ambiguities and contradictions. Although many young whites may choose to distance themselves from the circumscriptions of "race", the cultural bridges (Røgilds 1990, 1991) that they construct are volatile and temporary.

What I have shown is that white people find a passage through a social world that is full of publicly determined notions of personal identity. The strongly developed local anti-racism acts as a platform from which young whites get involved in intimate dialogues with their black peers. In this context young people inhabit and vacate identities according to their desirability. As I have shown, multiracial peer groups provide whites with new possibilities while at the same time presenting them with new dilemmas and limitations. It is here that whites find their notion of self. This process is expressed in a profoundly simple way in the following quote from Pauline, who is 16. She says:

> I mean I don't see myself as white in the same way as the National Front people do, and I don't see myself as black – I mean white in the same way as my friends see themselves as black. I suppose I'm an English girl from London – well Southgate.

Pauline cannot be white in the same way that her friends are black, yet she is not white in the same way that racists are white. This dilemma of how to develop, or reckon with, a notion of whiteness that is free of racism lies at the heart of the contradictions these young white people face (Ware & Back 1994). Pauline ends up by stating that she is "English but" from Southgate, a place that is somehow simultaneously both black and white.

Formulations of black identity and their meaning

In this section I want to outline the ways in which young people in this area formulate notions of black identity. Before going on to discuss the ethnographic material, I want to sketch its historical and political origins. Also, I want to place this discussion within some of the controversies over the use of the term in Britain.

Black identity has its historical roots in the "negritude" movement developed in Africa and the United States in the 1920s and 1930s and in the Afro-American civil rights and Black Power movements in the 1960s (Milner 1983, Hraba & Grant 1970, Davey 1987). In Britain it signifies the collective identity of people of African and Asian ancestry in their struggle against English racism (Sivanandan 1981–2). In this context, black becomes a political colour of resistance and an alternative to racially imposed definitions and identities. As Stuart

Hall points out, the struggle over the terms of identity is also linked to economic and social circumstances for black people, who were for the most part working class:

> Sometimes, the class struggle in language occurred between two different terms: the struggle, for example, to replace the term "immigrant" with the term "black". But often, the struggle took the form of a different accenting of the same term: e.g. the process by means of which the derogatory colour "black" became the enhanced value "black" (as in "Black is beautiful"). (Hall 1982: 59)

Thus the contestation over the meaning of identity labels is closely linked to the wider struggles over the economic and social conditions of black people living in Britain. Hall continues:

> It [identity politics] had become part of an organised practice of struggles requiring the building up of black resistances as well as the development of new forms of black consciousness. (Hall 1982: 59)

The assertion of blackness results in a re imagination of the black self, free from the stigmatized definitions formulated according to the logic of racism (Fanon 1968).

Numerous commentators have engaged critically with the concept (W. James 1986, Wilson 1987, Tizard & Phoenix 1989), suggesting that the reality of black selfhood is more complex than the political definitions mentioned above. In particular, a debate has occurred as to whether it is feasible to categorize people of "Asian" and "Afro-Caribbean" descent within an inclusive black definition (Banton 1987, Modood 1988). Others have commented that it is by no means clear that people who are designated "black" by political activists and intellectuals consider themselves in these politicized frames of reference. It is suggested that a whole host of factors may affect the formulation of racial identity, including social class, age, gender and locality (Tizard & Phoenix 1989, Mercer 1990b).

While being sensitive to these debates I want to focus in this section on how young people of Afro-Caribbean origin articulate a notion of blackness.[9] I argue that the debate should shift away from discussion of the existence, or non-existence, of a unitary notion of

blackness towards a perspective that can recognize multiple definitions of black identity. In this section I look at how black identities are
culturally constructed in the South London context.

Language and the musical cultures of South London are central to
the way young people express their blackness. The operation of black
linguistic codes is one way of marking historical connections with the
Caribbean and North America and identifying both with black peers
and with the alternative public sphere that can include young whites.
In the previous section I referred to the relationship between black
linguistic codes and white appropriations. Here I want briefly to discuss the role of black language in the expression of black cultural
identity.

In London a variety of Creole languages of Caribbean origin are
spoken. However, by far the most influential forms of Creole on
black languages in London are those that originate from Jamaica. It is
Jamaican Creole that has had most impact on the speech of black
young people born in Britain.[10] It is important to distinguish between
the Creoles spoken by people born in Jamaica and the derivations of
Creole employed by British-born black people. Unlike their parents,
young people do not operate Creole forms in a unitary or constant
sense. Michael, a young man of Jamaican parentage, explains in the
following quotation:

> The West Indians themselves, as in our parents and thing, no
> matter where they are, I don't care, they will always talk the
> same. But us now, there are certain little things that we pick
> off them and at the same time we could just be talking along
> with our friends and the rest of it – it comes out like that. It's
> not like I walking down the street thinking to myself I'm
> going to talk this way or I'm going to talk in that language.

It is this ability to switch between linguistic codes that distinguished
black British Creole from Jamaican or other Caribbean Creoles. Here
black young people have at their disposal a number of linguistic
codes. In most cases this includes both Creole and a regional English
(e.g. London, Birmingham or Yorkshire vernacular). Black young
people "switch codes" from regional English to Creole. There are a
number of discussions of "code switching" in the literature on the
ethnography of speaking (Sebba & Wooton 1984, Sebba 1986,
Hewitt 1986). Various conditions have been identified that trigger

switches from the regional vernacular to Creole and these include situations where speakers are expressing happiness or anger or greeting friends, in moments of assertiveness, in references to relationships with the opposite sex, where power is being contested and in defining black group identity (Hewitt 1989).[11]

In addition to these two black codes, urban black American speech is also being incorporated into the linguistic repertoire of black South Londoners. This development is closely related to the emergence and popularity of black American youth culture. The popularity of this language and music signifies a connection with the black diaspora in the United States. It is to the issue of diasporic connections in black identity formulations that I now turn.

The exploration of cultural heritage within the context of blackness

In this section I argue that young black people plot the interconnections within the African diaspora through the cultural construction of blackness. Blackness is defined not just in terms of Caribbean origins but through making connections with the entire diaspora. The prime medium through which this identification takes place is expressive black musical culture (Gilroy 1987). In the following account, Denise, a 19-year-old black woman, refers to the kinds of music that are played and heard in the area:

> Well, it's all from the same root innit. I mean you go to "All Nations" [a famous East London black club] and upstairs they play rap and soul and black music from America and downstairs they play reggae. But the music is all related and it's all like – you know, black music I suppose.

In this extract Denise shows how black music is connected to the same root. In doing so she is also identifying the link between Afro-American and Afro-Caribbean experience through the medium of popular culture (Back 1988a). I will return in a later chapter to the cultural motors that drive this process. For the moment I want merely to state that these connections are present in the way young black people talk about themselves and their community.

Another strong theme that emerges from the interviews that I have conducted is that blackness is not defined as a colour or "race" in a phenotypic sense. In the following quotation, Denise defines the meaning of "race". She states that she is black in feeling but not in colour.

> Of course I am black. I can't escape it. But I'm not black in colour, very few people are actually black or close to it. It actually doesn't describe the way I look but it's the way I am. It is like I haven't actually felt discrimination myself, I don't feel it every day because I live in an area where there are a lot of black people, no, not me personally but I don't have to feel it everyday to know that it is there – you know what I mean?

Denise's concept of blackness is not merely a reaction to discrimination. Her blackness is a felt sense of collective identity that is born out of the collective experience of black people. She does not have to feel racism every day to know that it is a potent force. Although her blackness may be defined against racism, it cannot be reduced to a response to it. Black identity is defined as a reaction to racism but also as the creative process of self-reconstruction. This is particularly powerful when expressed in accounts of black history and the rhetoric of "roots".

The concept of "roots" is extremely important within the black musical cultures found in South London. As Paul Gilroy points out:

> All these musics announce themselves as "roots", a complex term which combines the obvious organic similes of Garveyism – "A nation without its past history is like a tree without root" – with a belief in philosophical and political archaeology for which Alex Haley's book stands as both an example and a paradigm: "I was drifting away from reality, so far away from the roots in me". (Gilroy 1987: 207)

The "roots" concept is central to the way in which young black Londoners trace their history. In the following quote from Tony, who is 19 years old, we can see clearly how this young man separates the phenotypic notion of blackness from a cultural notion of "roots":

> To say I'm black is just to say something about a colour, right? But as you can see I am not black as in you look at my skin, right, and how would you describe it.

Les: Light brown, I suppose coffee.

Exactly. Now to say if you are black, now, that is to say that somewhere down the line you have been African – and if you are an African that has come from the Caribbean then chances are you must have been a slave and I don't care, people will never forget slavery.

Tony clearly connects African origins with both a Caribbean experience and the political legacy of slavery. African metaphors are a powerful means whereby young black people place themselves in history. It is, in a sense, the furthest back that their cultural heritage can be traced. The philosophical resources that young people use in these contexts include fragments of concepts borrowed from Rastafari. The impact of this philosophy goes much further than discussions of Rastafarianism as a religious system. They are registered in subtle ways in the conceptual language of black young people. The concept of "dread" is a good example of this.

"Dread" is a rasta notion that means the essence of the black experience. Thus it conveys the highest form of status and the most terrible experiences of exploitation. There are similarities between this notion and the idea of "soul" in the black American context (Hannerz 1968, 1969). Dread thus can be used as a substitute for blackness, and the word is widely used as a tag signifying commonness. The notion of "dread" should not be associated narrowly with the rituals of Rastafari. Although it is a core concept within rasta philosophy, it also signifies a condition of collective belonging. It is this wider sense of group belonging that has been missed by the established literature on the conceptual armoury of Rastafarianism (Miles 1978, Cashmore 1979). Rasta ethics and maxims are widely available and can form the basis of a metaphorical identification with Africa. Young black people plot the historical connectedness of black people throughout the new world by developing a "dread ontology" that provides the philosophical and practical matrix in which links are made within the diaspora.

Black young people develop the most profound connection with the African continent through identification with the political struggles in South Africa, particularly in the period under apartheid. In the following account recorded in 1988, a young black man – aged 24 – points out the significance of attitudes to South Africa and third world hunger.

When I see, when I look at South Africa, when I look on the telly and see a mass of starving black faces. I have never seen a mass country of white kids starving to death and God knows what, you know it is pathetic and they are throwing away food in America. Do you understand? And I don't want to see white people knocked down either, I don't want no kids like that, but them things get to me and hurt me and I relate to certain things, really check my mind out to see what is happening. Do you understand? I have to as a black person. Well, like Mandela, a lot of people in Britain see South Africa as a South African problem and they don't give a monkeys, but I'm not doing that because it is also part of me.

South Africa, third world hunger, over-development, British ambivalence to apartheid and, by implication, racism are all connected in the notion of blackness. In this sense, race is the modality in which these diverse social and political elements are understood and articulated.

National identity, ethnicity and "race"

Attitudes towards British or English nationalism varied amongst the black respondents. In the following account given by a 16-year-old young woman, the ambiguous relationship of nationality and race is made quite apparent:

It's like you identify yourself as a black person coming from – with West Indian parents. It's like we – they like to know that they are coming from elsewhere. A lot of black people don't see themselves as English. I think you should be aware of that. It is the way the country puts them down already. It makes you feel like you don't want to be from here. It's like when times are good, us – the people who are born here – are considered English, just like everybody else. But when things are bad, jobs are hard to get, we become black!

Here the fickle nature of the inclusion and exclusion of black people is exposed. This young woman understands clearly that, within political discourses, blackness and Englishness are viewed at best as problematic and at worst as mutually exclusive. However, this does not mean that young black people abandon the notion of British nationality altogether. Young people may on the one hand vacate a notion of Englishness while maintaining the right to British citizenship. Jenny – 15 years old – outlines this:

> Well I am British, I was born in London, but I am not the same as the English people, it's like I am a different kind of English – a different way. I mean we have different ways of – a different culture. But I am still British.

In this extract Jenny distances herself from being like English people but she characterizes herself as a "different kind of English". This points towards a reworking of the cultural aesthetic of Englishness and I will return to this later. Putting this question of cultural politics to one side for a moment, black young people find it easier to identify themselves with a notion of Britishness because it is more ambiguous in terms of its cultural definition. Black young people equate Britishness with citizenship. In Jenny's account above she separated the issue of cultural diversity and its relationship to Englishness from her identification with Britishness.

However, some young people abandon the concept of Britishness altogether. Geoff – 16 years old – shows how he has completely vacated the idea of British nationality.

> Well to me now I would define myself as a black person.
>
> Les: Would you also see yourself as British?
>
> [Laugh] Na, I mean I would take that as an insult. No, I see myself as a black person of West Indian parentage. I don't want to be classified on the British sides. I mean I feel sorry for them really. I mean [laugh] – no offence but there isn't much to attract me to it.

While there may be little in notions of Englishness and Britishness that seems attractive, accounts like this one should not be taken as evidence that young black people want nothing to do with Britain. Clearly, they are in the process of working out this relationship in a syncretic culture that is both black and British.

The island origin of the parents of these young people is also an important aspect of how they develop their identity. All of the young people of Caribbean origin I have interviewed utilize some notion of "island identity", and a common distinction that is made divides Jamaica and the rest, referred to as "small islands". However, these Caribbean identifications have to be placed in the broad process of the cultural construction of blackness. For example, I interviewed a young woman of Barbadian parentage who spoke a Jamaican-derived form of Creole in her peer group. In her account she identified with Barbadian origins but also with a shared sense of black Londonness. Thus within the cultural construction of "blackness" a diversity of origins can be made alongside the recognition of common links.

Present in many of the accounts of young black British people – particularly those whose parents came from Jamaica but not always confined to them – is the concept of "yard". "Yard" means home. It can relate to the house one lives in or the area one calls home territory. Particularly interesting is the flexibility of the concept when applied to Britain and the Caribbean. In this extract Elorna – 18 years old, Jamaican parents – talks about her identity via the concept of "yard".

> To me now England is my "yard"– that is to say I was born here. But if I went with my parents back to Jamaica they would check me as English. So I am English to a certain extent – but England is my "yard". If a Jamaican came to England now they would call him a "yardy". So things are complicated.

The claim of territory is an interesting feature of the accounts by young black people. They often speak of the "area" in the same way as they view "yard". I think there are a number of important appropriations being made here. One is a claim over territory (Hall 1988) and the other is a transformation of the meaning of that territory. To say that "England is my yard" not only is a statement about claiming rights but also transforms the meaning of England. The aesthetic of Englishness shifts from the English, white, racist triangle to a multiracial notion of Englishness in which a black English aesthetic can legitimately exist. At a local level these processes have reached advanced stages of development. This is not the case when one looks at the national discourses operated in the circuits of mass communication, where a new racism is abundant (van Dijk 1991). What I have shown in this chapter is that local definitions of inclusion and exclusion do not connect with "race" in the same way as their national equivalents (Gilroy 1987: 54). It is in these local spaces where new possibilities and identities are being explored.

So far within this section I have stressed the importance of understanding how black young people navigate their notions of identity across national boundaries to connect with New World African diasporas and the critical transformations that are taking place in English/British national identity. This analysis contrasts the literature critically reviewed in Chapter 1 that characterizes black youth as suffering from a crisis of identity. However, to suggest that racism does not provide black young people with dilemmas in terms of their notions of self would be to misrepresent the situation. I maintain that, although black young people may experience a tension between the ways their identities are socially defined, they are also actively resolving the racist identity riddle, i.e. that blackness and Englishness are mutually exclusive identities. In the following quotation from a 17-year-old young man called Michael we see that process in action. He starts off by articulating a notion of marginality:

> Buoy [boy] me? I'm lost! As much as it sounds bad, I'm lost. Because I am not Jamaican, as in, I couldn't go to Jamaica and say I'm Jamaican and I'm definitely not English – therefore I'm stuck in the middle.

Michael clearly identifies the source of the dilemma:

> But you know, out here, if I went for a job, I mean, I could be talking over the phone and I would sound a perfect Englishman and turn up for a job and they say – "but you're black"! Na mean? I look at them and say "Shush, don't tell everyone". Na mean? And buoy, I wouldn't even say it was even a racial thing but it is obvious to their eyes, yeah? You don't have black English people according to them.

He dismembers the racial common sense that sees blackness and Britishness as mutually exclusive. In an incisive way he identifies the shift in racist discourses away from "race" to the cultural definition of Englishness. For Michael there is no contradiction; the contradiction lies in those who think "black English" people do not exist.

While many have viewed accounts such as this as symptomatic of an identity crisis among the British-born black community, they can alternatively be seen as a driving force behind their creativity. It is in this way that young black people in this area have sought actively to define what their identities are and what their culture means.

Class, ethnic absolutism and the limits of cultural definitions of blackness

I began this section by arguing that, although the notion of "blackness" as a concept is ambiguous and problematic, it should be retained because it is often the medium through which connections to cultural heritage are made. However, there is a danger of privileging these particular cultural constructions as the only viable ones (Mercer 1990b), and thus slipping into a kind of "ethnic absolutism" (Gilroy 1987: 59). Some of the young people I have interviewed have clearly articulated a resistance to a unitary definition of "blackness". Here Julie, an 18-year-old black woman, describes how this syndrome has affected her life.

> I am black and I know what that means because I have learned to know what that means – people remind me. But like I don't want to have to wear that, to hold myself that way all the time. Like if you're black they expect you to act in a certain way – this big image thing.

She goes on to point out how these definitions can operate a double standard in relation to the cultural resources that are available to young black people:

> Well, it's not just the white people but – you know sometimes it comes from your own people. If you are not into dance-hall style and all that then you are not black enough for them. You know like it is hypocrisy. White people go down and buy a Bob Marley record and that is alright, but if I want to say get into, I don't know, Shakespeare or something then that is wrong. The white people see you as "Well, shouldn't you really be playing in a steel band" [laugh] and the black people check you as wanting to be white and I don't want to be white. I mean I don't have to be reminded that I am not white but I want to be able to take what I want and not have to – like these are the "black" things – these are for you.

Julie is aware of the ways she is limited by these expectations. It is in this way that absolutist notions of affirmative, syncretic black culture can act as a constraint on access to other cultural storehouses. Julie is a student at a local college and she is clearly aspirant. She points out the double standard whereby white people can buy Bob Marley records but she cannot have the same freedom to take what might be attractive in "white culture". This is very close to the examples Roger Hewitt has recorded where young black people are "marginalised both by white domination and by a culture they felt to be both theirs and yet simultaneously not theirs" (Hewitt 1986: 211–13).

Equally, Tony, a 21-year-young old man, explained to me in the youth club one night:

> You see upstairs now they've got a whole heap of books right [referring to the youth club library] and I mean they are all books about black history and so on. But right, what I want to find out about is art, and all kinds of other things you know. I mean I got this book out of there [passes over a copy of Ernest Cashmore's sociological text *Rastaman*] you know what I mean [laugh]. I want to know about China, Rome – read all kind of different things, rasta.

The black cultural identities I have reported are both powerful and, I would argue, positive. However, there are absolutist elements in popular talk. Thus people such as Tony and Julie can be defined as being "not black enough", or "Bountys" or "coconuts" (i.e. black on the outside, white on the inside). These forms of racial closure make moments of definition and identity possible. However, if affirmation leads to absolutism then the course of cultural development is blocked and may result in limiting the unifying potential of these identities.

Class differentiation within black communities is having significant effects on the ability of collective black identities to transcend class (Tizard & Phoenix 1989). The cultural definition of blackness I have described here is being formulated within a working-class context where many people are workless. Such culturally constructed definitions of blackness may not include middle-class black people. Michael comments:

> They [middle-class black people] makes me laugh. I mean I admire them for the fact that they have got there. They have

shown people – look at what I am, I don't care what you
think. I respect them for that but at the same time they make
me laugh. If I talk to them the way I'm talking now and they
come back with their educated accent, then I turn round and
come back with the Jamaican bit, they'd come back with
something and it would sound kind of limp [laugh] – kind of
limp against it. It's got no spin, it's got no – something's
missing.

Although Michael acknowledges the common experience of racism,
he also recognizes that middle-class black people do not share the
expressive culture so central to the definition of blackness in Southgate. Their language seems "kind of limp" and lacking in the prestigious codes recognized in his peers' group. In the following quotation,
Michael is also linking class with youth style:

I mean I know people like that [young middle-class black
people] and they're the ones who shave their heads in all kinds
of crazy styles, wear weird garments.

Les: Do you mean the hip hoppers?

Na. I mean they are alright, I means much as they look freaky,
they're alright because they are everyday, you see them on the
street, you know dem people. But I'm on about the ones who
ride the mauve bicycles with the straight handle bars and the
seats with the big fat springs – na mean.

In this extract Michael is talking about two locations of black stylers.
There are "everyday people" who are his peers, who adopt youth cultural forms rooted in reggae culture or hip hop and urban black forms
of style. Alternatively there are black people who wear "crazy style",
including those who attended a local art college. He recognizes common links yet at the same time refers to separate cultural spaces and
domains of cultural meaning. This is similar to what Labov identified
in the black American context, where black people who do not participate in the vernacular culture are classified as being "lame" (Labov
1972: 258). In this sense the type of black identity that I have referred
to in this section must be viewed as positioned within black working-
class culture.

In summary, living and working in Southgate one gets the feeling that young black people and their parents are consolidating their position in this area and at the same time defining the terms of their presence. In this sense the meaning of "blackness" is intimately related to this process and, although the symbolism that is used in constructing a black identity may originate from widespread sources, these become resonant and fit together in this time and place. Thus I am arguing that formulations of black identity in Southgate must be viewed as exhibiting both a local expression and a social articulation with black collectivities nationally and internationally.

"Mixed race" youth and identity

As Tizard and Phoenix have pointed out, there exists considerable evidence that people of "mixed race" will constitute a steadily growing sector of British society. The Labour Force Survey 1984–86 showed that 27 per cent of married and cohabiting Afro-Caribbean men under the age of 30, and 28 per cent of married and cohabiting Afro-Caribbean women of the same age, had a white partner (quoted in Tizard & Phoenix 1989). Although there are no current statistics for Southgate, I estimate that the level of inter-racial unions is at or above this level.

I have shown that a variety of categories exist for young people who are of mixed parentage: "mixed race", "light skinned", "coloured", "half caste". In the examples cited earlier, Chris and Cinta chose to vacate the notion "half caste" and in Cinta's case she chose to utilize a notion of blackness. I think these two instances show an important development that is going on in Southgate. There is a political and ideological move at the local level to redefine the notion of half caste and replace it with the concept of "mixed race". This is a conscious intervention on behalf of community workers and political activists to transform folk terms such as "half caste" that connote racial deficit and replace them with less stigmatized terms such as, for example, "mixed parentage". There has been a conscious attempt to try to change the assumption that children of "mixed race" are somehow caught "in between", in a state of marginality (Stonequist 1937).

In fact, a positive conception of the advantages of being "mixed race" is often used when the issue is raised in everyday talk. This is similar to the suggestion by Park (1937), that mixed-race people are able to move in and out of black and white communities. There is a movement away from the stigmatized notion of "half caste" but this movement has not yet dislocated its usage and the term is still prevalent. Indeed in both cases cited earlier the term was used as a means to hurt the young people.

In the small sample (six) I have interviewed, there seem to be two trajectories in identity formulation: one is a movement towards a notion of mixed ethnicity; and the other is a stronger identification with a notion of blackness. Their accounts offer evidence to support Ann Wilson's (1984) assertion that, in multiracial areas, "mixed race" is a viable identity. Joyce – 17 years old, with a white British mother and a black British father – outlines how she feels:

> Well I am mixed race and I am proud of that. I mean in many ways I am like this area – mixed. I mean sometimes you get people calling you "half caste" and all that but I don't think that is right – what does that mean any way. No I am mixed race.

Les: Did you ever feel that you wished you were more like either one of your parents.

> Na, not really. I mean I don't think about it in black or white terms – well I can't really can I?

Les: What do you mean?

> Well, if I was to favour one colour over another I would be favouring one of my parents over the other just because of colour – you know what I mean.

It is clear from Joyce's account that the way she speaks about her own notion of colour is closely related to the neighbourhood context. She sees herself as a product of this neighbourhood, where "racial things" are not important. Four out of the six young people I interviewed preferred this kind of orientation. These same young people also favoured mixed peer groups – although this had not always been the case for some. In multiracial peer groups, "mixed race" young people participated in the syncretic youth cultures mentioned in the previous sections. In this sense, the notion of "mixed race" and the emergent identities that are shared in multiracial peer groups are complementary.

In the other two cases the young people favoured a closer attachment to black friends and black identity. These two options are by no means mutually exclusive. In fact Matthew – 17 years old – shows that both of these identities can be inhabited without any contradiction:

> I am mixed race but I am also black. I mean there are many shades of black you know. I mean if a man sees you on the street and he is a racist he isn't going to come up to you and ask you exactly how much black blood you've got in you is he?

Clearly, the black–white dualism that racism enforces (Small 1986, W. James 1986) on young people is felt by them. Equally, some parents – especially those who have lived in the area and have learned about racism through their attachment to the black community – encourage identifications with blackness as a political response to racism. The following quote is from an interview with Debbie – quoted earlier – who has a "mixed-race" son.

> A lot of people say to me because he [her son] looks white, right, that um I must make him white you know. To me he has got that decision to make, but I feel that he should be black. Not necessarily that I want him to be black, but I know that as soon as they find out that he has got a black daddy, that he is going to have a lot of shit and the easiest way to go, I'm not saying that blacks will totally accept him, but more blacks will accept him than whites.

This view was held by some of the black people with whom I discussed this issue. Neville, a 23-year-old man, pointed this out:

> On my landing there is a friend, there is a Turkish girl who is living with a black guy and they have a child, right. Now she was saying to me how her child isn't black. I mean I had a long, long talk with her over this, right. And I said to her: "It might be alright you saying that now but when your little youth grows up and he starts to move around there is only one way that people will check him and that is as black!"

In this situation it is feasible for young people of mixed parentage to move closer to the highly syncretic black identities being forged in this area.

157

"Mixed-race" children can define themselves as mixed race and black. They can also be involved in the kinds of cultural dialogue that takes place in multi-ethnic peer groups. Equally, these young people espouse a racially inclusive local identity. Indeed the arguments that I have put forward for an understanding of youth identities as multi-faceted are equally applicable to young people of mixed parentage.

Conclusion

One of the most important contributions by anthropologists to the study of ethnicity is the insistence that ethnicity is produced in situations where two or more social collectivities are defined in relation to one another in a situation of contact (Barth 1969, Wallman 1979). Ethnicity is always about negotiations. In the account offered in this chapter I have moved the emphasis beyond the situational model of ethnicity towards something I refer to below as "negotiated ethnicity".

Here negotiation has two related but discrete meanings. In the first, negotiations are taking place between individual actors interacting in a specific micro context. The most important form of negotiation I have referred to is the dialogues occurring within multiracial friendships. What I have shown is that in the context of these friendship patterns young white and black people construct an alternative public sphere in which truly mixed ethnicities develop. In this space the divisive ideologies of race and racism can be unpacked. The language used in this context has a poly-vocality that reflects the diverse cultural materials being utilized by these young people. The result is the development of richly syncretic cultural forms that are open to young South Londoners regardless of origin.

The second meaning that negotiation has in this context is related to wider meanings; that is, between publicly generated definitions of identity and the way young people re-fashion these notions of identity. This results in a schism between the alternative public spheres of the neighbourhood and multiracial peer groups and a public arena dominated by national race discourses and racisms. The prevalence of racist discourses constantly undermines the negotiated forms of ethnicity being generated in multiracial peer groups.

The majority of white young people referred to in this study reject the terms in which white Englishness is defined. In this sense young

whites are searching for a notion of social identity free of the ideological underpinning of a racialized definition of Englishness. White
encoded identification with blackness offers a temporary solution.
However, identifications with their black peers are always desta-
bilized by the presence of racism and they are forced to confront the
meaning of whiteness and how their notions of selfhood are interpo-
lated through it.

Similarly, the construction of blackness as a cultural identity has to
be viewed in the specific context of Southgate where historical connections are being made with the New World African diaspora located in the Caribbean and North America. I have argued that black
identities in South London exhibit specific local qualities and national and international connections with black people elsewhere. As
Michael puts it in the following quotation, everybody has "their own
cut" (version):

> Out inna country, places like Birmingham, people speak the
> Jamaican in a different way – it cracks me up. Yeah, every-
> where you go it's different. You know what I mean, every-
> one's got their own variation to it, their own cut.

Equally, young black people are engaging with the way nationhood is
being defined and preparing the social ground where a reworked aesthetic of Englishness can exist free of racially exclusive terms of reference.

What I have shown is a glimpse into the new ethnicities and identities being explored by young people living in South London, such as
Michael:

> It's like if you are white living in a black area you'll have a
> little black in you, and if you are black living in a white area
> you will have a little white in you.

Young people living in Southgate are creating cultures that are neither
simply black nor simply white. These syncretic cultures produce
inter-racial harmony while celebrating diversity; they defy the logic
of the new racism and result in volatile cultural forms that can be
simultaneously black and white.

CHAPTER 7

Experiencing and parodying racism

Introduction

In the two previous chapters I have shown how the expression of racism at street level has been muted in Southgate. In this chapter I want to discuss the context in which young black British people experienced racism. I argue that this is affected by factors such as neighbourhood, life cycle and gender. I show that young black people are not passive recipients of racist discourses and that in the context of daily interactions black young people work on representations of race, parody racism and develop a critique of the racial structuring of British society.

The models of racism and the terms of definition of this concept are not always uniformly defined by the young people themselves. In some accounts racism is seen as including forms of both white and black prejudice. On other occasions a structural and abstracted model of racism is used. However, in most cases racism is talked about in the context of lived relationships, events and experiences. The young black people whom I have interviewed may not always see racism in a structural and abstract way, but they encounter racism as they move through educational, occupational and leisure spaces. I will show that this process is not static or unidirectional and that young people are not the passive recipients of racism.

The following discussion consists of two broad sections. The first addresses the contexts in which young black people experience racism and the content of racist discourses. In the second section I recount a series of incidents I recorded during participation in a black male peer group. Here I document the ways in which racial meanings were subverted and dismembered in the process of group interaction and verbal play. The aim of this chapter is to illustrate the ways young black people transcend racist discourses.

The experience of popular and institutional racism in Southgate

In this section I distinguish between two sites in which racism is directed at young people. The first refers to the experience of racism in daily contexts. This kind of racism is documented in Chapters 2 and 3 and I refer to it in what follows as popular racism (Cohen 1988a). Secondly, there are forms of racism that are operated within British institutions. The notion of "institutional racism" emerged from the Black Power movement during the 1960s in the United States (Carmichael & Hamilton 1968). A distinction was made between individual racism and covert racism operated by institutions. Robert Blauner developed this notion to include all institutional processes and the "the chains of unwilling actions" (Blauner 1972: 188) that result in the maintenance of racial inequality. Thus racism is understood as what white people do to maintain benefits that their "race" confers upon them (Wellman 1977).

A notion of institutional racism was introduced into Britain in the 1960s and early 1970s (Allen 1973, Dummett 1973, Sivanandan 1981–2, Miles & Phizacklea 1984). Since then the concept has been critically appraised (Mason 1982, Williams 1985, Phillips 1987, Miles 1989), particularly for not connecting with other processes of stratification such as class inequality. It is claimed that the notion of institutional racism does not allow for the fact that white people are not uniformly placed in powerful positions (Miles 1989: 54).

In the following analysis my concern is to report the contexts in which young black people experience racism. Here I utilize a conception of institutional racism that I define as the operation of racist discourses, which may be explicit or hidden, in an institutional context where these discourses *may* place their subjects in a materially subordinate position.[1] I am not suggesting that institutional racism is monolithic or all-pervasive. Rather I am concerned to identify the social locations where black people encounter racist ideologies and discourses.

Gender, racism and sexuality

Although all the young black people I have interviewed from Southgate said that they had experienced racism, many of them said that they did not meet much overt abuse in the area. They claimed that racism was most often experienced in districts outside of Southgate and in particular in more affluent neighbourhoods.

The identification of racism with areas outside of Southgate is clearly expressed in the following extracts from two young black men. This conversation took place in the Southgate Youth Club and the two people involved were Derek and Cookie. Derek – aged 22 – works in a clothes shop outside of Southgate. On this occasion he is describing an experience that happened while he was helping his father who is a self-employed builder. He had been working in an exclusive area of London's West End that day. He comments as follows and Creole switches are marked in italics:

Derek: I was working today up the West End with my old man – right – [whisper] in some big house. When we come in the house, this woman goes to her daughter [mimics an upper-class accent], "Make sure you bring the bags downstairs". You know what I mean?

Cookie: *Make sure you a?*

Derek: You know what I mean? [upper-class accent] "Make sure you bring the bags downstairs". I said *blood claht* [an expletive]. [Laugh]

Derek: I'm down there with my overalls and dirty trainer and dis and dat. Down Kensington I went into this shop, right, and this is them [mimics people turning their heads], "*Ras claht* [an expletive], what is he doing in here?"

Cookie, a bar clerk in a large court, commented that he has to deal with the expectations and prejudice of middle-class white people every day, and that he has to present himself to middle-class whites in an acceptable way in order to get on. He said that the people he works with have no understanding of working-class black people: "They think we are all muggers and tiefs [thiefs]." Derek then recounted his experience of walking around this affluent district of London:

Derek: Lunch time now I went down one road and there were all these small cafés.

Steve: Where was this?

Derek: Kensington . . . and all these small cafés down there and *you wanna see the people a look when I pass the door.* Like [posh voice] "I hope he doesn't come in here" – that type of look [looks down his nose]. You watch tomorrow now [group laughs] there is going to be some *rough business, rough business.*

Cookie: Hey D.[Derek] *you wanna say ragamuffin, innit.*

Derek: The *people them a look at me* and I give them some strong, strong look.

These two young black men are talking about their experiences of middle-class racism in the context of an affluent district of London – the West End – and in a professional community. In both cases they are recounting the kinds of prejudice that they meet as black people in these two social worlds. Derek comments on a class culture of affluence and the humiliating way he was treated as a young black man walking down a street in Kensington. The thing that is common to both accounts is their contempt for the "rich" who are unconcerned about black people whom they subject to racism. Here they are identifying class-specific expressions of racism. Although the accounts given reflect different situations, the language of description is a shared one. In particular, the code switches represent references to a common speech community. These switches mark statements with emphasis but also affirm the shared sensibilities of the speakers.

The stereotypes that are mobilized against young black people are also affected by gender. The reactions to Derek's blackness and maleness described above were probably informed by the racist representation of black young men as undesirable, violent, dangerous and aggressive. Many of the young men refer to instances in South London where white (adult) people with whom they come into contact "hold on to their bags tightly" or "put their heads down and walk away". Although the incidence of these kinds of reactions in Southgate is not as high as in other areas of London, they are still present. As Tim points out here:

> White people fear black people. Lotta people out there don't
> know black people. It's only what they hear and read in the

newspapers – that is how they know black people, that is how they see black people. Walking down the road you see white ladies holding onto their bags tight as you pass them, as if you are gonna rob dem.

In terms of racist common sense these kinds of stereotypes are less applicable to black women. Although they may experience racism in different ways, the young women I interviewed recognized the gender-sensitive nature of popular racism. This is highlighted in the following quote from a 16-year-old black young woman who identifies the ways in which maleness and blackness are constructed:

> Well, I don't experience discrimination all the time but I have friends that do. I mean I've never been picked up by the police or anything like that but I know a lot of people who have. Most of them were men . . . you know like if you are young and you're black they think automatically that you are dangerous, particularly for the boys.

Young black women may face different kinds of stereotyping but they are by no means exempt from racism. For black women, racist constructions focus on stereotypes of emotional volatility and sexuality. Trudy (15 years old) pointed out to me:

> I mean they might not come right out and say it but you always know that it is there . . . I suppose they expect girls to be more soft, you know what I mean? I mean they come out with, "Oh, the black girls are more emotional, they have short tempers. They have children quick – always having babies." You know what I mean?

Here Trudy gives a clue to the kinds of racism that the females face, i.e. they are seen as being "over-emotional" and "highly fertile". In the following extract two young women, Sharon (17 years old) and Delora (16 years old) talk through the relationship between racism and gender:

Sharon: Well, I suppose it is different for the boys. I mean they are the ones who the police stop but like for girls it is still –

Delora: Yeah, I remember one white boy saying about going out with black girls, it was like, what did he say – "Once you go black, you never turn back". Like black girls are supposed to be some sex machine.

Sharon: But I suppose that's the same for black boys, the thing about black men their big – you know [all laugh].

Sharon: Seriously!

In this extract two important issues are discussed. First, Delora points out the often quoted way in which racism makes black sexuality an element of white fantasy (Griffin 1960: 85–92). This particular strain of racist reasoning is applied differently to young men and women. Young men are characterized in this gendered racism as having "over-sized penises" and predatory desires, while young women's sexuality is viewed as all-encompassing yet addictive for white men. Hall has commented similarly that it is impossible to understand contemporary racism(s) without "crossing the questions of racism irrevocably with the questions of sexuality" (1988: 29). These concepts circulate in Southgate but they are certainly less prevalent in this area than in many other districts of London. Even so, while the numerical strength of black young people in Southgate may secure for them a space in which racist voices may be muted, or even silenced, it cannot shelter them from its wider prevalence.

"Taking liberties": The processes of racial structuring from school to work

The experience of racism in South London has to be placed within the contexts of the institutions in which young black people move. The young people emphasized that they mostly encountered racism at school. The experience of school has been well documented (Troyna 1979, Turkie 1982, Mac an Ghaill 1988) and here I want to discuss how relationships with others in the neighbourhood, including white peers, are affected by racial inequality in education.

There existed a common code of fairness in the way young people talked about interpersonal relations. Transgressing this code was referred to as "taking liberties". Tim (18 years old) outlines what this means in terms of his relations with teachers and his experience of school:

You don't have to be bad in school to get a bad reputation. I mean you used to go down to my school, right, and you see all the kids standing outside the Deputy Headmaster's room, it was pure black people, you know what I mean? And it wasn't as if at my school it was like white kids against black kids, it was more like we was all united against the teachers.

The common experience of school and locality meant that "race" as a divisive social parameter did not result in total separation at school. It was the way white teachers related to white pupils that was the significant factor. Tim went on to tell of an incident when he was discovered smoking with three other boys. Tim used the story to illustrate how the stereotypes operated by the teachers acted as means to divide them according to racial stereotypes. The boys were accused of smoking marijuana. According to Tim's account, the three black boys were expelled whereas the white boy was not. Tim suggested that this was a result of the teachers designating drug abuse as exclusively a black phenomenon in the school. He said:

I mean it's not my white spar's [friend] fault so I don't feel no way [resentment] for him, but it was the teacher who was being racist – na mean!

Racially unequal life chances were also something clearly articulated by the young black people I interviewed. This was in no way placed in contradiction with assertions of commonality with their white peers. Rather, it was a statement of the way in which "the system" ordered their ability to progress. Michael, 20 years old, comments in this extract on the divisions that are imposed by the existence of racial inequality in both schools and the labour market:

My white friends check things the same as me but at the same time they are in a better position than me, na mean? I wouldn't say that they were all working because they are definitely not all working. As much as they are not working – I mean – they are not being as scrutinized and followed by police in cars.

Here we see the direct conflict between the alliances that black and white young people develop and the existence of racism on the part of the police force and the labour market. Here the distinction between popular and institutional forms of racism is essential. Black young people clearly articulated that it is in the institutions of education and the police that racism is mostly encountered. It is not claimed that these institutions are monolithically racist. However, the racism that exists in these contexts introduces divisions that are being undermined by the cultural alliances being developed within the neighbourhood.

The importance of contextual influences on racial inequality was particularly salient for young people who attended a local university. In this context black young people were often exposed to the most crude forms of popular racism and ethnocentrism. In this predominantly middle-class context Greg, a 20-year-old black student, reported:

> You know one time I just couldn't believe it, right, we were in an anthropology lecture and the lecturer was talking about Rastafari. At the end the person in front of me turned around and asked me if I could speak African. I couldn't believe it. I was just flabbergasted by her ignorance.

White middle-class racism in this context was as virulent as anything these young people had encountered growing up in South London.

> You know some of the things that are written on the walls of this university are the kinds of things that you would expect a National Front person to think. Like in the toilet in the Geography Department: "What's worse than a dog turd? A white who sits next to a nigger in class" and "Nigger's [sic] go home". I mean I am tired of thinking about it, no offence, but it's not my problem, it is their problem.

This account challenges the popular characterization that racism is a white working-class problem. In the context of the university, young people were exposed to forms of ethnocentrism and ignorance that were uncommon in their own home locality.

It is in the institutional context of education that racism was identified as being the most severe. Equally, the activities of the police were typified as being the most common source of racism. This points to a series of important issues. One needs to temper any optimistic claims about interpreting the development of anti-racism by the youth community as an indication of the declining social prevalence of racism. Racist practices survive and to some degree militate against the cultural bridges (Røgilds 1991) being built by black and white young people. The institutional production of racial inequality introduces divisions even as young people are struggling to repel the divisive nature of "race". Institutional forms of racism do not directly undermine these youthful alliances. Indeed, black and white opposition to institutional forms of racism operated by teachers or policemen can further galvanize the cultural links already in place because racism is identified as being perpetrated by a white out-group (see Ch. 4). But it is clear from the texts I have included in this section that black young people are aware that their white peers are advancing economically at a faster rate than themselves. White peers are not themselves characterized as being racist but it is understood that racism places whites in a position of advantage. Racial inequalities in life chances subtly undermine the possibility of sustaining these alliances into adulthood. In short, there is a tension between youth egalitarianism and structural forms of inequality.

Parodying racism and subverting racial meanings

During the research I carried out long periods of participant observation with a group of black young men, aged between 16 to early twenties, who met regularly and played basketball together. I became a member of the team and for most of the time I was the only white player. In London it is quite common for sports teams to be predominantly white or black, but there were white teams that had one or two black players or vice versa. My participation was never threatened and rarely challenged. On one occasion my presence was questioned inside a youth club where we used to meet by a young black person not involved in the team. A member of the team immediately jumped to my defence: "The man's got as much right to be here as you, what's a matter wid you man!"

The team was coached by a black woman whose name was Pauline. The young men who played on the team were involved in a variety of educational and occupational activities. Phil was in his early twenties and he worked at the Department of Social Security. Beefy, also in his early twenties, was a qualified motor mechanic. Derek, again in his early twenties, worked in a local men's wear shop as a sales assistant. Stuart, who was of the same age, had recently been made redundant from a local printing firm. Winston worked as a financial clerk. The younger members of the team were attending either further education college, polytechnic or university. Tyrone and Clive were 18 and they studied at a local college of further education. Derek was 21 and was doing a degree course at a local polytechnic.

I became part of this peer group. I was even given a Creole name – "Satan Pickne" (devil child) – by one of the team members. This name was coined because I briefly took charge of training and got a reputation for running physically demanding sessions. I was also referred to as "Homeboy". As I showed in the last chapter, black young people use a range of classifications for white people. Amongst the most derogatory were "satan" or "devil". Thus in this context the Creole name applied to me could be read as an encoded form of abuse or rejection. However, the meaning of this naming claim is complex.

I was not called "Satan Pickne" by everyone in the group. It was Winston who gave me the name and who most often used it. On one occasion during an argument about the extent of racism that took place between Winston and an older man of Caribbean origin, Winston turned and pointed at me and said, "Well what about Les, he isn't a racist. *'Im black* on the inside." The older man replied to Winston's statement by suggesting that I was different because of my "socialization". This might seem extraordinary, but claims of this nature were often made about white insiders in the context of multiracial peer groups.

In the micro context of this peer group these two naming claims ("Satan" and being "black on the inside") signify two sorts of meaning. One meaning relates to the wider influences of racism and racial differentiation. The use of "Satan" acknowledges the different identities that racism forges for black and white young people. Although the name recognized my whiteness, the manner of its usage undermined the meaningfulness of racial divisions. The second meaning refers to the denial of the relevance of racial differentiation in the context of the peer groups and also acknowledges my identification with black people and blackness. This, as showed in Chapter 6, is the core of the dilemma that white people in this position face. The wider prevalence of racism outside of these friendships had to be reckoned with as we moved out of the "private" peer group setting (Suttles 1968).

As a white fieldworker I could develop only a limited appreciation of the ways in which racism impinges on these young people. The claims that I am making in this chapter should be viewed in the context of a white person developing relationships with black young people in a society that exhibits a multiplicity of racisms. In many ways I was entering relationships similar to those that white young South Londoners have with their black peers, and as a result there were occasions when I was close enough to racist practices to develop partial insights into the way popular racism was experienced.

There was limited evidence of racist behaviour from host teams in the local league in which we played. However, this was not the case when we travelled outside of London. This was illustrated when we went to Great Yarmouth to play in a tournament. We travelled to the tournament on a Friday night by minibus. The mood of the team was optimistic and excited. There were lively exchanges over the comparative merits of reggae and rub-a-dub versus soul and hip hop as competing opinions tried to influence the music played on the portable hi-fi.

When we arrived it was immediately apparent that we were entering a completely different social and political landscape. On Saturday we played two games, the second of which we lost by the smallest of margins. The young men contested the result and the team was disqualified from the tournament. I have no doubt that the decision was influenced by the racist images that the presence of these young men evoked in the minds of the white organizers. Winston, the team captain, saw this clearly: "I don't say this often, Les, but these people are racist. It is because we are a black team that they are being so hard on us." It was clear that the panic that the officials showed towards the team was not simply a result of the protests that we made. Pauline, the team coach, commented that exactly the same sequence of events had happened the previous year when a women's team from Brixton had participated in the tournament. She said, "The people here will do that if we don't behave properly. You see we make it easy for them to say 'What do you expect from them ghetto boys?'." Yet these young men were hardly "children of the ghetto"; they were all employed, some in "white-collar" jobs, or studying. It seemed clear to me that the fear that was so apparent in the behaviour of the white officials and organizers was the most important factor shaping the outcome of these events.

On the Saturday evening a dance was held to celebrate the tournament. The team attended with mixed feelings. We sat in a corner of the function room where the event was being held. I kept thinking of the extent to which basketball is predominantly a white game in Britain. Black players were perfectly fine as long as they remained just a few charismatic figures. It was a very different matter when black teams participated, as this experience had shown. The irony of the situation was that during the course of the evening the organizers ran a "best-looking player" competition, and it was won by one of our players. Just a few hours earlier the team had been characterized as a riotous group of black youngsters. Suddenly black became beautiful! There was a suggestion that Derek should not accept the prize as a protest against the earlier behaviour of the organizers. However, this did not happen and the team celebrated a strange victory. Paradoxically it seemed as if our white hosts characterized young black people as being individually glamorous and attractive while at the same time were fearful of them collectively. This comes close to what Stuart Hall calls the "doubling of fear and desire" (Hall 1988: 28) where contradictory feelings towards black subjects can be felt simultaneously. The contradiction is at the core of the construction of black otherness. The white organizers of the competition used the fact that a black person won the "beauty contest" as a way of denying that their prior actions had been informed by racism.

The problems of the weekend were compounded by the responses of other whites in this area. Before returning to London we decided to stop at a local McDonald's. We pulled up outside the restaurant. I was sitting at the front of the bus and furthest away from the exit doors, which were at the back. The McDonald's shop front consisted of a massive glass window. As I looked out of the bus towards the restaurant I could see all of the customers staring at the team. It seemed as if these people were mesmerized. Phil turned to me: "What's a matter with these people? Maybe they've never seen niggers before!" As we walked into the shop I said to him: "Who do they think they are looking at?" He replied "It doesn't piss me off, I just laugh at them. It was like when I went down to Wales, this little kid came over to me and said 'You're black'. I said, 'Yeah right, I know'." Phil laughed as we entered the restaurant. We got our food quickly then went back to the van to eat it. All of the young men were uneasy. Outside a couple of punks were walking their Rotweiler dogs. The dogs were barking ferociously at the van. Stuart collected up the rubbish from our meal and started to head for the rear door. Winston turned to him: "Stuart, man, it ain't safe for a black man to go out there. The dogs might like black meat. Let Les take it. It's alright Satan, *white blood na sweet* [white blood is not sweet]." We all laughed and I collected up the rubbish and took it outside to the bin.

We left for London soon after this incident. As we travelled home I said to the young men in the back of the bus that it made me feel ashamed because of the way the whites had reacted. Tyrone then added: "Yesterday, right, these two kids come up to me in the sports hall, right, and asked me where I was from. I said, 'Southgate'. They said, 'Where's that? Africa?' So I threw the ball and hit one of them right in the stomach. Agh, these kids were just being *facety* [cheeky]." Winston added: "You just don't let them mess wid you like that. They are pathetic, man. People take liberties wid you." Others thought that the best way to deal with this kind of ignorance was to ignore it. Alton said: "I feel sorry for them really you know. I just don't take any notice of them, they are just pure wickedness. That why some people won't come out of their yard [home or area] you know, Les."

It would, however, be premature to conclude that these young men's response was simply to ignore the ignorance of whites who operated racist ideas. This would capture only part of the sophisticated way in which these young men acknowledged racism and inverted racial meanings. The following exchange took place during a bus ride with the basketball team when we were travelling to West London. In doing so we passed through some of the affluent areas of the city. During the bus ride Winston performed a monologue for the entertainment of the team, and throughout the performance "race" ideologies were subverted and "commonsense" racism publicly ridiculed. Winston adopted the guise of a series of characters in order to make the performance work. The principal character was the crassly affected "Upper Class Twit".

The monologue

Oh, you see these buildings. My uncle owns them. I can't remember what it's called. I think it's Buckingham Palace. We rent them out to a rather nice family. In fact we own quite a lot of land in this area – um, I think it's called London. Yes, it's rather nice round here. We don't have any of you strange coloured people, except the Arabs. Nice people those Arabs.

I sold one of these buildings to an Arab. Do you know the
Hilton?

We don't have any of you West Indian people around
here. Of course you know you West Indian people eat rather
peculiar food. Oh yes, what is it called now. Is it the yellow
stuff – acke and salt fish? That's it. And there is another yellow dish, um plantain – that's it. Rather strange but it's very
nice. Of course, it is not like roast beef and Yorkshire pud-
ding but it is quite nice. And you listen to that music, what is
it called – regg? reggi? reggae? Yes, yes that's it. Frightfully
good, lots of rhythm, good to move about to. And you have
those fellows – ragga? ragamuffins? Yes, that's right. Mind
you I don't know what kind of fellows they are. And what is
that other kind of music you listen to – acid? The only kind
of acid I've seen is in a chemistry lab [laughter].But you people have got no class. I mean you don't even speak the
Queen's English, do you? I mean you West Indian people
speak what is it . . .

Switches character to the street-wise Ragamuffin, speaking out of the
corner of his mouth in Creole:

Whappen now star!!! Seckle, seckle now people. Cool, cool
na baass! [What is happening friends, settle down]

Switches back to the Upper Class Twit:

You see what I mean? I mean you West Indian people can't
speak the Queen's English, I can't even understand what he's
saying.

Switches characters to a Black Cockney:

I mean that's the way we talk like, na what I mean, innit?

Switches back to the Upper Class Twit:

That's better, I can understand what he's saying, but still no
class, no class at all. You see the way I speak, it has a certain
manner – class. Of course, it comes with education. I mean

where was you educated [looks at Les]. What did you say? Southgate High? Not bad but not very much class. I went to Cambridge then Harvard and that's why I can talk like this. You see it's all down to class. I'm travelling with you boys – incognito. Incognito! [Looks at Clive] Do you know what that means? I thought not – no class. I mean you have to watch these dark-skinned fellows. Of course, I've been all around the world – you know – with the army. In fact I went to a rather large place where they have a lot of these different colour[ed] people – it's called Africa. [Les, Alton and Phil laugh hysterically] In fact, I spent a lot of time in the Gambia. Yes, yes in the Gambia. Of course those Africans speak very strangely –

Switches to an African and says in affected "African speech":

I thank you very much. [Whole group laughs]

Switches back to the Upper Class Twit:

I know you fellows find it hard to get work over here and we all know that you're lazy, I might be able to get some jobs for you. In fact, I have a perfect job for you Beefy, wrestling lions. Yes, there are a lot of lions in the jungle and they need big boys like you to deal with the lions. And Phil, you can be Beefy's assistant. Clive, we have a special job for you – we'll put you in charge of the monkeys. You can be our monkey expert. [Looks at Alton] Of course, you know the jungle is a very dangerous place. [Whole bus laughs] And I've got a very special job for you Les. Yes, we'll make you a diplomat because you know you've got those white skins. You have a little more class.

The "Upper Class Twit" is the principal voice used in the narrative. He is presented as a product of his education and as "having class", a member of a wealthy, land-owning family travelling "incognito" with the group. He has a tourist-like curiosity about West Indian people and black British culture. He is fascinated by West Indian food, which is "rather strange but nice", likes reggae because "it's frightfully good, lots of rhythm, good to move to", but is perplexed about more recent

175

cultural phenomena (i.e. ragamuffin/reggae style and acid house music). The image parodied is a mixture of middle-class racism and colonial curiosity. Here the racist stereotyping is refined and subtle: "You people are interesting . . . but you've got no class."

Significantly, this monologue works because all the actors share the same semantic points of reference. The caricatures are drawn from the performer's constituency of meaning, which is shared with his audience. By utilizing various characters with contrasting "social voices" Winston addresses a wide range of issues including: a concept of class rooted in material and educational inequalities, the relationship between class, language and power, the "skin-sensitive" nature of the job market and the characterization of young black people as "lazy" victims of problems that are of their own making. The "culturally impoverished" (in this case black people) can't even speak the "Queen's English", a result of their lack of education. This version of reality is then challenged in the structure of the narrative by incorporating two black voices: a Creole-speaking Ragamuffin and a Black Cockney. The Creole voice is offered both as an example of "the way West Indian people speak" and as a linguistic adversary, both of which are incomprehensible to the Upper Class Twit. The Black Cockney appears as a partisan intermediary translating and defending black language against the claims made by the Upper Class Twit.[2]

For the Upper Class Twit, the relationship between educational inequality and social class is clearly stated and the reference to the army points to a British nationalism that is ideally white – not like "foreign places" that have a lot of "different coloured people". Those with class are educated, patriotic and white. Lastly, the skin-sensitive nature of the British job market is parodied in the section that documents employment possibilities in the Gambia. Here white skins are shown to have a "little more class than different colour people – not much more but a little bit more". Again my "whiteness" and the public meanings attached to it are being referred to and ridiculed at the same time. The constructs being applied to people in the group are not being attributed to individuals. Rather, the "race" of individuals is used to ridicule the way racist discourses confer attributes according to skin colour and origin. In this way my "race" provides a vehicle for criticizing the process that imbues "whiteness" with a superior status.

Young black people engage with racist terms. In play settings they use abusive words such as "nigger" against one another. The meanings of these exchanges are not simple. It is not merely a matter of black young people using racist materials to hurt other black young people. In the following extract the significance of these terms is explored. The exchange took place between two black young women, Donna (19 years old) and Jennifer (18 years old). Both women are from Southgate and they both work as secretaries in central London. Jennifer had been off work for two weeks with a viral infection. I was standing talking to Jennifer at a bus stop in Southgate when Donna approached us. The following exchange took place:

Donna: Are you still off work then?

Jennifer: Yeah, the doctor has signed me off 'til the end of the week you know.

Les: How long have you had this bug for then?

Jennifer: Two weeks.

Donna: Is it?

Les [to Jennifer]: You don't want to go back too soon or . . .

Donna: You niggers are all the same, you just don't want to work [starts to laugh].

Jennifer [sucks her teeth]: That's charming. [Laughing] I'll have you up for racism, you know. [All three laugh]

In this extract Donna is not applying an internalized racist stereotype (Fanon 1968) to a peer in an unaltered way. Rather she is exposing the content of this stereotype and ridiculing its meaning. My whiteness in this situation may have played a part in this interaction but I think that this did not necessarily alter or influence the outcome. Here a racist formula is simultaneously possessed and subverted. A similar phenomenon has been documented by Ben Rampton (1989), who shows how young British Asians "play to" stereotypical and racist constructions.

The question of the degree to which this process results in the mere reproduction of racist ideas has to be posed. However, I did not record instances where this was the case. I am not suggesting that critical encounters with racism always result from exchanges of this kind. The boundaries of significance and the semiotics of these interactions are ambiguous. But clearly they exemplify instances where ideological struggles over meaning are taking place. In this case it is perhaps more accurate to speak about the *extent* to which racist ideas are subverted. In a sense there is a tension between, on the one hand, the reproduction of racist images within this process and, on the other, the potential to subvert the content of racist ideas through parody.

Conclusion

I have shown how the collective struggles of the black community in Southgate have in effect curbed the public expression of racist sentiments. As a result, the social geography of popular racism is divided into areas where it has flourished in a uncontested way and areas such as Southgate.

The accounts included here show the importance of dividing our understanding of racism into *institutional* and *popular* variants. It is in the institutional contexts of school and work that racist practices are most important. Popular racism, on the other hand, is viewed as unevenly developed amongst peers and fellow residents. The awareness of this division is very important when considering how to locate the understanding of racism both spatially and institutionally.

Popular racist ideas experienced by black young people were also differentiated by gender and in particular by racist constructions of black sexuality. Within these discourses, black masculinity is identified with aggressiveness and sexual potency, while black femininity is associated with emotionality and fecundity. Thus racist common sense is not "gender blind". But, equally, the experience of racism is not always gender specific. In this way racist discourse differentiates between gendered black subjects and at the same time unifies them in racialized social groupings.

Black young people do not passively experience racist discourse. There exists a level of experience in which racist ideas and meanings are worked on, subverted and partially transformed. I have shown evidence of this process in action. However, the meaning of these practices is ambiguous and the outcome of the engagements with racist ideology does not always lead to the dismembering of racism. However, I maintain that the play exchanges I have described in this chapter are examples of how black young people develop a micro critique of racial inequality.

Before moving on to the final part of the study I want to draw some comparisons between Riverview and Southgate. Despite the fact that these neighbourhoods are geographically close to one another, I maintain that they exhibit very different qualities. With regard to the community discourses discussed in Chapters 2 and 5, it is clear that similar notions of community are being circulated in these districts. However, in Southgate the racially inclusive notion of community that I refer to as the "our area" semantic system was ascendant. There were similar notions of community in circulation in Riverview, but the dominant discourses in this district result in a racist construction that connects the decline of the district with the increasing presence of racially defined others. In both cases residents spoke about "race" through the language of community.

In Riverview, young people are not passive recipients of the local racism. Young people deny that race is important and almost unanimously condemn racism as being wrong. Yet, at the same time, incidents of racist name-calling continued to occur and Vietnamese refugees were vilified along with black people from other areas. Thus the identities of young whites in this area are subject to competing sets of definitions, i.e. between the local inclusion of selected black peers and racialized definitions of nationality that define Englishness and blackness as mutually exclusive phenomena.

In contrast to Riverview, in Southgate the inclusive notions of local belonging enable a greater degree of cultural syncretism to develop amongst young people. Racism is almost universally condemned by the youth community. The rejection of race as a significant division led to rich and ambiguous cultural exchanges. Alongside this process the cultural construction of blackness is developed. Thus young people move from a youthful rejection of race towards a profound appreciation of the meaning of racism. For young white people this propels them towards a search for a notion of identity free of racism; for black people this results in both an exploration of the interconnected nature of the situation within African diasporas elsewhere and a critical reworking of the relationship between Englishness and blackness. These two developments combine to result in a reformulation of the meaning of nationhood and belonging at a local level. England is defined as a multiracial and culturally hybrid society that is free of racism.

I have argued that the expression and experience of racism are dependent on local factors. However, the cultures of young people living in areas such as the ones I have described cannot be understood simply in the local context. The cultural forms that are produced exhibit local versions of a cultural process that has international reference points. In the next part of the study I want to explore this more fully with regard to the musical cultures found in these areas. I will argue that the cultural production of young people living in South London should be "nested" within international networks of cultural exchange. It is to the nature of these exchanges that Part III is devoted.

PART III

Black music, youth culture and syncretism

CHAPTER 8

"Inglan, nice up!": black music, autonomy and the cultural intermezzo

Introduction

Throughout Parts I and II, I argued that complex syncretic cultural forms are developing within urban settings. These ethnicities need to be understood in specific local contexts where traditions are being re-invented. Although an appreciation of the importance of local factors is essential to the argument put forward so far, these cultural processes also need to be understood in the context of an international traffic in cultural meanings and meaningful forms.

Ulf Hannerz has attempted to conceptualize such a "macro-anthropology" (Hannerz 1989a,b). Hannerz maintains that holistic notions of bounded cultures cannot have explanatory power in a world that exhibits high degrees of transnational connectedness. He discusses the transportation of cultural forms – what he refers to as "flow" (Hannerz 1987, 1990c) – in a global ecumene (1989b, 1990a). Cultures are assumed to be not cohesive and self-perpetuating, but complex and unevenly developed networks of symbols constantly being reworked and "creolized" (Hannerz 1987, Barth 1989, Glissant 1992). Thus complex urban cultures are viewed as dynamic entities that may tend towards stability or innovation, depending on their organizing principles (Hannerz 1990b).

Paul Gilroy has developed an approach similar to Hannerz's notion of cultural networks. However, for Gilroy the driving force behind these movements is a response to the scattering of Africans throughout the New World (Gilroy 1987, 1993a). The expansion of the modern world system (Wallerstein 1974) and the peculiarities of international labour demand have governed the transnational movement of humans throughout the capitalist and antecedent periods. The human consequences of slavery and abject forms of exploitation stripped African peoples of their historical being. Orlando Patterson (1980) suggests that this resulted in a state of "social death". Yet slavery paradoxically "unite[d] what it divide[d] . . . producing new phenomena of religious syncretism and cultural crossbreeding" (Bastide 1978: 67). This process of collective reconstruction echoes throughout the musical cultures of the twentieth century within what Gilroy refers to as the Black Atlantic (Gilroy 1993a).

Theodore Adorno (1978), an early twentieth-century cultural critic, warned that the mechanical reproduction of art and culture would result in the standardization of cultural forms and the inhibition of critical reflection. Mass culture was aimed at merely making the "inescapable easier to bear" (Adorno 1967: 126–7). However, within the context of the musical cultures I will refer to, the technologies of mass consumption have facilitated the re-drawing of the historical and political map of the African diaspora (Drake 1987, Gilroy 1987). The lack of separation between art and life integral to African traditions of music-making (Keil 1972, Sithole 1972, Hoare 1975) has been applied to mechanically reproducible music (Frith 1986).

The histories and cultural politics of the Caribbean and black America form the raw materials for a creative process that defines what it means to be black within a distinctively British setting. This results in a sequence of syncretic cultural processes in which "[b]lack culture is actively made and re-made" (Gilroy 1987: 154). However, the process of constant fashioning and re-fashioning is occurring within the ecology of particular urban contexts and social relations. In this sense these musical cultures have particular local features, yet they cannot be explained in these terms alone. Conceptually the metaphor of the crossroads provides an appropriate tool here (Gilroy 1992). Within the context of diaspora cultural production, the challenge is how to keep sight of the histories that propel these cultural flows while remaining open to the new possibilities that emerge at the crossroads where unforeseen things happen. The concept of the crossroads alone cannot provide an adequately detailed theoretical tool to unpick what happens at the conjunction of cultural routes. Here I want to introduce the notion of rhizome as elaborated in the writings of Gilles Deleuze and Felix Guattari (1986). For Deleuze and Guattari, rhizomes offer an alternative to the vertical root and tree structure of dichotomous arborescent thinking. Through adventurous growths and rhizomes, horizontal connections can be developed between things that have no necessary relation with each other. *Cultural rhizomes* (see also Mercer 1992) form places where political and cultural connections can take place through the creation of a "throng of dialects, patois, slangs and specialised languages" (Deleuze and Guattari 1986: 7). A rhizome has no beginning or end, it is always in the middle. The usefulness of the notion of rhizome is that it provides a way of describing forms of cultural inter-being.

I want to concentrate on the musical cultures from the perspective outlined above. The emphasis on cultural routes over a fixed or essential concept of culture has serious implications for the way in which tradition, music and identity are theorized. The crucial question thus becomes how to theorize forms of continuity within these cultural practices without invoking a notion of primordial essence.

This chapter has two major purposes. I will show that white working-class cultural institutions rejected black workers in post-war London, resulting in the creation of autonomous black forms of leisure. I further argue that black leisure forms provided an alternative for young whites to those of their parents. Whites have negotiated access to black culture, culminating in a partial recomposition of working-class leisure. Additionally, I examine how these processes are also occurring within other British cities outside of the capital. Here I shall look at the musical cultures of young South Asians and the forms of cultural dialogue that are being embodied within these musics. Secondly, I demonstrate the connections that are being made between the dispersed elements of the African diaspora in these musical cultures. Musical genres have converged on South London from the Caribbean and North America and black culture has been created with European specificities and transatlantic connections. This process takes on further transnational nuances when South Asian lexical and cultural elements are introduced into these syncretic processes. The modes of expression that are produced possess a kind of triple consciousness that is simultaneously the child of Africa, Asia and Europe. In the language of black vernacular cultures, the music has gone *outernational*, simultaneously inside and beyond the nations through which it passes. In this way contemporary musical cultures are fuelled by the creative tension between tradition and improvisation (Gilroy 1991).

Racism and working-class leisure

The movement of Afro-Caribbean workers to Britain in the post-war period and the racism that they encountered were a symptom of a radical change occurring in the social structure of urban Britain. The result was the construction of a racially demarcated class fraction (Gilroy 1982b). Although this was felt most starkly by black workers in the housing and labour markets, comparable fragmentations took place in the nature of working-class culture and the institutions of working-class leisure (Sivanandan 1981–2). As Simon Jones points out:

> The same racism that operated in the job and housing markets also operated to bar black workers from many white working-class leisure institutions, such as pubs, clubs, dance palais and bingo halls. (Jones 1988: 33)

White workers had been exposed to the expressive culture of black people for some considerable time – black culture had impacted on white workers from the nineteenth century onwards.[1] However, a "colour bar" operated in post-war working-class life and black workers had to find alternative forms of leisure.

The emergence of black-owned clubs provided a context in which black workers could socialize without encountering racism. According to Dilip Hiro (1971), during the 1950s and 1960s over 50 clubs opened in South London. The music played in these night spots reflected the diverse origins of South London's black settlers. In addition to public leisure spaces, sociability was also connected to family celebrations, house parties, sports functions and the church (Gutzmore 1978). Music was central to many of these leisure activities (Hinds 1980).[2]

Within these autonomous black leisure spaces, black working-class life was recomposed in Britain. In particular, the numerical dominance of Jamaican migrants – who constitute over half of migrants coming from the Caribbean – was echoed in the cultural forms adopted as leisure. The sound system and gambling house became focal points for association and communication. According to Darcus Howe, these institutions were introduced by the second wave of migrants who came largely from urban working-class areas in Jamaica (Howe 1973).

The popularity of black music during the 1950s and 1960s meant that black forms were not confined to autonomous black spaces. As the music evolved, the context, quality and social constituency changed. The popularity of rhythm and blues in the early 1960s led to a boom in the number of nightclubs in central London where Jamaican music and Ska were also popular. Jamaican DJs (disc jockeys) were integral to this scene. Duke Vin, reportedly the first sound system operator,[3] was resident at the Flamingo on Thursdays and Count Suckle played at the prestigious Roaring Twenties in Carnaby Street.[4] Soho had a thriving club scene and other major venues including Paradise, the Alphabet and Tiles. In South East London the Ska Bar in Woolwich was an important venue. It was in these contexts that black and white youth associated.[5]

The emergence of a black British sound system scene is linked to the exclusive practices operated in white working-class leisure. Ribs, of Unity sound system, comments:

> So where is there for black people to go on a weekend? Where is there for us? We don't go to the pub, so we go a dance. (*Echoes*, 11 August 1984)

By the beginning of the 1980s sound systems operated in all the major regions of London where black young people lived.[6] A politically engaged form of Rastafari was the dominant ethos within a reformed black working-class culture. This in turn was to have an important impact on the culture of white working-class youth. While the established institutions of the white working class had operated an effective colour bar, a segment of white youth grew up alongside black peers and embraced the music and culture. For whites this transformed the nature of what being working class meant to them. From the big band jazz of the 1930s and 1940s to "mod" in the 1960s and "soul" in the 1970s, these movements allowed the emergence of contexts in which the meaning of "race" and the transmission of racism could be inhibited. Within the alternative public spheres where black music was played and danced to, collective sensibilities could be shared and new ones forged. The various musical cultures found in British cities did not produce identical outcomes or a uniformly transracial culture. However, metropolitan dancefloors shared a potential to develop a vision of the "state of the nation" that contrasted sharply with the public rhetoric of Thatcherism, which dominated the political climate of the 1980s and beyond.

Technology and sound system performance

The playing of prerecorded music is central to the musical cultures of black London. The "sound system" is at the core of these expressive cultures. Sound systems are massive hi-fis, usually owned by one person or by a partnership, but they are too big to be operated alone. Some owners deal with the business side themselves, while others have managers to organize bookings and financial issues. The sound system itself is run by a group, within which a division of labour operates. This is seldom rigid; there is often overlap and people will do more than one task. Some sound systems have a whole host of helpers to drive vans or "box boys" to shift equipment. Other aspects are more specialized.

The technology of reggae sound systems is called the "set". This can range in size. The idea is to construct a system that can give a unique mix and musical quality. The power of the sound is one part of this equation, but equal to this is the highly diverse range of speakers that sound systems use.[7] The music is transformed as it passes through the set. Different effects are used to give the records played a new "mix". Most common is the use of echo, usually reverb, which adds an atmospheric sound quality. Some sounds use digital delay units that have the capacity to repeat the signal from the microphone or the mixer. In addition, small synthesizers, or "noise boxes", enable the operator to add processed sounds. Power amps may be used to boost the output of the set. Some of the larger sounds use mixer boards to achieve a high range of equalization and to co-ordinate the use of signal-processing devices. The person who deals with this sophisticated equipment, who puts the sound system together and maintains it, is the operator. The operator has to be the sound technician, electronics expert and engineer rolled into one; dotted around London now are people who specialize in constructing power amps, equalization units, effects boxes and speaker cabinets.

On the early sounds there was no distinction between the person who played the sound and the DJ who provided vocal introductions and augmentations via the microphone. However, with the development of more sophisticated forms of vocal performance, a further division has occurred between the operator of the set and the MC (master of ceremonies or "mike chanter").

The operator complements the MC's vocal track. Thus the operator plays the sound like a musical instrument in order to alter the tempo of the music through rhythmic increases in volume. The MC, on the other hand, is in direct contact with the crowd, not just introducing the music but performing and directing the dance. Each sound will have its own "stable" of MCs, paid by the owners to "chat" lyrics on the set; some also have singers to sing over prerecorded backing tracks.

In many ways the most important person in the sound is the selector, who chooses the running order for the music and decides when the MC should come to the microphone. A good selector will be able to judge the mood of a crowd and know which types of music it will react to. He has to know when to liven up the crowd and when to calm it down. The selector and operator may be the same person.

It is important to stress that these forms of leisure are continuous with the culture of the parents of these young people. Denis Roe, who owns the South London sound system Saxon Studio with his partner Lloyd "Musclehead" Francis, shows how his own experience illustrates these cultural continuities:

> All my family have always had sounds from when I've been a boy. When I was younger one of my cousins used to have a sound and he used to let me play it, you na mean. He used to like give me the records and I used to put them on and from

Figure 8.1 Denis Roe (left) and Lloyd "Musclehead" Francis "stringing up" Saxon Studio sound system, Notting Hill Carnival, 1984 (photograph by Anna Arnone)

there everyone used to praise me as a little sound man from a little boy. All my family, my family used to have parties . . . My uncle Felix like he had a sound. I used to be with him all the time, if it was a family thing I would be there with him, learning how to play it.

Les: How young were you?

From seven and I've come up over the years. I was in sounds with other people, na mean, like Sky Rock, Imperial Rockers and then Saxon so I've always been in sounds from like school days, always been in sound business, never been out of it. There was a load of us in sounds and everyone chip in to buy things, you know, went to get a paper round and that and get some money together, buy some records, get a couple of old ten inches and twelve inches.

One key to success is having original music; it is hard to overemphasize its importance. Dub plates, or recorded rhythms, are original acetates and they are usually the only copies. (Dub is essentially an instrumental form of reggae.) They often have the bass and drums remixed with a more resonant, eerie emphasis, underlined by a snatch of vocals and other instruments sporadically dropped back into the mix. The records are made by artists specially for the sound. I Roy, the Jamaican toaster, celebrated the London-based Sir Coxone Outernational sound system in his recordings "Coxone Affair" and "Lloyd Coxone Time". "Sound called Coxone is the first, sounds that control the universe and quench our musical thirst" (I Roy, "Coxone Affair").

Original music enables the sound to develop a unique style of putting over the music. A sound will be "rated" for the number of versions it has of the same record (or "counteractions"), and so different mixes of the same tune are highly sought after. Denis Roe points this out:

The usual sound just played one or two new records, not like us. We are playing records, after two weeks the record is old. We get music from anywhere, anyone, no partiality and that's what terrifies other sounds when we play with them. They can never know what we've got. I can tell you what other sounds have got before we play them on the night. I know what they are coming with. But a man can't tell you what we've got. You can't keep you eyes on Saxon man, better you watch something else, better you watch TV and try and get track of politics and what Margaret Thatcher is going on with.

The smaller sounds, who do not have access to these original pressings, might well use popular reggae hits on general release. During the 1970s a lively soul scene had paralleled the growth of reggae sound systems. The composition of the crowds was multiracial and in this vibrant scene soul became equated with black and white social mixing (Hewitt 1986: 100). However, the influence of reggae and other Caribbean music was in the ascendant during this period. This situation changed by the middle 1980s when funk, soul, go go, hip hop and house increased in influence and the dance-halls were no longer the domain of reggae. In the same way, sound systems were passed on to a new generation interested in new forms of music-making that utilized the technology of the sound system. As Donovan explains, there is a continuity that underlies this process and its evolving trends:

> I've given my sound to my brother – he's dealing with soul and rap them things. I gave him the sound because he's like me. Do you understand what I am saying? Black like me.

The "warehouse party" and "hip hop jam" had signalled a new and vital development, but what remained was the use of recorded music in a creative and dynamic performance. Hip hop is a music that is created out of re-mixing two records on a double turntable. Unlike the reggae sound system it is possible to produce completely new music from the live intermixing of records. In the United States this form of music developed out of the street culture of young black Americans and their urban associates (Toop 1984).

Hip hop was clearly in the ascendant during this period. As Chris comments:

> With our two turntables . . . that will just jealousise the reggae DJs, because we do something that they cannot. When we used to play reggae, DJs would come from all the surrounding areas and I would hear them say – boy I have never seen a man touch knobs them ways.

With the emergence of hip hop and soul, new forms of cultural syncretism became possible. The fact that hip hop DJs used records as their instruments meant new combinations and styles were possible. Max of Mastermind sound system explains the innovative character of hip hop technology:

> With reggae sound system battles, the winner is generally the one who has the most exclusive records, or just the greatest number of versions of the same music. With the soul scene, it is basically technical skill and imagination on the turntables with any record, whether it's electro, classical, new wave, rock or whatever. It is the way you use it, not the actual record, that is important.

The music is dependent on the rearranging of musical fragments intermixed by the DJ. This is called break-beat music. The DJ is close to what Levi-Strauss (1976) called a cultural "bricoleur", or a crafts-person who makes use – in this case – of musical fragments in order to create new music. Here a beat or passage is identified by the DJ and, using two copies of the record, it is intermixed, enabling the seamless repetition of a percussive section of a particular record.

Break beats are not the only technique utilized by DJs. A whole range of styles have been developed to create unique sounds through mixing records and sound effects on twin turntables. The most well known of these is "scratching". This involves moving a record backwards and forwards while the record is being played and amplified. This results in a percussive effect that augments the rhythm or provides musical punctuation. Other effects include the "stab" and "drop in", which are rushes of sound created through playing an extract of a record over the rhythm playing on the first turntable. The DJ can create new music or unique mixes of an existing record.

These expressive musical cultures are produced through the interaction between the audience and the performers. In hip hop and reggae cultures the consumption of the music becomes a collective celebratory event where listening is an active process (Gilroy 1985). These expressive forms are close to what Walter Benjamin identified as possessing the qualities of a "story teller" (Benjamin 1968b). The lyricists and DJs, like the storyteller, take their experiences and relate them to the practical concerns of the audience, who respond to their creations. The call and response, or antiphonic, nature of this culture

Figure 8.2 "The Decks", Mastermind Roadshow (photograph by Anna Arnone)

has its roots in a long history of folk art originating from Africa (Oliver 1970, Finnegan 1970). The end result is a democratic process of mechanically reproduced art (Benjamin 1968a) that converges with the participatory elements in lyrical performance: "Lines between self and other are blurred and special forms of pleasure are created as a result" (Gilroy 1991: 13). The dance provides a unifying context for the sharing and celebration of collective experiences. In the following section I want to examine in detail the content and form of the culture's lyrical elements.

Lyricism in sound system performance

The sound system and the microphone provide a platform from which black Londoners can rewrite and document their own history. What makes them so effective in this is the lack of distance between the performance and the audience. When Papa Levi "chats" lyrics about the 36b bus ride and his experience growing up as a black Londoner, everyone in the dance knows what he is talking about. The physical and social reality common to the audience and the performers alike makes the music relevant and accessible.

The nature of this relationship has led Paul Gilroy to apply Gramsci's (1971) notion of the "organic intellectual" to these lyricists. The lesson from the mike is "check yourself", don't fight among yourselves, see the "bars and chains" that confine. These messages relate to black history, black unity and struggle. This "didactic populism" is accessible to a community of listeners who come together within the dance-halls. The owners, operators and performers share a determination to speak about the issues that affect their audience. This ensures that the music embodies a cultural politics that is relevant and accessible.

"Kinetic orality" and the Jamaican tradition

Dance-hall lyricism has its origins in Jamaican "toasting", or what Paul Gilroy (1987, 1991) refers to as "kinetic orality". In Jamaica the emergence of toasting was characterized by a schism in "roots culture" between the political programmes of singers and toasters/DJs: "Jamaican DJs steered the dance-hall side of roots culture away from political and historical themes towards 'slackness': crude and often insulting wordplay pronouncing on sexuality and sexual antagonisms" (Gilroy 1987: 188). The ascendancy of slackness in reggae music led

Figure 8.3 Tipper Irie and Daddy Colonel on the mike, Saxon Studio sound system, Brixton Youth Club 1984 (photograph by Anna Arnone)

to the waning of political emphasis in Jamaican reggae, which shifted from the engaged politics of Rastafari to an assertive individualism. It was this turning away from politics in Jamaica that opened a space for English MCs such as Tipper Irie, Papa Levi and Leslie Lyrix to take the musical and oral practices of the sound system and change the agenda on the microphone. The result was a fusion of the assertive style of the "slackness" DJs (Yellowman and General Echo are prime examples) with a grounded dissection of the social consequences of Britain's economic and political crisis for young black Britons.

New styles emerged that were much more than plagiarized versions of their Jamaican counterparts. Tipper Irie:

> The three wise men are Daddy Colonel, Papa Levi and me
> If you want to learn the "fast style"
> Check [Papa] Levi
> If you want to roll your tongue,
> Check Colonel T
> [if] You want intelligent lyric
> Check Tipper Irie.[8]

The concept of "style" has a number of meanings. It is both the content and originality of the lyric but it is concerned with innovations in form within the genre. One of the most important innovations in England during the mid-1980s was developed by Peter King in what came to be known as the "fast style" or "rapid rappin". This was an important development because it meant that English MCs were no longer dependent on their Jamaican counterparts for inspiration. As Peter King explains:

> A lot of English MCs was chatting like yardies [Jamaicans], they weren't trying to be original. I heard a lot of MCs copying and pirating, not entire lyrics – just the style. It all became rather the same . . . I did the fast style in 1982. People was already coming to Saxon but they used to love the fast style . . . People from other sounds used to say the "fast style" was bad. They come to me and say "drop it in now", in the dance so that they could hear it. Everybody was doing a style off a it – just said, well, cool runnings, at least they know who originated it. (*Echoes*, 4 May 1985)

In this way an originator will add to the spectrum of available styles. This is quite different from literary culture where authorship of the individual artist is the focus. In this sense this lyrical form is simultaneously about individual creativity and collective expression (Lord 1958).

During the mid-1980s MCs moved self-consciously away from chatting "slackness". The refusal to chat slackness was linked to an emphasis on addressing the everyday situations of young black people in Britain. The emphasis on "culture lyrics" embodies this move. Smiley Culture describes this:

> Culture lyrics comes first. We weren't brought up the way nuff men probably thought we was brought up – or the way nuff men pretend they was brought up. I wouldn't chat slackness. I wouldn't like my mother to hear me chatting slackness . . . When it comes to styles . . . you've got to be educated to say the things that are necessary. (*Echoes*, 26 May 1984)

Papa Levi emphasizes the point and says of slackness:

> It's not beneficial, I know that because it is not uplifting. The most you can really say if you're not revolted by it is you can laugh. That isn't beneficial neither, cos, we are living in a very serious time, where there is a whole heap of educational things what are directly happening in South Africa, in Jamaica or whatever. (*Echoes*, 28 April 1984)

The emphasis on "culture lyrics" signifies the way in which rasta political language enters into the culture. The political sensibilities of Rastafari provide analytical and ontological resources within the form.

The lyrics of the dance-hall are not simply concerned with the specific plight of black youth in Britain. Although they always speak from this perspective, a wide variety of topics are scrutinized in dance-hall style. In the following performance we see how a disaster that affected white working-class football fans was recorded and offered to the dance-hall collectivity.

The lyrics are taken from a local MC competition that featured Michael Ranks. The rhythms were provided by Spectra and Mantis sound systems. I was involved with Tim, who is mentioned, in making a film of the competition. The performance begins with Michael taking the microphone, and a barrage of whistles and acknowledgements from the crowd.

> Easy man, easy now man. Seckle up, seckle na, chaa.
> Cool na star.
> Hitch up the style now selector, 'itch it up. Yeah, kinda hot ya know.
> Dedicated to all Senator posse, C. C. Ranking. Now seckle, Andy cool na.
> Now them style is dedicated to all them Lewisham Way posse.
> Dedicated to girl called Carol.
> Dedicated to the youth.
> Dedicated to Saxon posse, Musclehead – hey
> Hear me now.

[The music starts and the crowd dances, shouts approval and whistles]

> Seckle, understand me na man, seckle, itch it up there grandad.
> Lif it up, lif it up there grandad.
> Lif it up.

[Music stops – crowd whistling]

> Too much noise. Seckle now people chaa.
> Mantis posse.
> Timmy – now just flash the camera chaa.
> Now drop it down fine.
> Now them style is dedicated to each and everyone.
> Yeah here is style, fashion and origination – seen!
> Hear me now.

[Music starts again]

> Cool now sa understand me na man.
> Cool now sa understand me now man.
> Now this is dedicated to every dance fan.

This Michael Ranks esquire on the microphone stand.

[Whistling shouts of approval from the crowd]

Itch up them style – too much noise man!
So much noise that me cyan [can't] remember the lyrics –
   seen [emphasizing tag] [laughing].
Seckle them style now.
Slacky yout give me a fine mix.
Dedicated to a youth called Trevor, man called Daddy
   Skrawler, I man bredder, man called Desmond.
Everybody jus cool.
Style!
Hear me now.

[Music starts again and a barrage of whistles comes from the crowd]

There's a fire in the football stadium, about a Fire in the
   football stand – jah man, jah man.
And there's a fire in the football stadium. About the fire in
   the football stand.
Hear me now.
Just de other week me watch the television.
Well me like a sport, me a watch Grandstand.
So when me take a look there was an interruption.
And a show Bradford from the third division.
But I man can't remember the opposition.
Well it seem a lickle fire started in a grandstand [. . .] so
   that they could not move everyone.
Well it didn't take a minute, didn't take few seconds.
Call for ambulance and de fireman.
The flame kept rising.
The fireball struck and within a couple minute it did get
   outa han[d].
Dem people did a suffer and also mutilation.
Be it policeman, hooligan or football fan.
Well it seems that everybody did get their portion.
Now there's only one thing, one question was it accident
   or was it arson?

[Repeat chorus]

Now fires not a joke, it's not a laughing matter.

To be burned by a flame is the worst torture.
Well the air was full of smoke.
There was a high temperature.
It was clear for you to see that it was a scorcha.
Well dem people panic you could hear it in the voice of the
    commentator.
The flames were burning rapid, they were burning faster.
In a short space of time it pull down the 'ole shelter.

[Music stops]

After dat, 'pon the news lickle while later.
Who 'pon the screen?
It was a Margaret Thatcher.
She a push her face in front the camera and she a talk to
    the mike and each and every viewer
And her voice so hoarse like she smoke ganja.

[Switches to Thatcher impersonation. Music stops, whistling and approval from crowd]

"I feel sorry for the victims of this disaster. It's a shame
    and disgrace that these people should suffer. In to this
    situation I must enquire."
Now that's the same thing she said 'bout the New Cross
    fire.
And what she done chat – they never went na furda.
About the fire in the football stadium about the fire in the
    football stand.

[Whistling, shouts of approval]

The performance goes through a number of phases. The lyrics are
dedicated and made collective, which results in the space between performer and listener being dissolved. Integral to this is the starting and
stopping of the performance. The MC pulls the audience in so that
their participation in the event overwhelms the performer: the performance breaks down only to be re-started with another dedication.
The collective nature of the performance results in the affirmation of
shared political and social principles. This is explicitly useful knowledge (Benjamin 1968b) and in periods of political strife the sound systems become both a source of alternative news and an arena for black

unity and autonomy. In the dance-hall, politics and pleasure coexist.

This particular lyric addresses the tragedy that occurred in Bradford where white working-class supporters were burned and killed. Michael uses linguistic code-switching as a creative resource. When he switches to impersonate the response of Prime Minister Margaret Thatcher to the disaster he is criticizing the hypocrisy of political interventions in disasters of this kind. The dance-hall is reminded of another situation – the New Cross fire – where the authorities paid lip-service to the loss of young lives. The style connects this event with the experience of young black people and their white associates. The interactive quality of MC performance is crucial in understanding the power and meaning of the music. Vocal punctuations signifying approval are offered from the crowd and resonate around the dance-hall accompanied by whistles. The power of the music feeds off this antiphony. These production and consumption relations create social criticism that is both authored and controlled by young black people.

MC-ing remains a predominantly male activity. However, this is not uniformly the case. From the mid-1980s a growing band of women MCs – Ranking Ann, Lorna Gee, Sister Candy – introduced a critical perspective from the point of view of black women. Sister Candy commented:

> All kinds of things are said about women by male MCs and singers. When you hear women sing about men, all you hear is that they love them. Like Lovers' Rock [ballad-orientated reggae] women are expressing their feelings, whereas a man tries to play hard. He always likes to be domineering and doesn't like to show his feelings, because he might be getting soft. (*Echoes*, 22 December 1984)

All-women sound systems such as Silhouette and Ladies Choice no longer accepted "being the 'pied pipers' of the dance-hall: girls attract men, and men want Rub-a-dub". They had different priorities, as Sonia from Silhouette explained:

> Men seem more interested in finding out how big you amp is. We don't feel that we need to compete with anyone, it is just a waste of time. (*Echoes*, 22 December 1984)

Figure 8.4 Sister Candy at home, January 1985 (photograph by Anna Arnone)

Figure 8.5 Lorna Gee, Fulham Town Hall, April 1984 (photograph by Anna Arnone)

The emphasis in female sounds varies with regard to genres of music; soul, rap and hip hop have all been incorporated. One problem they face is that women MCs are often accused of being "slack", that is running down men in their lyrics. Sister Candy denies this, and defended lyrics about women's experience:

> This is a reality that is not often expressed in MC-ing. Everything is said about women – she looks disgusting, she has been with ten thousand men or whatever. I have chatted lyrics about battering women, I had a lot of guys coming up to me laughing. They would say, "Yeah, you are saying something about me there".

But however much men may dominate sound systems, the microphone does provide these women with a platform for their version of reality. The dance-halls are important because they provide a microcosm, controlled by black people, in which young black men and women work through in symbolic form the variety of their experiences, conflicts and desires.

Developments in black American music have added to the stylistic resources available to London MCs (Gilroy 1987: 192–7). The hybrid nature of this form of oral art reinforces the connections between black America, the Caribbean and the black English cultural system. Chris, from Deck Masters sound system, outlined the continuities between hip hop and reggae music:

> Rappin' and the reggae scene has got a lot in common. Yesterday, Wednesday night, I thought of breaking up the crew, innit. You know who changed my mind? Levi! The Saxon MC, Levi! I was killed, man. I said, "What you?" Then he started going – "You Talk Too Much" [a lyric by Run DMC] and I said, "You what". He said that he loves hip hop and that it's not like soul. He said soul music was all about "I love you" and party style and everything. He said, "No!" He said, "Hip hop is different". He said, "Listen to this record, it is about reality, life" – you know what I mean?

It is to that influence of hip hop and rap that we now turn.

Word: rap in the UK

Rap was the most important development in dance-hall lyricism to occur during the 1980s. A wide range of black American lyrical styles were adopted by young performers, and oral percussion called the "human beat box" was adapted to the English setting. The "human beat box" enabled rhythms and beats to be produced by amplifying the voice itself. Rap and hip hop were the most influential innovation to emerge during the decade. This form stripped popular music down to the components of voice and rhythm (Gilroy 1985). Rap music was quickly and enthusiastically adapted to London's cultural landscape.

Rap music has been developed out of pre-existing traditions of communication within urban black America, particularly what is referred to as "playing the dozens" and "signifying" (Abrahams 1970, Labov 1972). These are verbal games that involve boasting and counter-claiming on the nature of a particular event or issue. The most successful signifiers are those people who construct what are referred to in the culture as the "biggest lies". "Inversion" is another common element (Sims Holt 1972), i.e. where a word is used when an opposite meaning is signified. An example of this in relation to hip hop culture is the use of "bad" meaning "good". Rap music has to be located within the context of these codes.

To read the boasting and bravado used in rap is to believe that which is intentionally a lie. This is particularly important when assessing the rap music in terms of gender. In America, the controversy over 2 Live Crew's hit record "As nasty as they wanna be" is a good example of white incomprehension of black cultural codes. Henry Louis Gates Junior, writing in the *New York Times*, commented:

> In the face of racist stereotypes about black sexuality, you can do one of two things: you can disavow them or explode them with exaggeration. 2 Live Crew, like many other "hip hop" groups, is engaged in sexual carnivalesque. Parody reigns supreme, from a take-off of standard blues to a spoof of the black power movement; their off colour nursery rhymes are part of a venerable Western tradition . . . 2 Live Crew must be interpreted within the context of black culture generally and of signifying specifically. (*New York Times*, 19 June 1990)

The insistence on placing rap music in a social context does not necessarily mean that "anything goes". Paul Gilroy points out that "academic or journalistic commentary on black popular music in America has failed to develop a reflexive political aesthetics capable of distinguishing Two Live Crew and their ilk from equally 'authentic' but possibly more compelling and certainly more constructive peers" (Gilroy 1991: 7). The simple point here is that rap lyricism is not just about "telling lies". Working in the form are artists engaged in the promotion of gender equality, e.g. Jungle Brothers, De La Soul and A Tribe Called Quest. A range of competing discourses on gender are operated within rap lyricism. Although there may be a relationship between the racist construction of black masculinity, it is clearly dangerous to suggest that all references to gender in rap performance are merely parody because of the cultural heritage of signifying. Such an analysis undermines the possibility for rap to exist as a serious medium of social criticism. Rap cannot be characterized simplistically; there is ample evidence that the form is more than parody. Politically engaged rap lyricism is concerned with generating an accessible form of social criticism. In short, rap is more than fictional boasting and attempts to tell the "biggest truths" about the state of black America. Equally important, women are not silent within rap discourse.

The very participation of women performers provides a critical perspective that seems to go unnoticed by the critics concerned about what they characterize as the "black, proud and sexist syndrome" (Chambers 1985: 148). There are no fixed outcomes within rap music because the form itself is about altering cultural resources in order to produce new forms of expression. In a way comparable to the reggae tradition, women performers have used the microphone to determine their own agendas in music. They are also determining what is objectionable within men's lyrics.

Some women MCs have taken on a black cultural code – such as signifying – and turned it back on itself. Mystery MC, a white 17 year old, is one example. She is quite clear about the position of women in rap music:

> If men are going on about how they can fuck all night, then you do it too – it shocks them. It is no good slagging them down. You have to be funny. Otherwise they just go away in a rotten mood. You might think that a lot of things men say are

sexist but most of it doesn't offend me. Occasionally something does offend me, then I think that it is a shame because then the rap is spoilt . . . People often say that I am good for a girl. Sometimes they say I am good considering that I am white, but not that often since I hang around with black guys.

She raps with the Islington-based Family Quest. In her lyrics she parodies the masculinism of some of her male peers and inverts masculine bravado and posturing:

> It ain't Christmas day or New Year's eve. Here's something
> for your eyes and your ears to believe.
> It's not marriage or a one night stand. It is Mystery MC
> with a Mic in her hand.
> I am going to make it clear so that you can understand.
> It's not the man in my life but the life in my man.
> It is not what you are drinking, it is what it does.
> Cos it not worth drinking if it has got no buzz.
> It is not how I walk it is how I can wriggle. Not the way I
> laugh but the way I giggle.
> I am a female Casanova, one that comes to the beat.
> I climb on it and ride until I reach my peak.
> (*City Limits*, 24–30 January 1986)

Mystery MC raps with a crew of men, while other women rap in pairs, like the famous duo, the Cookie Crew. The Cookies developed their own UK version of high-speed rapping. They emphasize their professionalism and their independence:

> We do everything ourselves. And we are not interested in running people down, we just want to be really good.

Hailing from Battersea, the Cookies lead a stable of women MCs including the She Rockers (from Harlesden), Monie Love, Mistaken Identity (the Cookies' younger sister), the Gemini Girls, and the Angels. They looked to the American women MCs for inspiration and found ample examples from the Real Roxanne to Souljah. As Sonia sums up:

> It is no good sitting around and moaning about boring and

offensive lyrics from men. There is only one solution – grab the mike and show those sucker MCs to get on their bike. (*City Limits*, 24–30 January 1986)

These young women set their agenda despite the way their music has been championed and appropriated by liberal commentators. Remedee and Siouxie Q are clear about the expectations of their male peers and the wider audience:

A lot of guys didn't think girls could rap, but we've won respect now. We didn't say anything about women, we just rapped about ourselves and people we know. (*Observer Magazine*, 27 October 1985)

Remedee continues:

They say talk about women's rights or rap about the problems of the world. We are not into that. We rap about ourselves, about the scene, what is going on the floor. I think they are spoiling it, really squeezing everything out of it. We are trying to keep away from all that, we have got our own nations and we are having our own thing. It is our world, our hip hop world and I am not going to let them destroy it like they destroyed everything else. (*City Limits*, 17–23 May 1985)

The maintenance of "their world" was clearly seen to be threatened by any radical acquisition without consent.

The politics of their music cannot be confined to those lyrics that address overtly political subjects. From Lorna Gee to Monie Love women are asserting their own claim to speak and rhyme. The point I am making here is that the music of women MCs should not be understood as merely striking back at a male-dominated music subculture; it is about setting the terms of their own aesthetic in which to make fun, provoke thought and generate a lyrical reflection on themselves and their environment.[9]

The sexual politics of the agenda on "the mike" has intensified with the emergence and popularity of West Coast gansta rappers such as Ice Cube, DRS and NWA (Niggers with Attitude) and the complex carnalities of Snoop Doggy Dog and Dr Dre. Andrew Ross commented:

The fantasy and theatricality associated with the gangbanger role was a dramatic space for reconciling the tension between public enemy stereotypes and masculine images of strength and agency for ghetto youth. Among other things, the overwrought sexism and homophobia associated with this theatre was an intrinsic product of the physically threatened conditions under which black male youth negotiated their social survival. (Ross & Rose 1994: 5)

Others have criticized the squeamishness of such positions with regard to engaging critically with the sexual discourses of rap. Paul Gilroy has warned against the ways in which these shifts within black music are producing a fixation with the body politics of racial alterity. The emancipatory potential of sound is no longer pre-eminent and it is the visual aesthetics of skin and body that dominate contemporary black music (Gilroy 1994b). This discussion warns against the revolutionary conservatism that is abroad within hip hop but at the same time points to the places where the moral agent within rap undermines the certainties of racial absolutism. The American media in particular have been quick to condemn the homophobia and misogyny of gansta. As bell hooks has argued, this conservatism is a product not of racial otherness but rather of the assimilation of the maxims of white supremacist capitalist patriarchy:

When young black males labor in the plantation of misogyny and sexism to produce gansta rap, white supremacist patriarchy approves the violence and materially rewards them. far from being an expression of their "manhood", it is an expression of their own subjugation and humiliation by more powerful, less visible forces of patriarchal gangsterism. (hooks 1994: 122)

Beyond this she argues that in such a context feminist critiques of sexism must remain vigilantly against all the manifestations misogyny and avoid adding to the "sensationalist drama of demonizing of black youth culture" (ibid.: 115).

In its initial stages at least, rap in Britain focused on particular British circumstances. Dizzi Heights, a veteran British rapper, puts emphasis on staying true to both a spirit of tradition and a commitment to innovation. Dizzi, a hairdresser of Guyanese origin from Kensing-

ton, started rapping at the Language Lab, a weekly club in London's
Soho, in the early 1980s. Prior to his participation in the rap scene he
experimented with reggae music. He commented:

> Now I think English rapping could . . . be a combination of
> different accents. I'm sick of English rap kids saying "fresh"
> and "def" and "hard". Those words come from America.
> We've got – "it's well 'ard" and "it's cool" lots of slang
> words. South, East, West and North London have got all
> their own words – not cockney but slang what people use in
> the street everyday. People lose their identity because they're
> so into listening to the next American idea that they've for-
> gotten all the other things that would rhyme. You can listen
> to people talking on a bus and hear funny things – they do it
> in the clubs, but not on vinyl, so the records just come across
> as bad imitations of what the Americans do. You can make
> much better raps using words you know and that's where we
> could really come in. (*City Limits*, 17–23 May 1985)

Dizzi thus points to keeping the music relevant to the environment in
which it is produced.

Another rapper, Lovebug, from South London, focuses his
attention on lyrically inflating and exaggerating the humour in ordinary life. His performance uses the language of the South Bronx,
which is transported and applied to the British context with unique
results. In the following lyric, "Bug" documents a royal visit to his
home town:

> Now I told you many stories told you many tales
> But did I tell how I met the Princess of Wales.
> Well now she was on a visit she was making the rounds
> When I heard she was coming to my own town.
> So I wanted to see what was going on so I dressed up
> warm.
> So I moved to the front so that I could see
> And the next thing she pointed at me.
> She said "You're the Lovebug".
> I said "Yes I am".
> She said "Glad to see you, I am Lady Diane".
> Well most guys would panic wonder what to do next

So I pinched her on the ass for a fifty pence bet.
But like a true gentleman with etiquette
I said glad to meet you but have we met? Because I know
  you will be married for about four years to the ugly
  looking dude with the giant ears.
Well what happened next there is no need to explain
Because you can find out for yourself if you remember the
  name.
Because I am in the yellow pages under L for love
And any time that you want me just give me a buzz.

This is the language of black New York being used to document and mythologize happenings in South London. Importantly, Bug is talking about his home town, which anchors this cultural expression in a geographical space. Yet his lyricism defies being settled in one context and has a transnational and Janus-like quality. It looks out and plots cultural connections with African Americans, while at the same time looking in and reconstituting the local aesthetics of South London. The language and style of South London are thus laced with symbols and cultural fragments from urban America and the Caribbean that are rearranged in a unique way. Such performances are clearly situated within the forms of masculinism and bravado mentioned earlier. However, they also show the ways in which figures within the English establishment are parodied.

Symbols of England, such as the "Royal Family", are used in these expressive cultures to poke fun at definitions of Englishness that are racially exclusive. For example, in a dance I once heard a black female rap duo perform a lyric entitled "What would happen if the King was Black!". It constructed a scenario where the black British heavyweight boxer Frank Bruno married Princess Diana, after Diana got rid of the "ugly looking dude with the giant ears"! The whole dance laughed as the story unfolded, but beneath the humour was a profound tension. The allegory served to cut straight to the heart of British racial discourse where blackness and Englishness were being reproduced as mutually exclusive categories. The point is that the very existence of the culture I am describing defies the racist logic of this discourse. Even Britain's most sacred institutions such as the British Broadcasting Corporation, have not escaped parody. The black-run pirate station DBC (Dread Broadcasting Corporation) referenced this bastion of Englishness and provided the voice of a very different nation (Hind & Mosco 1985). These cultural syncretisms express a new kind of cultural aesthetic. These forms "belong to England" but they cannot be confined in the boundaries of the nation. This culture is simultaneously local, multinational and transcultural.

Summary

As the sound system "plays out" and the bass registers of the music occupy the dance, the venue is marked with the aesthetics of the diaspora. Thus English church halls, clubs and town halls house new sensibilities and forms of expression. As Paul Gilroy notes: "As the sound system wires are strung up and the lights go down, dancers could be transported anywhere in the diaspora without altering the quality of their pleasure" (Gilroy 1987: 210). The sound systems establish an entire acoustic environment that transcends any simple notion of merely playing records. The field of sounds, or soundscape (Shafer 1977, Jarviluoma 1994), is established within which trans-national references can be registered. The dance is about making connection with the denizens of the Black Atlantic (Gilroy 1993a). In making connections with the New World black diasporas, something also happens to the site where connections are made. The result is that local aesthetics are transformed by this process. A good example of this is the way Jamaican geographical taxonomies have been applied to Britain. "Country", associated in Jamaica with rural parishes, is used by Londoners to refer to anywhere that is outside the capital. These alternative meanings are adopted by white peers. In one situation I remember telling a white young woman that I was going to Birmingham and she said "Oh a country". The dance is thus about affirming historical connections but it is also about transform-ing the conditions of the present.

The larger London sound systems also tour internationally. Denis Roe explains:

> Saxon has been to America. You know, we were the hottest thing around since wagon wheels in America. Been to Jamaica, now that was a different runnings 'cause Jamaica was somewhere where we had to go. You know we had to go no matter what. I've always known that my sound was going to end up in Jamaica one day. More than go anywhere else we had to go there. Don't like to be biased or nothin' but we

done really well and because of that fact that England is so forward on music we was a big surprise in Jamaica. The surprise that we came down in Jamaica, man, they couldn't believe that an English sound like us was going on in this way.

The cycle is thus completed only to be started again. A cultural form developed in Jamaica is transported to Europe, re-made, and then, reconnected as a tradition, becomes re-cast in the present.

The lyricism I have referred to provides the context in which young people can dissect the social and political forces that affect their lives. It provides a microcosm controlled by young people where the conflicts in their desires and aspirations can also be explored. Equally, the dance is a place to celebrate and have fun. But this does not mean that the audience is there to induce a soporific state of political fatalism. The dance provides a powerful unifying context and a congregationalist ethic (Ross & Rose 1994). The overriding aesthetic of the dance-hall is black: black is host. Whites in this situation gain access to the political agendas of black culture. For black young people the dance provides a context where experiences can be shared and history rewritten.

Although all the above statements hold true for the musical forms I have referred to so far, it is also important to appreciate that the social constituencies of black music vary in terms of the degree of transracial sociability. In the following section I describe these variations and explore their implications.

Groove allegiance: the social constituencies of black expressive culture

I want to explore the social constituencies of black music by looking at the degrees of inter-racial contact that take place in the reggae dance, soul and hip hop jams and the late 1980s' innovations referred to as the dancefloor movement.

The reggae sound system dances are a predominantly black social constituency. Whites are certainly not excluded from these leisure spaces but their participation is closely monitored. Like the discussion of white Creole use offered in a previous chapter, the participation of whites in this space is dependent on peer approval. The dominant ethos of the reggae dance is black unity, and the lesson from the microphone is informed by black experiences and constructs a specifically black agenda.

Central to the social collectivities of reggae dances is a notion of followers or "posse". A posse need not be defined solely by allegiance to a sound. It can also refer to a geographical area or merely to a group of friends in a dance. The boundaries of the group are not absolute. It involves a sharing of loyalties, of origins, of identities.

This constituency or "interpretive community" (Gilroy 1987) is not exclusively black. It is within this context that whites can gain access to the sensibilities and programmes of black England. Denis Roe, of Saxon Studio sound system, explains the nature of his audience and states that he does not want his music to be confined to black youth:

> I am not going to categorize it like that and just say black
> youts because 'em. I mean look at DominiK [a white reg-
> gae DJ], DominiK is not actually black and you asked him
> about the dances he's gone to where he's got the most leni-
> ency he has gone with us all over. He'll tell ya so it's not a
> matter of what raccs and that, its Afro-Caribbean but
> everyone is involved now and everyone wants a piece of
> the cake. It's not who's listening, it is what is being said.
> There is some really conscious music out there, with some
> really solid meanings.

As Denis explains, the emphasis is on those who are willing to listen. What is distinctive about reggae music is that the political agenda of the music is set by the black performers. The sensibilities of the music are opened to whites within the dance who are committed to the sentiments expressed in the music.

Despite the fact that reggae was open to white people, social mixing between black and white was primarily associated with soul music. The split between reggae and soul cultures was more pronounced during the 1970s. In this period, intense rivalry existed amongst reggae sound systems and in particular between those hailing from North and South London. The reggae scene was very competitive, especially during "cup dances" or competitions, or where sound systems played together, called "clash dances". These sometimes ended in physical confrontation. For some dance-goers the soul and Lovers' Rock scene offered an alternative. To some degree the distinction between the soul and reggae scenes was also about contrasting social and political agendas:

> Reggae was more tied up with black nationalism and certain rigidities of sex and race – tough masculine left politics. Soul on the other hand, allowed inter-racial relationships and challenged some of the structures of black masculinity. (Julien 1991: 2)

The contrast in political sensibilities was not quite as clear-cut as Julien suggests here. The popularity of Lovers' Rock, a melodic ballad-based genre of reggae (named after a South London record label run by the luminary producer Denis Bovell), adds a further complicating feature in this political cartography of taste. Lovers' straddled both soul and reggae and included such artists as Caroll Thompson, Donnie Elbert, Louisa Mark and Janet Kay, who produced a string of broken-hearted songs focusing on the perils and euphoria of love found and lost. The importance of Lovers' is in the way it both disrupted the simple distinction between soul and reggae and allowed a whole generation of black female artists to establish themselves – however temporarily – in reggae music (see Hebdige 1987).

In the 1970s' soul scenes, the musical agenda set by Funkadelic's anthem "One nation under a groove" was echoed in the social composition of the dancefloor. Tony Johns, the pioneer of soul pirate Radio Invicta, broadcast soul music across the capital from 1970. Other white DJs such as Robbie Vincent and Peter Young were also seminal London blue-eyed soul figures. Weekend soul festivals such as the legendary Caister Soul Festival provided an opportunity to move out of the city and partially escape from the circumscriptions of race. Pirate radio through stations such as LWR, Invicta, Horizon and DBC provided an enduring testament to the maxim "you can't segregate the airwaves" and broke down racial soundscapes as they broadcast black music to an ever-widening constituency of listeners. Invicta also pioneered the introduction of new techniques of mixing and hip hop and electro DJ-ing. The Harlesden-based Mastermind Roadshow performed on Invicta. Heralded as the best rapping, scratching and mixing crew in London, Mastermind absorbed hip hop and electro influences and developed their own unique sound through featuring four record decks in their live shows (Hind & Mosco 1985).

During the early 1970s the soul scene was in large part steered by

Figure 8.6 "We send the sounds – you cut the beat", Master-mind Roadshow, Notting Hill Carnival, 1984 (photograph by Anna Arnone)

white impresarios. Norman Jay, a seminal figure in what was to emerge out of this scene, remembers:

> In '75–'76, it was unheard of for Black kids to be into R'n'B. R'n'B was, in this country, part of the white way of life. That whole scene here was run by white people, people with that English conservative-eccentric attitude, that when you're into something deeply you treasure it, collect it and you're very protective about it. The stereotypes were set, you know – if you're black, you're into reggae; if you're white, you can be into what you want.[10]

Such observations need to be seen as warnings against any slippage into a premature optimism with regard to the cultural politics of 1970s' soul. However, what is equally true is that London's soul scene and the weekend migrations that were integral to it did provide an important space in which inter-racial sociability was fostered. The soul and hip hop scenes of the 1980s shared many of the characteristics of the 1970s' soul scene referred to above. By the early 1980s, warehouse parties and West End clubs like Gullivers, the Casses Club and the Wag provided the context for 1970s' funk and soul to be exhumed. Norman Jay – aka Norman Joseph – coined the phrase "rare groove" and his legendary shows on the London pirate KISS-FM made it possible for this music to be played to new audiences and established audiences. During the 1980s the rigid barriers between the various genres of black music that had established themselves in London were starting to break down. Saxon sound system in particular was influential in innovating new styles of reggae lyricism and performance, and through DJs such as Mistri broke new ground in playing soul and black American genres. Hip hop was designated a "culture for the kids" where black symbols and emblems were equally accessible. The "hip hop nation" had a black culture but its citizens were multiracial. The themes of unity and inter-racial contact were effectively transported to a new generation of young people who had a profound understanding of what it meant to live in a multiracial society.

The development of the dancefloor movement in the late 1980s saw a significant shift in the racial politics of black culture. This was also connected to the unique innovations emerging out of British soul. A new interest was revived in rare soul music that coincided with an enormous growth in the London club scene. At the core of this movement was a series of black DJs who were finding and circulating classic yet obscure soul tunes.[11] Pirate stations had been important within the reggae scene for a long time but, with the emergence of a new "soul underground", pirate radios such as KISS-FM shared an equal position with the sound system as the platform for cultural development. Some of the real innovators were Norman Jay, Steve Jerviere, Trevor Shakes and Trevor "Madhatter" Nelson. For a generation of young black DJs the raregroove "vinyl trade" provided alternative employment. While the ignorance of opportunist white DJs was sometimes exploited, a flood of classic soul was revitalized within a new dancefloor style.

The philosophy of the movement was born out of the multiracial character of the warehouse parties of the hip hop and later the house movements. House music originating from the black districts of Chicago had been enthusiastically applied to the London dance scene. On the dancefloor the nation could really be re-invented with new rhythms. As in the soul movement of the 1970s, the dancefloors were profoundly multiracial and composed of a mixture of middle- and working-class young people. New leisure spaces emerged that brought together Soul II Soul and the white sound system Family Funktion. Jazzy B, of Soul II Soul, explains:

> Classes as well as races started to mix. And I believe that we were the instigators: a black street crew and a white, middle-class bunch. People checked us as a form of rebelling. (*City Limits*, 5–12 November 1987)

Black styles operated as a socially cohesive force that unified young people within these alternative spaces. This was particularly profound for young whites who found themselves owning black cultural forms.[12]

The dancefloor movement constituted a vast and mostly unnoticed group of young people who avidly followed the pirate stations and waited for news of the next "rave". Trevor "Madhatter" Nelson commented in the summer of 1988:

> People who aren't part of it can't imagine the size the whole scene has grown to. Maybe they should just stand around Cambridge Circus at 3.00 am. They'd see hundreds of people go by, all eating dodgy takeaways, hustling to get the night bus. They're all under twenty, all dressed the same. And they're black and white, and Chinese and Greek and Indian. (*New Statesman and Society*, 17 June 1988)

The movement constituted a youthful and truly multiracial culture embodied within style, fashion, design and music that, while primarily working class, also included middle-class soul rebels (Rose 1991). The British dance movement was led by crews such as Good Times, Rappattack, Fresh Beat, Madhatters, BT Express and, most notably, from behind the turntables of Jazzy B's – aka Beresford Romeo – Soul II Soul sound system. Soul II Soul developed a distinct musical and political identity through blending black self-help with transracial unity.

These cultures are not merely about rhizomorphic dialogue across the colour-line. A sense of diasporic connection is precisely what is manifested within the loaded planes of black cultural expression. When asked about the traffic in black music at a gathering of black artists in Montego Bay, Jamaica, Jazzy B replied:

> I saw the broadness that it [cultural exchange] added to your whole perspective of life and you are meeting other people and sharing each other's cultures like that – it can only help to enhance your own and it makes you respect exactly what you are. I think it is a really good thing, especially when you are growing up and you are looking for identity.[13]

The search for identity is synonymous with a cultural reconstruction of the history of the black diaspora. Black expressive cultures are characterized by the coexistence of a number of cultural codes, ranging from the spirituality of Rastafari and dread ethical maxims to the fast style of London MCs and the sensibilities of hip hop and rap. The process of creating and participating in these cultures provides the crucial defining moment in

> . . . what becomes a determinedly non-traditional tradition for this is not tradition as closed or simple repetition. Invariably promiscuous and unsystematically profane, diaspora challenges us to apprehend mutable itinerant culture. It suggests the complex, dynamic potency of living memory: more embodied than inscribed. (Gilroy 1994b: 212)

These outernational processes are reflected in the profoundly plural and recombinant nature of these creative musical processes.

The boundaries between these cultural forms are fast becoming more difficult to identify. They do not exist as mutually exclusive "subcultures" but rather provide a variety of resources that can be switched into and out of by black young people. The result is the development of a kind of *diasporic code-switching*. In the dance-halls one can see this process in operation. As the rhythms change and the musical genre switches continents from Europe to the Caribbean and on to North America, young people slip into the appropriate style of dance, i.e. from two-step soul moves to the jockey of the reggae dance-hall. These complex cultural forms cannot be separated from

217

one another because they are utilized by the same young people and in increasingly mixed permutations. The separation between reggae and soul found in the 1970s is undermined as boundaries are breached. A good example of this is the style – Funki Dred – associated with Jazzy B's sound system Soul II Soul.

The Funki Dred style is a mixture of roots culture, dread politics and the rhythms of soul. At the core of Funki Dred style and philosophy is the Soul II Soul sound system and a division of labour associated with the material culture of reggae. The philosophy guiding the collective is self-help infused with a combination of roots and soul imagery, "a happy face / a pumping bass / for a living race". The point here is *not* to attempt to disentangle the component parts of this culture, but to appreciate the richly syncretic and multi-faceted nature of the culture as a whole. Cynthia Rose concludes that "Soul II Soul symbolises a populist, post-modern black aesthetic" (Rose 1990: 169). The multiply inflected, translocal nature of these forms provides compelling evidence that – as the Brazilian pop singer Gilberto Gil has suggested – we live in an age where roots have been replaced by aerials.

These complex cultural forms are not only found in London. Bristol boasts On U sound system, which is a multiracial collective headed by Adrian Sherwood and Gary Clail. Clail, a white native of Bristol, spent his childhood following reggae sound systems, and during the 1980s he built his own sound. Clail played his sound system alongside some of the most notable in Britain. Paul Bradshaw, editor of the black music paper *Straight No Chaser*, remembers a dance-hall confrontation with the veteran London system, Coxone Outernational Hi-Fi:

> They all turned up and it was "Oh, were going to mash him up". And they just made a racket. Meanwhile Coxone's stringing his bass-bin, gets the sound balanced, plays sweet reggae music, no fuss and wipes the floor with him. (*The Crack*, June 1991)

However, Clail and On U sound system have enjoyed considerable success by blending reggae and house music. Mass Attack and Tricky provide more recent examples of transcultural music emerging from the Bristol scene.

Complex fusions of reggae and south Asian rhythmic and lexical elements and sound system culture have also started to emerge. In

particular, the popularity of the MC Apache Indian has given prominence to these dialogic forms of expression. Apache, a sheet metal
worker from Handsworth, combines reggae performance delivered
in Creole and Punjabi lyrics spoken over a range of rhythms. The
popularity of Apache in Birmingham points to new and significant
dialogue going on between Asian and Afro-Caribbean youth. Equally,
in London's East End, Bengali youth are operating sound systems
and appropriating rap and reggae lyrical styles. British Bengali rappers such as Sharif Rothman have chosen rap as a medium critically
to unpack what it means to be of Bengali origin and living in the East
End.[14] Sound systems such as the Asian Dub Foundation have
utilized sound system culture as a medium through which to inter-
twine the south Asian references with the rituals of sound system performance.

X amount of sat siri akal!: sound system culture and south Asian music dialogue

There are direct parallels between the development of sound system
culture and the emergence of new south Asian musical cultures in
Britain during the 1980s. The dance and song genre *bhangra* origi-
nates in the Punjab and it "[c]elebrates the robust and energetic punc-
tuated rhythms and Iambic meter of the double-sided drums dhol and
dholki, the supple directness of Punjabi language, and the pleasures
associated with its main social occasions, the harvest festival
bhaisakhi" (Baumann 1990: 81). Within the context of Britain,
bhangra music has been re-invented. Bands such as alaap in West
London's Southall district incorporated sound sampling, drum ma-
chines and synthesizers to produce the new form called *bhangra beat*,
also known as Southall beat. In the Midlands other influences from
hip hop and house music have been incorporated producing *northern
rock bhangra* and *house bhangra*.

The development of these robust and rich new forms has been
read as a focal point for an incipient British Asian youth culture
(Baumann 1990). Bhangra created an over-arching reference point
cutting across cleavages of nationality (Indian, Pakistani, Bangladeshi
and other), religion (Sikh, Muslim and Hindu) and caste or class. One
distinctive feature of this culture was the so-called "daytimer", a live
event that took place during school hours to compensate for the

young Asians' inability to attend night-time clubs. The function of the daytimer is described here by Mac, singer with the group Dhamaka:

> Daytimers reinforce our culture and values, girls dress in sulwaars [salwaar-kamiz, the traditional dress of Punjabi women], boys can come in turbans and get no hassle. The music is our music, and it's their show, not a "goray" [white] gig or a "kale" [black] show. Do parents want for kids to go out to gora shows? Would they rather have Asian kids disowning and abandoning their culture, to become Sharons and Garys tomorrow. (Quoted in Baumann 1990: 87)

The connection of bhangra with a youthful sense of Asian unity is also expressed in the following quote from Komal, one of the lead singers of the East London bhangra group Cobra:

> I can remember going to college discos a long time ago, when all you heard was Reggae, Reggae, reggae. Asians were lost, they weren't accepted by whites, so they drifted into the black culture, dressing like blacks, talking like them, and listening to reggae. But now Bhangra has given them "their" music and made them feel that they do have an identity. No matter if they are Gujaratis, Punjabis or whatever, – Bhangra is Asian music for Asians. (Quoted in Baumann 1990: 91)

The emergence of bhangra in the 1980s signalled the development of a self-conscious and distinctively British Asian youth culture. The result was the development of an autonomous alternative public sphere for young Asians that was comparable to the reggae dancehall. However, the dance has also enabled further processes of cultural syncretism to flourish. Complex fusions emerged during the early 1990s – both inside and outside of bhangra music and its culture – bringing south Asian artists to an unprecedented prominence.

Apache Indian – aka Steven Kapur – embodies some of the most interesting examples of creative traffic within recent musical cultures. Apache Indian was raised in the multi-ethnic area of Handsworth, Birmingham, born of Hindu Punjabi parents from Jalandhar. He performs and expresses himself through snatches of Jamaican patois, Punjabi and a unique form of English that is being generated by groups of young people who are growing up alongside each other in

Birmingham. His first record, entitled, "Movie Over India", released in 1990, topped both the reggae and bhangra charts. The new form was dubbed in the media *bhangramuffin* after its ragga counterpart. The first point to make about Apache's biography is that his relationship to reggae music cannot be separated from his broader involvement in multiracial peer groups and the wider black community.

Apache was inducted into sound system culture by a young black man of Caribbean parentage called Sheldon who ran Siffa sound system. Sheldon introduced him to important people within Birmingham's reggae scene and later he became his brother-in-law. By the time he was 16 Apache was working with a sound system in the Birmingham area. He invested in his own set, calling it Simeon, the dread name given to the month of May – the month in which he was born – by Rastafari and the Twelve Tribes of Israel. Apache joined forces with Sheldon under the name of Sunset. By the age of 18 he had his own amps and speaker boxes and was learning the culture of the dance-hall. The next crucial step was his decision to become a "van man". He raised the money to buy a Luton van and ended up driving some of Birmingham's premier sound systems all over the country. At this time he had also followed his male relatives into a job in a local engineering factory where he was employed as a welder.

His involvement with dance-hall culture intensified when he met a prominent Birmingham soundman called Wooligan, who ran Orthodox 38 sound system.

> When I met Woolly I realized that I met someone who was as crazy about the music as me. If you go to his house he eats off speaker boxes. He sleeps in a speaker box. It is in his blood. I was the van man and I just loved to drive to the dance – just to be around the sound. What happened was that one night, it was in Slough, his DJ and the people who were supposed to chat never showed up. So I started chatting on the mike. Somebody said "Who is that chatting? It's the van man, van man doesn't chat, van man drives the van."

This marked the end of a long induction into the culture. His identification with reggae and black style was taken to serious lengths.

At 16 he started to grow dreadlocks. Reflecting on this, he explains his desire to grow locks as an extension of his love and identification with reggae music and dance-hall culture. His experience of having locks was highly formative with regard to his own sense of politiciz-ation. He describes an incident surrounding a shopping expedition on Handsworth's main street – The Soho Road.

> I remember I walked in [to a shop] and as soon as I walked through the door people started to talk in Punjabi. They saw my locks and they checked me as a black guy. I can't remem-ber exactly what the shopkeeper said, but it was something like "Watch out, this black guy is going to tief [thieve] some-thing" . . . This made me realise, that opened my eyes to what was happening in the street and what people like Bob Marley were saying about what black people go through and what tribulation meant. What made it worse was that it wasn't white people who were saying these things.

Apache talks about a period when he felt that he was in effect liv-ing out or claiming a kind of Afro-black identity. This was part and parcel of an identification with a culture but also a wider community. It was also about learning what the culture stood for historically and politically.

> I know it is a serious culture, I know it is a serious thing. I look around and see people playing with it today and I tell them this is a serious, serious thing. It has roots which go back a long way and you have to respect that. It means a lot to black people and I found that out being around black peo-ple. Me having locks was nothing cultural, it was me just try-ing to get closer to the music that I loved. I cut off my locks out of respect but I will always have my *locks in my mind* [my emphasis].

The significance of this story is that it shows that Apache's initiation into this culture was part of a long-standing dialogue. Similar experi-ences have been documented elsewhere with regard to black culture and white young people (see Ch. 6).

Towards the end of 1992 Apache Indian and the black South Lon-don reggae singer Maxi Priest collaborated on a tune called "Fe Real". The tune constituted an extraordinary and historic moment because not only did Apache Indian perform in his combination style but Maxi Priest sung part of the lyric in Punjabi, taking the motif of cultural translation to new heights. They performed a small number of PAs (i.e. a live vocal performance rendered over a backing track) together. The first show was scheduled to take place in the unlikely setting of a provincial town called Peterborough. Peterborough has a small Afro-Caribbean and south Asian population and it is about 100 miles from Birmingham.

I set off from Birmingham, where I was living at the time, with a friend about 9.30 pm. As we drove through countless stereotypically English villages – which were complete with church spires and lines of cottages – I reflected on how the places I was travelling through related to what I was going to see at my destination. It struck me, here I was, a white Englishman with a profound love of the sensibilities of black music, passing through caricatures of England on my way to encounter another version of what "Englishness plus" might mean. We arrived at the La Vistos nightclub just before midnight. The description that follows of what I saw there should not be read as a simple realist narrative. My intention here is to attempt to represent – albeit in an inevitably flawed and partial way – the sublime energy and joy of what it was like to bear witness to the appearance of a new transcultural congregation. I am not asking you necessarily to believe me; but rather to read this as an urban poem:

La Vistos is a classic seventies nightclub with a full complement of glitz and neon. It could have been in any provincial town. The club was complete with revolving light rigs, strobes and a terminal that breathed dry ice over the heads of the people on the dancefloor. The multi-coloured lights revolved and the dry ice flowed – it could have been 1976 and John Travolta might feasibly have been preening himself in the toilets. But this was not just a white disco scene. Probably about 40 per cent of the audience were black and Asian dance-hall goers. It was almost as if the rituals of the dance-hall and the kitsch disco cultures had seamlessly fused. The fault lines showed but they were not totalizing, as if for one brief moment the divisive identities of race and nation were up for grabs. It was a carnival of identity, a place where time and social designation seemed temporarily suspended under the omnipresent groove of the drum and the bass. One could feel things opening up.

Before Apache and Maxi took the stage, the DJ proclaimed a dance competition. "I have a bottle of champagne for the best dance-hall shaker." He stood on top of a stack of speaker cabs and rode the

Figure 8.7 "Fe Real", Apache Indian and Maxi Priest, November 1992

rhythm, finger outstretched, scanning the dancefloor for crucial moves. Shabba Ranks offered a rhythm and it was almost physically impossible to stand still. The DJ presided over the swaying mass of people. First up was a black woman in her forties. In the corner a white woman moved to the rhythm in a way that was indistinguishable from her black friends. Her white boyfriend looked on disapprovingly. She turned her back on him and moved with a mass of people of all shades. The DJ recognized the shattered black/white binary and proclaimed her as the next winner as the dance-hall massive tore up racial boundaries. "Yes, yes, nuff respect – come here sister!" The white sister picked up her prize, she took it over to her disapproving boyfriend and put it on the table in front of him.

Three black women had been dancing with their white friend when one of them beckoned an Asian man. The pair moved in unison, locked in motion at the hip yet not touching. Another division was exploded in an expression of Afro-Asian unity. The DJ called them. The black woman took the bottle, she turned, a path was cleared on the dancefloor and the two partners slowly worked their way towards one another as if the music drew them together.

Last up was a black man in his thirties winning his bottle through sheer commitment rather than style. The DJ passed judgement – "This man has been dancing his ass off all evening, come here brother." As I scanned the dancefloor I could see some white men on the periphery trying to find a groove, stiffly jerking their bodies like a car that turns over but will not start. Others stood unimpressed, demanding that the DJ "Get on with it and play the music". For both those whites who embraced the rhythm or those who were unable to be possessed by it there was no escape. The Next fashions and the Dorothy Perkins' dresses all moved – however awkwardly – to the beat of a different drum.

The lights went down and Apache took the stage. "This one is dedicated to all the Indian ragamuffin posse – X amount of sat siri akal, X amount salaam alakum for all the Muslim posse." Although the microphone failed him, Apache led the crowd through a tour of his hits. A group of Afro-Caribbean young men looked on unimpressed. One young man wearing a turned-around baseball cap with "X" showing, stood arms folded, surveying the scene. His friend moved and swayed with the dance-hall massive composed of Asian, black and white, but he stood motionless. Apache paused, "I am going to bring out a friend of mine now". Maxi Priest strolled on stage. He proceeded to sing snatches from his hits through this awful sound system with a beauty that would have melted the "whitest heart". After the vocal overture Maxi addressed the crowd: "This tune that we have recorded is for the India people. In it I try to sing in Indian." "Fe Real" begins. Apache acclaims Maxi in Punjabi – "Maxi Ji". As the tune draws to an end Maxi sings his Punjabi lines over and over again. The black young man standing on the side of the dancefloor is still unimpressed but as one of his friends grabs him and pulls him onto the floor the group moves in unison to a new style. The tune draws to an end to frantic whistling as the crowd shout a chorus of approval "Bo, bo, bo!" I looked at my watch and it was 2.30 am.

I want to argue that what results from this is the opening up of new identifications. These processes are not completely autonomous from external forces and divisions but I am arguing that these dialogues can result in the development of new intermezzo cultures. The notion of intermezzo features in the work of Deleuze and Guattari (1986: 25) and draws appropriately on a musical metaphor. Its literal meaning is a short dramatic musical performance serving as a connecting link between the main divisions of a large musical work. Here I am using this as an analogy to refer to a space that links social collectivities, producing cultures of inter-being and mutual identification. The prime one I am concerned with here is the fusion of elements of south Asian culture and the rituals of the reggae dance-hall.

Through the call and response between performer and audience these new cultural forms are endorsed. Two examples from Apache's musical collaborations demonstrate this process. During the promotion of "Fe Real", Maxi Priest and Apache performed at a celebration held in Leicester of the religious festival Divali. The event drew an audience of 8,000 Hindus. Apache, remembering the show, comments on its significance:

> It was a nice warm kind of evening. They had 8,000 Asian kids on the streets. We never realized it was going to be that big. When we went on stage Maxi did his Indian [Punjabi] chorus, when they saw him singing that, it meant so much. The Maxi Priest thing was a huge thing, it is all to do with us being a very self-contained people and thinking that people around us don't want to know what is happening. They see a black person wanting to use the language, wanting to come aboard what Apache is doing. Then it is like Maxi is an international star singing in Punjabi and then the Asian youth check it as – yeah people do want to know about us. It was special.

The music in this setting addressed a specific Asian constituency, and was embraced and in turn legitimated. Similar processes occurred when Apache performed at prestigious reggae venues. Notably he was acknowledged during a televised performance at the celebrated black London venue, the 291 Club, where he won over many of his detractors. In 1991 he was voted Best Newcomer at the British Reggae Industry Awards. In these kinds of contexts the music is being authenticated by a distinctly Afro-Caribbean constituency.

Apache comments here on an experience of playing an Afro-Caribbean venue in Southall where he performed his tune "Arranged Marriage", in which he takes himself through a marriage, and the dancefloor rouser "Chok There" (which means "raise up" or "lively up"):

> I did a show, a reggae show for Daddy Ernie from Choice FM at Tudor Rose, Southall – black crowd, 99 per cent black crowd. Before I did "Arranged Marriage" I said, "Buoy I am looking for a girl for my arranged marriage who will dress up in a sari and come to Delhi" and all the black girls threw up their hands. When I was singing "Chok There" I had two thousand black people singing out "Chok There".

These constitute powerful moments where social and musical conventions are being played with and transgressed: an Afro-Caribbean performer singing in Punjabi to a south Asian audience, and an African Caribbean audience singing Punjabi with an Asian artist. The result is an exciting tangle of rhizomorphous connection, a *sound block* that no longer has a point of origin but forms a conjunction. Borrowing from the conceptual language of Deleuze and Guattari, these intermezzo cultures constitute a kind of *cultural body* without organs.[15] A state of fusional multiplicity is established and music provides a smooth surface on which the distinctions and social divisions within the dance-hall can be blurred. Complex and challenging cultures reside in this *sonorous interjacence* that cannot be comprehended in term of simple racial binaries.

The culture that I have tried to describe in this chapter refuses to be located within the either/or ism of "identity". This music manifests itself in a connective supplementarity – ragga *plus* bhangra *plus* England *plus* Indian *plus* Kingston *plus* Birmingham. The culture that is produced relies not on entities of selfhood but on the process of becoming more than one. Here I want to return to the metaphor of the crossroads. At the beginning of this chapter I suggested that the utility of this notion was the way it captured a sense of convergence, particularly in the wider context of the global passage of cultural flows. The crossroads, however, is not just a place where routes converge, it is also the point where choices have to be made and directions plotted. I want to focus on this issue and examine the political bearings that are being established within these polygot cultures.

It is important to stress the plurality of south Asian musics and the variety of resources and inflections that young Asians have embraced. There is a serious dearth of insightful writing into the long history of the involvement of British Asians in musical cultures. The limited comments offered here are intended only to point to some of the important developments.[16] Signs of these dialogues can be seen with the swelling numbers of Asians following established reggae sound systems such as Jah Shaka (*The Voice*, 28 May 1991). Equally, the Coventry-based producer Bally Sagoo is combining bhangra beats, ragga and hip hop in his "Wham Bam" collections, with richly syncretic results. His work includes swing beat mixes of the Muslim Qawwali singer Nusrat Fateh Ali Khan and ragga versions of classic Punjabi folk. His album *Essential Ragga*, which sold 50,000 copies, featured singers such as Rama alongside the white MC Cheshire Cat. A whole wave of Asian musicians is beginning to emerge and includes Bradford's Fun^da^mental, Leicester's indie rock band Cornershop, the Kaliphz (meaning messenger in Arabic), Asian Dub Foundation, Hustlers HC, State of Bengal and Sasha, a major contributor to Multitone's best-seller *Ragga for the masses*. The diversity of these forms of expression confounds the simple characterization that *bhangra* is the prime form of south Asian youth culture. These musical cultures provide a context to challenge dominant stereotypes, express translocal connections and find a voice that does justice to the social location and agenda of their British Asian exponents. These artists both lay claim to Englishness while parodying the racial exclusivity present within the cultural rhetoric of national belonging.

It is equally important to realize that Afro-Caribbean musicians are answering the call of the musics of the south Asian diaspora. For example, a young band called XLNC from Birmingham's neighbouring town of Wolverhampton is developing a unique "combination style". At the core of their music is bhangra beat, yet their bass player Derrick is born of Jamaican parents. They cover the reggae classic "Red Red Wine" but in the form of a traditional Punjabi song "Lwt Ke Le Gaye" (meaning "she swept me away"). Similarly, the Southall-based African Caribbean singer Mixmaster Ji combines lyrics sung in impeccable Punjabi with dance beats. This antiphonic exchange makes the music a junction box for cross-cultural flows resonant with the sounds of reggae, house, techno, soul and Indian folk.

A sensitivity to the politics of inter-diasporic connections may well provide the potential for developing new *historical blocks* (Gramsci 1971) of political commonality. At an analytical level, such an approach promises to remain sensitive to the particularities of local cultures while being alert to the global matrices of diaspora cultures.

Sacrificing certitude for fragmentation may bring about new political as well as cultural possibilities. Rhizomes of anti-racist agency are being formed in the cultural intermezzo that reject both ethnocentrism and the psychic shackles of the "either/or" model of identity. The urgency embracing this politics is all the more immediate in a context where racist violence is rising along with the electoral success of neo-fascist groups in Britain.

Ragga tip and jungle vibe: dance-hall culture in the 1990s

> Warehouses [unofficial parties] taught young Britons of different classes how to be social together outside of the confines of work, clubs and football terraces. Taught them there didn't have to be rules – or expensive bars doormen telling you what you could and couldn't wear. We freed people's imaginations. (Norman Jay[17])

> A whole literary fiction of the festival grew up around the plague: suspended laws, lifted prohibitions, the frenzy of passing time, *bodies mingling together without respect*, individuals unmasked, abandoning their statutory identity and the figure under which they had all been recognised, *allowing a quite different truth to appear*. (Michel Foucault 1977: 197; my emphasis)

The expressive musical cultures of Britain's cities provide a context in which political autonomy and self-representation can be realized alongside profound forms of transcultural dialogue. Michel Foucault, in the above epigraph, describes the carnival of transgression that occurred during the plagues of the medieval period. There are important similarities between Foucault's telling description and the suspension of the social divisions that takes place within the alternative public spheres of the dance-hall, club and house party. The liminality of the dance-hall allows a similar process of cultural transgression and change. The infectious rhythms of the music suspend the social divisions that exist outside the dance and enable new forms of expression. Within these subaltern soundscapes (Gilroy 1994a) different truths about the politics of race can be spoken, nurtured and circulated.

The politics of the dance-hall are complex and it would be a gross misrepresentation to present the expressive cultures that are fostered here as unambiguously transgressive. Syncretism is a two-way process. While the aesthetics of "small nationalisms" are parodied and carnivalized within these spaces, one can also identify the cultural traces of imperialism and the echoes of slavery within these styles, dances and sounds. Recent controversies over the celebration of misogyny, homophobia and "gun iconography" in dance-halls provide key moments where the rupture and violence of white supremacy are registered in black culture in seismic proportions. Following bell hooks, mentioned earlier, one must see these phenomena not as the product of racial alterity but as the assimilation of modernity's inheritance replete with hierarchies of race, class and gender. Linton Kwesi Johnson commented 20 years ago that reggae was a music that "beats heavily against the walls of Babylon, that the walls may come a-tumbling down; a music that chucks the heavy historical load that is pain, that is hunger, that is bitter, that is blood, that is DREAD" (Johnson 1976: 397). This inheritance feeds the powerfully critical and transcendent qualities embodied within these cultures that I have discussed at length in this chapter. Yet it can also harbour some of the destructive features of racial supremacy within the culture itself. Fanon, in his seminal discussion of colonialism, suggested that the violence deposited by the colonizer "in the bones" colonized would be first turned inward against themselves and their peers (Fanon 1963: 40). The gunshot deaths of almost a generation of Jamaican DJs needs to be seen through the lens of these wise words.

The resurgence of slackness during the late 1980s and 1990s shifted the agenda on the mike. Jamaican DJs such as Shabba Ranks, Lovindeer, Chaka Demus and Buju Banton led the sensibilities of the dance-hall into unparalleled "sex talk", word-play and controversy. This reached its height in the summer of 1992 when Buju Banton's "Boom Bye Bye" proposed taking a gun to gay men and Shabba Ranks, appearing on British television, denounced homosexuality through invoking the Bible. These incidents feed the British and American media's appetite for racial demonology. However, their implications cannot be easily dismissed as merely another white supremacist moral panic. These attempts to marshall and define the relationship between sexuality and blackness produced a form of authoritarianism aimed to compensate for the devastation being experienced by black people in the Caribbean, America and Europe (Gilroy

1993b, West 1993). Within this line of argument, contemporary music, dance and oral cultures are viewed as an "after-shock" of slavery in which the body becomes the prime text of authenticity and recompense for an enduring lack of freedom.[18]

Others have argued that, within the hyper-sexualized settings of 1990s' ragga, one can find a politics of subversion missed by those who see slackness as culturally conservative. The most ardent exponent of this line is Carolyn Cooper who argued that in Jamaica slackness can be seen as a "downtown" revolt against the pious morality of fundamentalist Jamaican society:

> Slackness is not mere sexual looseness – though it is certainly that. Slackness is a metaphorical revolt against law and order; an undermining of consensual standards of decency. It is the antithesis of Culture. To quote Josey Wales: "Slackness in di backyard hidin, hidin from Culture". Slackness as an (h)ideology of escape from authority of omniscient Culture is negotiated in a coded language of evasive *double-entendre*.
> (Cooper 1993: 141)

Cooper maintains that the moralist critique of slackness misses the power that dance-hall possesses for flouting the moral conservatism of the Jamaican uptown elite. However, such an assessment produces a barren ethical position that merely celebrates everything within the dance as "resistance", no matter what the consequences.[19] More convincingly, Cooper points to the opportunity that the dance-hall offers women to have control over their bodies and express their sexuality. Sexually expressive forms of dancing such as "wining" allow "female power to be exuded in the extravagant display of flashy jewellery, expensive clothes, elaborate hairstyles and the rigidly attendant men that altogether represent substantial wealth" (ibid.: 155). The emergent fame of "dance-hall Queens" such as Carlene Smith provides important examples of where women have achieved status and economic power through such means. For Cooper, women's power within the dance lies in the control over their sexuality and men's dependence upon them.

Others have argued precisely the opposite – that women's power lies in their autonomy from men within the dance-hall. Daniel Miller has argued in relation to Trinidad that the auto-sexuality of "wining" engenders for women something akin to a Hegelian form of absolute freedom. Here sexual fulfilment becomes the dancer's own autonomous object: "It is an expression of a free sexuality which has no object but itself, and most especially it is a sexuality not dependent upon men" (Miller 1991: 333). This momentary and transient individuation produces a self-absorbed and self-sufficient sexual fulfilment in which the dancer is free from everything that binds her to the world. Inge Blackman, director of the film *Ragga Gyal D'bout*, argued further that the dance-hall offers a context for black women to celebrate their sexuality. Unlike any other form of black popular culture, ragga in Britain allowed black women to be sensual with each other beyond narrowly heterosexual terms of reference.[20] The sexual politics of ragga is clearly complex. Opportunistic media racism characterized these forms of music and dance as crudely homophobic and misogynistic, yet these evaluations produce little more than the latest in a long line of racist moral panics. Despite this, serious issues remain in the future regarding the ways in which the echoes of slavery and imperialism resurface in the loaded planes of dance-hall culture and music.

The technologies and traditions of sound system performance have totally transformed the production and consumption of music. The effects of these changes are extraordinarily wide ranging. DJ Kool Herc transported sound system technology from Kingston, Jamaica, to the South Bronx in the late 1960s and in doing so provided the crucible in which new forms of music-making could be established within hip hop and its flamboyant sibling, rap lyricism. In Britain, the sound systems ethos has transformed youth culture. Any young person growing up in a British city – regardless of their parental origins – will in some way be touched by this inheritance. From the popularity of the 12 inch single, to the vinyl culture that still doggedly refuses to be overtaken by "superior" recording formats and the collective sensibilities associated with "playing out", this technology has enabled a whole range of young Britons to "string up" and chat their own directives. The democratic forms of antiphony produced in live performance are no longer as common as they were in the hey-day of the fast-style MCs. "Specials" (one-off recordings) from popular artists now monopolize sound system prestige as the most sought after items. But new and richly syncretic forms of music have inherited "sound system theory" (Rose 1991) and taken their music into uncharted territories.

One direct descendant of this culture is London's jungle scene. In the late 1980s a complex fusion occurred between techno and house from Detroit and Chicago respectively, the break beat music of hip hop, ragga DJs and the reggae sound systems. The full story of this complex form should be left to someone more qualified, but I want to point to some of the continuities that this music has with the forms discussed in this chapter. Through the early 1990s, jungle sustained itself as an underground music controlled by principally black DJs and their white and Asian associates. As Moose, original DJ at the legendary Sunday Roast sessions at London's Astoria, puts it, the musical ethos is transcultural: "It's not a black thing and it's not a white thing – it's a vibe thing. What we're running – it's Jungle, a multicultural thing." Like its predecessors, this new music takes icons of Englishness – such as the roast dinner – and puts them in the service of an emergent re-signified dance-floor nation. The term "jungle" first emerged on a Rebel MC sample in 1991. This term is associated with an area of Kingston, Jamaica, called Tivoli Gardens, known as "the Jungle" and frequently cited in "yard tapes". A whole infrastructure of clubs and radio stations emerged. Labels such as Ibiza and Reinforce Records played a crucial role in the early development of the music. At the core of the culture are DJs such as Fabio, Grooverider, Goldie, DJ Ron, DJ Kenny Ken, LTJ Bukum; club sessions at Sunday Roast, the Paradise Club, and Thunder and Joy; and a host of pirate stations – Kool FM, Eruption FM, Fantasy FM and Chaos FM. Like its soul and reggae predecessors, this music is being fostered within an alternative public sphere and broadcasts to its followers from the top of tower blocks via pirate radio. The computer and sampler are added to the technology of the sound system, but the fundamental ethos and social structure remain intact.

In 1994 the ragga MC General Levy and M Beat's "Incredible" broke jungle into the mass marketplace. The success of "Incredible" in the charts was much to the chagrin of the scene's devotees and earned accusations of opportunism and widespread suspicion. The jungle DJ is more central than the MC of the past, although figures such as MC Navigator and UK Apache are important exceptions. Jungle lyricism is marked by a return to the minimalism of dub DJ commentary combined with the intermittent injection of throaty ragga delivery and fast-style rappin'. The sampler provides the means to simulate virtually any voice from the pantheon of ragga DJs. The verbal gymnastics of Supercat, Buju Banton, Cutty Ranks and Barrington Levi are thus injected with fresh energy at the rate of 160 beats per minute. The music is also promiscuous with regard to its sampled material, utilizing sources as diverse as Pink Floyd, Lonnie Liston Smith and Tenorsaw. By using programs such as Cubase or Creator, sampled sounds can be represented visually on the computer screen, providing an inexhaustible amount of options for the junglist composer. This process is further enhanced by techniques such as "timestretching", which enable percussive or melodic sounds to be speeded up and slowed down without altering their pitch. Jungle is fast fracturing in a whole corona of sub-genres from ragga-jungle to ambient and jazz-inflected forms.

The central elements in sound culture are also retained within jungle, including the dependence on dub plates and exclusive music available only to DJs. Equally, "lif it up selecta" interruptions have been retained in the dance, where they are referred to as "rewinds". In jungle the same processes of antiphony discussed earlier in relation to the fast-style MCs apply, as the crowd demands that the DJ "wheel" a tune back to the start. The "digital steppers" produced through these means have resulted in some unique music emerging from the capital.

Jungle demonstrates a diaspora sensitivity that renders explicit the Jamaican traces within hip hop culture along with a radical re-alignment of national images. Black, white and Asian junglists all claim that the music uniquely belongs to Britain, or more specifically that jungle is "a London somet'ing". For these citizens, jungle is a music "to feel at home in", profoundly heterotopic and simultaneously local, national and transnational. The nascent patriotism found in jungle is all the more surprising given that the genesis of the scene was in some part due to a hardening of racism within rave, combined with a racially exclusive door policy in London clubs. This refashioning is part of a profound process in which the politics of race and nation is claimed and redefined by young people, a project that still possesses a vitality and urgency within Britain's cities. DJ Kenny Ken explains:

> Another reason why I'm involved in jungle music is because it's brought a lot of people together – you know what I mean – like certain men a few years ago wouldn't have dreamed of talking to a white person and same the other way around. But now we're under the same roof ravin', laughing and joking together – you know what I mean?[21]

In this alternative public sphere, the aesthetics of the nation are recomposed, resulting in more inclusive translocal notions of what it means to reside within UK boundaries. The ideologies developed within these musical cultures offer a stark alternative to the racialized views of nation circulated in the wider public arenas of British political life: England has been "niced up". Returning to Norman Jay's comments, which opened this final section, the enduring power of these musical forms lay in their ability to imagine new types of association that transcend the divisions of race, class and gender. In this cultural intermezzo, the map of nationhood can – however fleetingly – be re-drawn under radically different terms.

CHAPTER 9

Future reality: racisms, new ethnicity and the millennium

Take me through a time machine, so that I can ease my
  mind
Take me through those lovely places, that I would really
  love to find
Travel through space and time, blow my mind
Ex-ceed-ing-ly beautiful, Ex-ceed-ing-ly beautiful . . .
Travel through a time machine, future reality
                    (Chocolate Milk, *Time machine*[1])

I, the man of colour, want only this:
That the tool never possess the man. That the enslavement
  of man cease forever . . . That it be possible for me to
  discover and to love man, wherever he may be.
The Negro is not [able]. Any more than the white man.
Both must turn their backs on the inhuman voices which
  were those of their respective ancestors in order that
  authentic communication be possible.
                              (Fanon 1968: 231)

I begin this concluding chapter with these two quotes because they
point towards some of the optimistic trends that are present within
contemporary urban cultures with regard to the valence of racism.
Some of the young people I have referred to, as Fanon suggests, have
turned their backs on the inhuman voices of their ancestors. The
dehumanizing consequences of racism do not flourish uncontested in
the metropolis. Young people are attempting to build a culture, and
defend a space, beyond the circumscriptions of race. Yet progress

towards this vision of unity is not simple or linear. It is here that I return to the question I posed at the beginning of the book. How does racism enter into the lives of young people growing up in urban contexts? A short, and perhaps banal answer is that the impact of racist discourses on young lives is partial and complex. In the following discussion I want to explore what this means and how this book furthers an understanding of England's multiracial and multi-racist character.

This final chapter is organized around two themes. First I attempt to restate the central concerns of the book and summarize its major findings. Secondly, I want to extend some of these arguments and outline their implications for the theorization of culture, identity and ethnicity.

As regards the central themes of the book, I will confine my comments to three core areas: the nature of "community" in these districts, the social identities of these young people, and their experience of racism.

Although Southgate and Riverview were very close together, they revealed very different social and cultural characteristics. I explained the differences in ethnic composition in terms of the housing allocation procedures operated by the Greater London Council and the local borough. The selective tenancy letting policy adopted by the GLC meant that Riverview was allocated to a relatively affluent white working-class community of residents. The numerical dominance of white workers was challenged in the 1970s when the management of this unit of housing was handed over to the local borough. From this point onwards Riverview progressively became a more heterogeneous space. Southgate, on the other hand, was not settled according to selective procedures. As a result, from its beginning the neighbourhood became an intensely multiracial place. Particularly important was the development of black cultural institutions within the area.

These basic inequalities in housing provision provided the base for my analysis of "community" in these areas. In order to comprehend the complex notions of community expressed in these two neighbourhoods I employed a concept referred to as "community discourse" and I showed that, within these areas, competing definitions struggle to project meaning out onto the ebb and flow of social life. Thus communities do not exist *sui generis*, they are created and imagined on a, more or less, daily basis. In Chapters 2 and 5 I outlined the array of community discourses in these two districts. What was common to both areas was that residents spoke about race and racism through the language of community. I showed how sets of these discourses were organized in relation to one another, whereby notions of community were produced from what I referred to as a "semantic system". The most widely operated semantic system would thus become the dominant definition of community.

In Riverview, the predominant semantic system was what I referred to as "white flight". This system is composed of three discourses, and their organizing themes ranged from the assertion that the area had lost its sense of community, to the idea that the neighbourhood was being swamped by minorities and that as a result established residents were being forced to move away. The three discourses were placed in a metonymic relationship, i.e. reference to one element of the system automatically evokes meanings related to the other two. It was in this context that local racism was expressed. The decline in the housing and economic circumstances of these residents was "explained" by correlating these changes with the presence of variously defined "problem families", black people and Vietnamese refugees.

The "white flight" semantic system was not the only resource used to project community, or more correctly the lack of it, on to the Riverview context. There was a partially developed discourse that characterized the estate as a harmoniously multi-ethnic district where belonging was determined by commitment to the area. I showed that this discourse was developed by the young people living in the area, resulting in an racially inclusive localism that I called "neighbourhood nationalism".

Southgate, by contrast, was characterized by the "our area" semantic system. Here the district was viewed as a place where harmonious relations existed. The "our area" system was composed of two discursive elements, whose organizing themes I referred to as the "harmony discourse" and the "black community discourse". White and black people used harmony discourse to reject the legitimacy of racism, in effect banishing it from the district. Here racism was both acknowledged as socially significant but rejected as inapplicable to the situation found in the neighbourhood. Black community discourse, on the other hand, laid claim to the area as a site of black organization. Thus the district was viewed as a place where black people had successfully defended their position. These two discourses were in a mutually reinforcing relationship. The harmony discourse opened up a space where black organization was seen as legitimate and also facilitated inter-racial contact and communication.

Although the "our area" semantic system predominated in Southgate, it was not the only formulation of community found in the district. I also found a "white flight" semantic system – similar to that reported in Riverview – present in some accounts. Thus I conclude that these semantic systems constitute available resources that compete to project meaning out on the urban landscape. Each of the systems has an attendant racial agenda, which either posits racist explanations for the economic and social ills of the area or asserts the existence of a racially inclusive localism. In this situation some semantic systems prevail, or win out, while others are suppressed.

The existence of these systems is very important with reference to the nature of social identity amongst the young. These discourses provide social resources that can be used in order for young people to find a place. As a result the expression of identity found amongst the youth of Southgate and Riverview also varied significantly. I documented these variations in Chapters 3 and 6.

I developed a model of identity definition that was concerned with the identities that young people chose to inhabit, but also with the public notions of self that were abandoned – a process I referred to as "vacating". In both districts the young people denied that colour was important and asserted that racism was "out of order". In Riverview this led to a racially inclusive notion that I have referred to as "neighbourhood nationalism". Here the definition of who belonged in the national community was shrunk to the size of the neighbourhood. "Belonging" was thus determined by length of residence and commitment to the area. Particularly important here was the assertion that black and white young people had grown up together in this area. As a result, it was asserted that "we are all the same". Black young people thus became contingent insiders. Along with this process was the development of a youth culture that called upon a variety of symbolic resources, many of which stem from black forms of expression and music.

This did not lead to a situation where racism was completely banished. The identities of young white people in the area exhibited a divided quality. On the one side of this conflict was the assertion that racism is wrong and that their black friends belong, and, on the other, were the local racist discourses found in the "white flight" semantic system and racism located within a wider public arena (i.e. the media and politics). Black young people too maintained a commitment to neighbourhood nationalism, yet at the same time they were conscious of the limits that racism placed on their relationships with whites. Thus their notion of self was a product of shared identification with the locality and also the exploration of links with black people outside of the neighbourhood.

Although there was evidence of dialogue between black and white young people, Vietnamese youth in the area were not included in these processes. The volatile anti-racism promulgated in multiracial peer groups was of little significance to their situation. The Vietnamese were vilified as an unwanted out-group and subjected to the worst forms of racial abuse.

In Southgate the existence of an inclusive local philosophy meant that more profound and rigorously syncretic cultural dialogues took place between black and white young people. Whites vacated concepts of whiteness and Englishness. This resulted in a cultural vacuum into which a host of black idioms of speech and vernacular culture were drawn. Embracing these forms resulted in an encoded identification with black people and blackness as a culturally defined set of actions and modes of thinking. White young people took this form of identification very seriously, even to the degree that some talked about the desire in mid-adolescence to "want to be black". Their black peers allowed this identification in all but its most extreme form of expression, with the result that within the alternative public sphere of peer activity a negotiated form of identity and ethnicity was generated. It was in this space that whites could claim legitimate ownership of black linguistic and cultural forms that offered an alternative identity option. Locally, then, whiteness, racism and national chauvinism were identified as connected in a triangular and mutually reinforcing way. The negotiated access to black practices meant that the former notion of identity could be vacated in favour of a mixed ethnicity that was shared with black peers. This form of identification could not always be sustained, because ultimately young people were brought back and forced to reckon with the meaning of their whiteness and the significance of racism in the lives of their black friends.

The situation for black young people in Southgate contrasted with that found in Riverview. Here there was a significant reconstruction of a notion of blackness that was defined in cultural terms. In South London, black identity must be viewed as having a specifically local expression, but it is also concerned with developing connections with the African diaspora, both nationally and internationally. Through the cultural construction of blackness the history of the black Briton is rewritten and identifications are made with black people throughout the New World. Blackness is the medium through which historical connections are made. However, black young people also questioned whether this should be privileged as the only viable notion of self. Some of the young people in the study warned of slipping into essentialist definitions of black culture.

Black young people also maintained that Southgate was a place where racial harmony existed and many of them identified strongly with South London. At the same time, they abandoned a notion of Englishness in favour of the classification British. This was seen to be a statement of citizenship, rather than involving a cultural aesthetic. Yet, the presence of black young people in South London has transformed the aesthetic of the locality. The claiming of South London, and ultimately England, as home could produce a reworking in the definition of what Englishness means. The definition of blackness and Englishness as mutually exclusive identities cannot be sustained in the situation I have described. I suggested that the dialogues occurring in South London could result in a truly multiracial aesthetic of working-class Englishness. In Chapter 8, I showed that these developments were also consistent with developments occurring within the musical cultures found in London and elsewhere. This discussion of musical cultures also showed the transnational frameworks within which both south Asian and African diaspora cultures operate and pointed to the potential for understanding both transcultural alliances and inter-diasporic connections.

The situation for young people defined as "mixed race" was also affected by transformations occurring in the locality. For example, here was a move to abandon stigmatized definitions of "mixed blood" or "half caste" and replace these notions with a concept of "mixed race". "Mixed-race" young people could both identify themselves as having a mixed-race identity, and locate themselves within a notion of blackness. In this sense the richly syncretic cultures that were being made and re-made in communities of young people provided a context where mixed identity and blackness could be held simultaneously and not challenged.

I divided the discussion of how racism entered into the lives of these young people into two areas. One I designated popular racism, which referred to how white youngsters used the racist discourses in their everyday lives. The other meaning referred to the institutional process of racial discrimination. Thus unequal allocation of housing was designated an institutional form of racism, while the "white flight" semantic system provided an example of popular racism. In Chapters 3 and 7, I discussed how racism was expressed by white people and experienced by black youngsters. It is this issue that I want to reflect on.

White people do not experience racism in a monolithic or total way. It was clear from the analysis offered in Chapter 3 that white youth use popular racism as a strategic resource. As a result, apparently contradictory assertions can be made. Racism is understood as illegitimate ("out of order") but it is used precisely because it can be hurtful to a black peer. In the situations I described as duelling play, whites gained advantage through using racism. In the aftermath of the incidents of racist name-calling, whites uniformly said that their racist practice was meaningless and a form of play. Here the insider status of black peers was restated. Equally, there was a division between black people who live in the area, who are defined as belonging, and racist constructions of black people from outside the area. However, black insiders could still have racist discourses mobilized against them in ambiguous play contexts. As a result their insider status was always contingent. Vietnamese youth did not benefit from the ambiguities in white common sense. They were constructed in crass racist ways and subjected to attack and abuse. Thus popular racism was unevenly developed in the lives of white young people in Riverview. As a result, particular forms of racist discourse could be muted while others flourished.

The situation in Southgate was very different. The relative numerical strength and street power of black young people in this district meant that popular racism of the kind mentioned above was all but banished from the area. Having said this, black young men, in particular, said that they were conscious that some white adults were fearful of them. Equally, young black women gave accounts of gendered forms of racism that characterized them as "over-emotional", "highly fertile" and possessing "exotic sexual abilities". However, these young people also said that popular racism was something that they did not encounter on a daily basis in Southgate. They located the experience of racism in two institutional and, to some degree, geographical spaces. Racism was experienced within educational institutions, the police and at work. Thus racism was mostly experienced outside the area. Here black young people were careful to assign racism to a specific set of actors and to the institutions of society. For example, white peers were seen to benefit from the existence of racial inequality in job opportunities, but were not blamed for the existence of these inequalities.

Having summarized the book's major arguments, I want to suggest a model for understanding the nature of the dialogues found in these two districts. In particular, I focus on how the ethnicity of these young people should be theorized. I argue that the syncretic cultures catalogued in this study can be seen as liminal forms of ethnicity.

Roger Hewitt has argued that the apprehension of culture should be viewed "not as 'tradition' but rather, as the bricoleur's bag, [where] meaning [is] created as much as given" (Hewitt 1991: 15). This has implications for how we theorize ethnicity. In much of the work influenced by Frederik Barth (1969), there is a tendency to underplay the importance of the creation of cultural meanings and to concentrate on the way ethnic emblems are used to mark boundaries between social actors (Wallman 1978a, 1978b, 1979). Hewitt's emphasis on the creation of new cultures, in short the remaking of tradition, undermines the assumption that ethnic identities are primordial (Wallman 1986). I want to attempt to resolve this tension by suggesting a model of ethnicity that is able to cope with the complexity of the cultural innovations documented in this book.

I draw on two concepts as the basis of this model. The first is the concept of liminality, drawn from the work of the Franco-Dutch folklorist Arnold Van Gennep (1960) and the anthropologist Victor Turner (1969). Liminality in their work refers to a state of separation from the mundane aspects of life. The stage of liminality was the conjunction between a previous status – such as childhood – and a new public identity. As Turner points out, liminality is not merely about assigning identity, it can also relate to the inversion and transformation of public roles:

> . . . liminal phases and states often are more about the doffing of masks, the stripping of statuses, the renunciation of roles, the demolishing of structures, than about putting them on and keeping them on. (Turner 1984: 26)

It is in this sense that I maintain that the alternative public sphere occupied by black and white young people in South London constitutes a liminal space.

Secondly, I want to incorporate Deleuze and Guattari's (1986) notion of the rhizome and my adaption of this concept through the idea of the cultural intermezzo. In the previous chapter I showed how these concepts allow forms of cultural inter-being to be comprehended without recourse to a notion of primordial essence. The logic of the rhizome is always about doing and making connections between things that have no necessary relationship to one another. It is for this reason that the connective supplementarity of the rhizome is always about affiliation: "Rhizome is alliance, uniquely alliance" (Deleuze & Guattari 1986: 25). This abstraction allows for the complex identification discussed within the book to be placed within a theoretical frame. However, the rhizomatics of contemporary youth culture are not stable and the potential for invoking racism remains within these vernacular cultures. It is with this in mind that I want to develop a model that can allow for the congregationalist ethos of the rhizome, while being alert to ways in which racial division can continue to be potentially active within these polyglot cultures.

I am arguing that new forms of ethnicity are emerging where identities and public meanings are suspended in this liminal phase. The result is exactly what Hewitt (1991) refers to as the destabilization of tradition. Here "kaleidoscopic formations of 'trans-racial' cultural syncretism are growing daily more detailed and more beautiful" (Gilroy 1988–9: 37). There are, however, stresses placed on these syncretic cultures. These result from the fact that the alternative public sphere cannot remain fully autonomous from forces that are external to it. Thus potential lines of fissure run through these cultural spaces.

For clarity I am going to represent the boundaries of this cultural intermezzo diagrammatically in the shape of a diamond. Inside the diamond, young people interact within multiracial peer groups. In this space a transformation in meaning can take place as symbols and identities are re-made. However, the content and quality of these liminal cultures are dependent on the social context (community discourses and the racial or ethnic balance of peer groups) and the pressures that are placed on it from outside (racist discourses and the existence of racial inequality).

I want to focus on two sets of tensions, or fault lines, that run through these intermezzo urban cultures. The first relates to the processes that either curb or promote the local expression of popular racism. Here the local semantic system that produces images of community is important. These discourses act as resources with which young people can validate the terms of the liminal culture. In

Southgate the predominance of the "our area" semantic system facilitated rather than prohibited inter-racial dialogue. These local circumstances stand in stark contrast to national definitions of belonging. Thus I am suggesting that running through this liminal culture is a tension between local and national definitions of inclusion. In Figure 9.1, I have represented this as a broken line. The line remains broken because there is no congruence between local inclusive definitions and racialized definitions of nationalism. The "our area" system prevails and the terms of liminal ethnicity are secure.

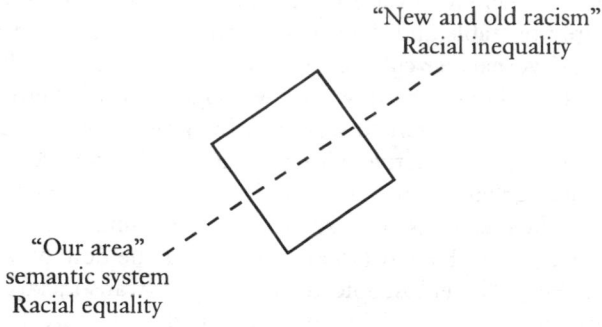

"New and old racism"
Racial inequality

"Our area"
semantic system
Racial equality

Figure 9.1   Racism and liminal ethnicity

The situation is very different in Riverview. The formulation I referred to as "neighbourhood nationalism" has all the qualities of a liminal ethnicity. The situation is complicated by the fact that black people within the locality can be included but Vietnamese migrants are excluded. However, a fault line runs through this localism. The racism expressed in the "white flight" semantic system and other forms of racism circulated within the press and media can be strategically used against black peers, for example where an incident of racist name-calling occurs. The use of racist discourses by whites violates the terms of this liminal ethnicity, the line between local racism and national racism is completed and a black–white segmentation results (see Fig. 9.2).

The maintenance of these liminal forms of ethnicity is dependent on the expulsion of racism. Where racism is present, the terms of inter-racial dialogue break down. Racism operates as a form of closure, where racialized boundaries are evoked that define black people as outsiders.

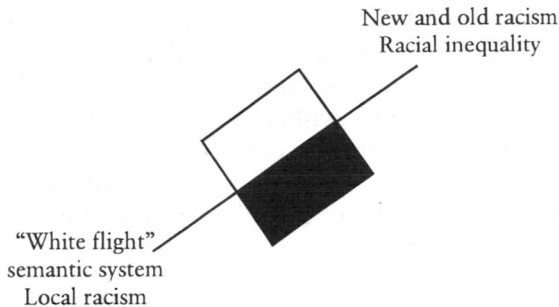

New and old racism
Racial inequality

"White flight",
semantic system
Local racism

Figure 9.2 Racist name-calling and neighbourhood nationalism

The second fault line exists for very different reasons. This relates to black forms of closure. Here black elements of the culture are re-appropriated and imbued with specifically black meanings. This form of closure is not comparable to those discussed above. Black closure is not synonymous with white racism. The impulse that stimulates the owning of black symbols varies. It includes situations where whites are seen to be parodying black culture, or where whites take their identification with blackness beyond the limits of black consent. In Chapter 6, I documented an exchange in which a white young man proclaimed to his black friends that he wanted to be black. Prior to this claim the three boys were acting out the liminal form of ethnicity I am referring to here. However, the explicit desire to be black, on the part of the white youngster, violated the terms of this ethnicity. The distinction is between sharing symbols and cultural resources, which is admissible within the terms of the culture, and a form of emulation that abandons the equality on which the culture is based. White youngsters acting "as if" they were black violates the ethos of "doing" and participation in culture as a shared activity and reduces the transcultural dialogue to a rapacious attribution of racial "being".

In addition, proximity to and experience of racial inequality may also lead to a defensive form of black closure. In these situations black symbols are owned in order to combat racism. This kind of closure was surprisingly rare. The extraordinary thing about these liminal ethnicities is that they can exist despite the tensions that are placed upon them. It is for this reason that they deserve to be analytically comprehended.

The fault line in the model I am suggesting has two poles. At one end is the phenomenon of black closure, where cultural and linguistic

247

resources are owned by black young people and white use is censured. At the other end are the processes that open up elements of black culture to common use in multiracial peer groups. The continuation of cultural syncretism within communities of young people is thus dependent upon the absence of black closure.

In Figure 9.3 I represent the complete model. The maintenance of this liminal form of ethnicity is dependent upon the two diagonal fault lines remaining broken.

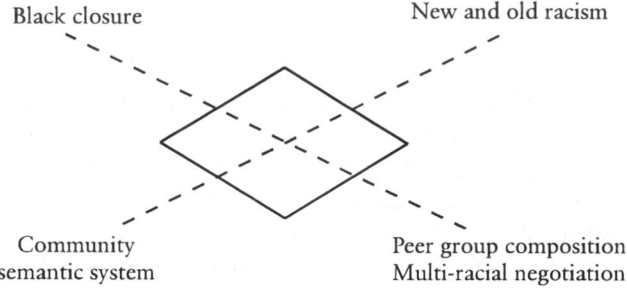

Black closure

New and old racism

Community
semantic system

Peer group composition
Multi-racial negotiation

Figure 9.3 A model of liminal ethnicity

In this model of ethnicity, boundaries are viewed as being evoked from outside and not intrinsic or primordial. This is the crucial difference between this view of ethnicity and previous theoretical work. The liminal and mixed cultures that I have described defy boundaries of race and ethnicity. They are racially and ethnically inclusive cultural forms.

A legitimate question to raise is the durability and significance of these liminal ethnicities. As I have shown with reference to whites, young people are always called back to take some account of public definitions of their culture and identity. I have argued that these mixed cultural forms offer young whites a sense of "difference" that provides an alternative to the public meanings associated with whiteness and Englishness. In this liminal culture, white young people reckon with the meaning of their whiteness and the place of racism within their experience. This results in social knowledge, in the sense that this word is used to mean the range of one's information about the nature of the social world. Thus participation in these liminal forms of ethnicity can result in the creation of a critical perspective resulting in a knowing effect. Similarly for black young people, the historical connections that are being made within these syncretic cultures produce social knowledge about their place in an African diaspora. Equally, black young people use these means to create a cultural space in Britain that is not confined by the aesthetic of Englishness. In both cases this knowledge may lead to new forms of identity and consciousness.

However, it is important to evaluate these developments with some caution. Liminality is by definition unstable because it is a conjunction. In this respect, it is possible to document where liminal forms come from and their current qualities, but it is more difficult to project what will be delivered as these young people grow older. It may be that in some districts of South London a truly new form of entitlement and iterant belonging, free of racial absolutes, is about to come of age. It is impossible at this stage to substantiate these claims and there is a need for research that will monitor these trajectories longitudinally.

What is certain is that any progression towards a "new England" will not be linear or simple. As I have shown in this study, it is possible for egalitarian processes to exists alongside the most brutal forms of racism. Returning to Fanon's comments, racism is not just about inhuman ancestral voices; new forms of racism emerge as old ones are muted. This is classically reflected in Riverview, where the partial suppression of racism directed against black people can exist simultaneously with the application of racist discourses to Vietnamese young people and black people outside the neighbourhood. The configuration of racism seems to be more complex than ever. Although there is some cause for optimism, this must be set against other harsh realities.[2]

The rich and hybrid nature of what I have described is very threatening to those who defend a definition of Englishness imbued with an imperial past. Enoch Powell's comments of some time ago are still germane:

> There is . . . [a] problem where a native culture has already begun to disintegrate under foreign influence, where a native population has already taken in more of the foreign culture than it can ever expel. There is a problem, as in some of the West Indies, where several uprooted peoples have been haphazardly mixed. And these problems are insoluble.[3]

The fears of the contemporary supporters of old England – expressed in the above quote from Powell – relate to the withering popularity of T. S. Eliot's vision of English culture. The England I have described includes much more than "Derby Day, Henley Regatta, Cowes, the twelfth of August, a cup final, the dog races, the pin table, the dart board, Wensleydale cheese, boiled cabbage cut into sections, beetroot in vinegar, nineteenth century Gothic churches and the music of Elgar".[4] I have shown that young people in British cities are embracing diversity in seemingly inexhaustible combinations of form and content in ways that make Britishness or Englishness almost meaningless. Yet, we cannot dispose of national identity altogether. On both the left and the right, the beseiged British way of life and its attendant logic of cultural purity still provides an organizational skin to be stretched over the frame of the state. The vibrant cultures I have described in this book constitute a polyphonic explosion of this narrow and shallow version of our national heritage. As the twenty-first century approaches, these little nationalisms are no longer a tenable social container for forms of association and sociality. Perhaps in this context, the nation is important only in the moment where its cultural imperatives are being carnivalized, subverted and challenged.

Salman Rushdie, in his book *The satanic verses*, suggests that the problem with the English is that their identity has always been defined in terms of imperial exploits abroad. Images of England are created as if in the mind's eye of a colonial bureaucrat, sitting in some distant outpost of the Empire, nostalgically thinking of home. It is this sense of remoteness that Rushdie captures through his characters.[5] I have shown in this study that the meaning of England is being recomposed in the heart of its cities. The young people I have written about are finding out for themselves what it means to be English in a multiracial society.

These issues transcend the narrow confines of Britain. The fragmentation and reassertion of national identities are a global phenomenon. From the United States to Europe, young people are claiming a new racial hybridism (Bernstein 1994). But there is no uniform connection between this phenomenon and the withering of white supremacy. Chocolate Milk's dream-like vision of a beautiful future beyond racism seems destined for some period ahead to be confined to the time-traveller's utopian muse. Our future, with all its complications, will be caught within what I have referred to as a metropolitan paradox, where momentary escapes from racism are contiguous with ever more complex forms of racial power and domination.

If multiculturalism is to have any meaning in the context of the twenty-first century, the idea of the existence of homogeneous cultures and identities must be undermined irrevocably. Edward Said concludes that, as we approach the millennium, identity labels provide little more than a departure:

> Muslim or American are no more than starting-points, which if followed into actual experience for only a moment are quickly left behind. Imperialism consolidated the mixture of cultures and identities on a global scale. But its worst and most paradoxical gift was to allow people to believe that they were only, mainly, exclusively, white, or Black, or Western or Oriental. (Said 1993: 408)

Here he points clearly to the connection between racism and the reification of cultural difference. Historically, in Britain at least, multiculturalism has operated within such absolutist models of "minority culture". But such cultural hermetism ignores the intense contact that is also a part of the largess of imperialism. If multiculturalism is to be politically re-configured, the strange comforts of cultural absolutism must be abandoned. It is only then that we can fully embrace and reckon with the intense relationship between modernity and multiculture.

APPENDIX 1

The ethnographic sample

Between 1985 and 1989 I collected ethnographic data from 99 young people who visited Riverview Youth Club and whose ages ranged from 12 to 25. All of the young people I spoke to were born in South London or had lived there for more than five years. The ethnic origin of these young people is as follows: 10 black Britons of Afro-Caribbean origin (6 M, 4 F), 11 Vietnamese (7 M, 4 F), 15 mixed parentage Afro-Caribbean/white English (6 M, 9 F), 4 Turkish or Greek Cypriot (1 F), 56 white English (26 M, 30 F), 3 N/S Irish (2 M, 1 F). The richness and depth of individual cases varied within this sample. For some individuals I collected only the most basic of accounts, while other young people were interviewed repeatedly, in combination with lengthy periods of participant observation. This was dependent in the main on the quality of individual relationships. Because of the difficulties in doing fieldwork in this context, the core sample was 54 young people.

A similar situation operated within Southgate. Here the ethnographic sample consisted of 104 young people between the ages of 11 and 25. The ethnic composition of this sample is as follows: 72 black Britons of Afro-Caribbean origin (40 M, 32 F), 18 white South London (8 M, 10 F), 6 mixed parentage (4 M, 2 F), 4 Turkish Cypriot (2 M, 2 F) and 4 Vietnamese (2 M, 2 F). Again the quality of the data produced within this sample varied greatly. In the Southgate situation I was forced to make more contacts outside of the youth club because of the fluctuating attendance at the youth club during the research period. However, there was a core of 51 informants whom I met repeatedly and for whom I recorded life histories and informal interviews.

In addition to participant observation with young people, I also conducted a series of interviews with adults (between 26 and 60 years of age) from within the two neighbourhoods, including parents of key informants. The rationale behind this was to develop an appreciation of the nature of the parent culture and in particular the way race and racism were talked about within the home setting. This sample consisted of 30 people in Riverview and 26 people in Southgate.

1981 and 1991 census data and ethno-demographic structure

The research period spanned 1985–89. As a result, census material for 1981 and 1991 can provide only a guide to the overall demographic structure of these areas during the period of the research. In many respects the demographic structure of these districts during the period of the research lay somewhere between the statistics for 1981 and 1991. Geographically defined census data for both Riverview

Table 1 Riverview Estate: ethno-demographic structure, 1981 census.

Country of birth	Males	Females	Total	% of total*	
Total	1,201	1,291	2,492	–	
England	906	1,011	1,917	77	
Scotland	26	22	48	2	
Wales	13	12	25	1	
Rest of UK	10	10	20	1	
Irish Rep.	51	47	98	4	
Old Commonwealth	4	2	6	–	
New Commonwealth	103	113	216	9	
				% NCW	
E. Africa	4	6	10	5	
Africa	30	26	56	26	
Caribbean	41	59	100	46	
India	7	8	15	7	
Far East	5	0	5	2	
Mediterranean	15	12	27	12	
Remainder	1	2	3	1	
Pakistan	1	1	2	–	
Other EC	9	8	17		1
Other Europe	23	16	39		1
Rest	55	49	104		4

* To nearest %

and Southgate are discussed in what follows. The details of the ethno-demographic composition of these two areas for 1981 are repro-duced in Tables 1 and 2.

There are a number of points that need to be emphasized regard-ing these figures. First, the predominance of the figure for "English" residence (77 per cent) provides an indication of the predominantly white nature of this area during the research period. Only 9 per cent of the population were born in the New Commonwealth and of that figure the largest minority were of Caribbean origin, although there were considerable numbers of people of African (26 per cent) and Mediterranean origin (12 per cent). The situation in Southgate in 1981 was significantly different, with a much higher proportion of residents born in the New Commonwealth (23 per cent); this pro-vides an indication of the more profoundly multi-ethnic nature of this estate in contrast to Riverview. Here people of Caribbean origin were by far the largest minority (70 per cent).

These figures give only a guide to the overall ethnic composition of these South London neighbourhoods because they in effect subsume

Table 2   Southgate Estate: ethno-demographic structure, 1981 census.

Country of birth	Males	Females	Total	% of total*	
Total	1,528	1,624	3,152	–	
England	1,057	1,166	2,223	70	
Scotland	25	20	45	1	
Wales	3	6	9	–	
Rest of UK	14	12	26	1	
Irish Rep.	26	27	53	2	
Old Commonwealth	4	1	5	–	
New Commonwealth	371	354	725	23	
				% NCW	
E. Africa	3	0	3	–	
Africa	55	62	117	16	
Caribbean	252	259	511	70	
India	9	6	15	2	
Bangladesh	1	0	1	–	
Far East	10	8	18	2	
Mediterranean	31	16	47	6	
Remainder	10	3	13	2	
Pakistan	6	2	8	–	
Other EC	3	14	17	1	
Other Europe	7	9	16	1	
Rest of world	12	13	25	1	

* To nearest %

any London-born ethnic minority residence within the English category. This situation changed in 1991 with the inclusion of a question on ethnic groups within the census. The data for Riverview and Southgate are included in Tables 3 and 4. These data are as open to question as the information for 1981. In particular the categories used here reify identity categories and it is important to view these data with qualified suspicion. However, they do give some indication of the changing make-up of these South London communities.

Table 3   Riverview Estate: ethno-demographic structure, 1991 census.

Ethnic group	Males	Females	Total	% of total*
Total	1,347	1,352	2,699	–
White	771	730	1,501	56
Black – Caribbean	113	122	235	9
Black – Africa	277	289	566	21
Black – other	44	75	119	4
Total	434	486	920	34
Indian	2	7	9	–
Pakistani	3	0	3	–
Bangladeshi	4	5	9	–
Chinese	27	39	66	2
Asian	59	36	96	4
Other	47	49	96	4

* To nearest %

Table 4   Southgate Estate: ethno-demographic structure, 1991 census.

Ethnic group	Males	Females	Total	% of total*
Total	1,204	1,213	2,417	–
White	525	515	1,040	43
Black – Caribbean	261	281	542	22
Black – African	250	211	461	20
Black – Other	34	59	93	4
Total	545	551	1,096	46
Indian	6	4	10	–
Pakistani	7	5	12	–
Bangladeshi	7	15	22	–
Chinese	51	58	109	5
Asian	36	42	78	3
Other	27	23	50	3

* To nearest %

By 1991 the changing nature of Riverview's population had re-sulted in a radical transformation. The trends discussed in Chapters 2 and 3 seem to have continued into the 1990s. Only 56 per cent of the population in 1991 was designated "white" and 34 per cent of its population fell within the three black categories used in the census.

Another important demographic feature is the large growth in Af-rican residence (21 per cent) – over twice the number recorded in the Black–Caribbean category. The Vietnamese population is not prop-erly represented in these statistics. This is in large part owing to the inadequacy of the ethnic group categories. Some indication of their numbers can be adduced if the "Chinese" and "Asian" categories are amalgamated (i.e. 6 per cent). The implications of these shifts are only hinted at within this study because these changes occurred in large part after the period of fieldwork was completed. A full discus-sion of the impact of these changes can be explored only within a separate and subsequent project. However, this change should be kept in mind when evaluating the analysis of community discourses and youth culture.

For Southgate it is equally true that the trends discussed in Chap-ters 5 and 6 continued in the 1990s. Here the multi-ethnic quality of this area deepened. By 1991 only 43 per cent of the overall popula-tion was white. The black groups taken together constituted 46 per cent of the overall population. Similarly to Riverview, the African population within the area had grown significantly, to a level (20 per cent) that was almost equal to the Caribbean presence (22 per cent).

This may well have far-reaching effects on the cultural landscape. However, it is beyond the reach of this study to discuss with any con-fidence what these changes will bring regarding the issues of identity formation and cultural production. The Vietnamese presence in Southgate is obscured by the census categories and the best guess is that this population was somewhere around 8 per cent of the total residents.

These changes were particularly felt in the composition of the youthful populations in both Riverview and Southgate. In both cases a more thoroughly plural youth community emerged. In Riverview the ethnic breakdown of the 5–15 age group was as follows: white 45.5 per cent, black groups 41 per cent (African 23 per cent, Carib-bean 9 per cent, Other 9 per cent), Chinese 4 per cent and Asian 4 per cent. In total, visible minorities constituted 50 per cent of the overall population of this age group. Here again these figures need to be read in relation to the account of youth culture and social identity discussed in Chapter 3. Southgate showed similar patterns within the 5–15 age range: white 37 per cent, black groups 45.5 per cent (Caribbean 24 per cent, African 12.5 per cent, Other 8 per cent), Chinese 6 per cent and Asian 4 per cent. The ethno-demographic trends identified in this book have all progressed in the 1990s.

Notes

Chapter 1

1. R. Kelly is a black American rhythm and blues singer who is extremely popular in London. Thanks to my niece Vicki Back for this insightful comment.
2. There is a need to develop an approach that combines the theoretical sophistication of writers such as Hebdige and Gilroy and the empirical rigour of British sociological studies of youth (Jephcott 1942, Wilmott 1966, Patrick 1973).
3. Particularly interesting in this area is the recent work conducted by Phil Cohen (1988a,b), who is seeking to understand the relationship between race and youth in the context of the race, gender and class triad.
4. This approach has been developed within the wider context of ethnogenesis by Roosens (1989).
5. A factory owner, Thomas Letts, requested a lease to build a leather goods and printing factory in 1898 and reminded the local landlords that those employed would be "all of respectable class" (cited in Crossick 1978).
6. It is my view that the integrated notion of working-class community present in the functionalist writers of the time led to a fixing and ossification of dynamic cultural processes, and a conservative and static definition of community.
7. Quoted from Hewitt (1986: 14).
8. By 1987 there were approximately 7,000 Vietnamese residents in the district and these people were mainly concentrated in the council estates in the north. For a full discussion of Vietnamese migration to London and their socio-economic location see Lam & Martin (1995).
9. This took the form of cussing and wind-up exchanges (see Ch. 4). I have discussed these issues in full elsewhere (Back 1993).

Chapter 2

1. Although Castells has been criticized for the general, all-encompassing nature of this concept (Saunders 1979), I feel it is useful because he points out the role of the local state in managing social reproduction and identifies the potential for conflict over these collectively consumed resources. The general nature of the concept needs distillation and refinement, and in order to do this it is necessary to locate historical and qualitative relations of collective consumption in specific cases.
2. John Rex and Robert Moore (1967), in their classic study of race relations in Sparkbrook, Birmingham, utilized a Weberian class analysis to show how racial antagonisms mirrored the location of migrant and non-migrant in different housing classes. In the Riverview situation, the notion of housing class is of little use since tenants on the estate do not occupy different class locations in a Weberian sense. They are all tenants. However, what they do struggle over is the question of being given access. This is why I find the notion of collective consumption more applicable to this situation.
3. It is important to remember that during this period central government was engaged in a campaign to encourage council tenants to buy their own homes. This meant that people occupying high-standard council housing bought properties that were not returned to the pool of public sector housing. This had a "creaming off" effect, which meant that local authorities lost much of the better-quality housing stock.
4. The order of priority in the lettings system is as follows:
   Priority Group 1
   Homeless persons
   Applicants living in properties subject to Closing Orders/Demolition Orders/ Dangerous Structures Notices
   Tenants subject to racial harassment
   Secure tenants being required to move to enable extensive remedial works to be carried out
   Priority Group 2
   Rehousing to enable redevelopment or improvement works to proceed
   Nominations from the Director of Social Services to prevent children from being taken into care or for families in the Battered Wives' Refuge, or for potential foster parents for the council
   Priority Group 3
   Housing waiting lists special medical recommendations
   Highest-priority medical transfer cases
   Management of individual committee decision cases
   Priority Group 4
   Secure tenants registered on the primary transfer lists for reasons of overcrowding, under-occupation, or low medical priority
   Secure council tenants on secondary list for good tenants
   Owner-occupiers selling individual properties to the council
   Priority Group 5
   Applicants to the housing waiting list
   Nominations from other authorities under the Inter-borough Nominations

Scheme/Greater London Council's Mobility Scheme
5. These figures are the official crimes reported and it is estimated that only 50 per cent of crimes are reported to the police.
6. At the 1984 annual general meeting of the Riverview Estate Community Centre Association (composed of the Tenants' Association and the Sports and Social Club) there was barely the quorum of 30 people needed to make the meeting legal.

Chapter 3

1. There are many examples where whites have adopted black cultural codes in situations of multiracial contact. For example, Roger Bastide (1978) has reported that, even in the post-slavery Brazilian context, the de-Africanization of black people occurred simultaneously with a less profound Africanization of whites.
2. The equivalent insult in the Chinese community is "banana", used for those who are seen as being too white in cultural terms.

Chapter 4

1. Skinhead style is no longer popular within Riverview. However, the "skinhead" is still a powerful symbol of whiteness. Its reproduction here is evidence of its resonance in the minds of young whites. The skinhead movement attempted to construct a working-class identity out of the chaos of post-war urban change (Cohen 1972, Hebdige 1981). It tried to salvage an imperial notion of national pride in a period when Britain was barely hanging on to its "first world status". The Skins in this sense can be characterized as a "ghost dance of white ethnicity" (Mercer 1987: 50; see also Mercer 1994: 123–4).

Chapter 5

1. Like the Riverview development, the estate when completed consisted of a mixture of low-rise (4 storey) housing blocks and high-rise towers (24 storey). In the centre of the estate there were a number of small terraced streets that pre-date the Southgate development.
2. Although it seemed to be almost standard practice to build community centres within the council estates in the area, Southgate did not receive such amenities until the latter half of the 1980s.
3. This construction is not simply a caricature. In a study commissioned by the local authority of 200 people throughout the borough as a whole, it was found that 60 per cent of "Asian" people (this was taken to include both descendants from the Indian subcontinent and recently settled refugees from

Vietnam) said they stayed in after dark and nearly 55 per cent invested in security devices. This was in contrast to Afro-Caribbeans, who were least likely of all groups to take any special measures with regard to security. This clearly has implications for how one understands the nature and experience of racism in this area.

4. I cannot disclose the source here, but it is worth noting that it was also suggested in the same report that the security of black people in the area would "tend to protect Afro-Caribbeans from being victims (as they have by now been 'accepted' in the territory)".

5. From the 1981 census data the age structure of the estate shows that 65 per cent of the population are aged 5–35 and this reflects the youthful nature of the community. Research conducted by the council in Southgate in 1987 showed that 1 in 3 males was unemployed, with close to 40 per cent unemployment amongst 16–19 years olds, two-thirds of the households received housing benefit and the average household income for council tenants in 1985 was only £5,242. Also the employment structure shows, from data returned in the 1981 census, that a high proportion of those employed were registered under the "others employed" bracket and not in supervisory posts; in Southgate this figure was 40 per cent whereas in Riverview it was slightly lower at 37 per cent. Southgate also compared slightly less well with Riverview in relation to people employed in supervisory positions: in Riverview, 12 per cent of those employed were in jobs where they supervised others, whereas in Southgate the figure was 9 per cent.

6. Michael Keith (1993) developed this kind of approach in relation to debates around public order. He identifies a discursive field, or series of interrelated constructs, that operates around the question of public order. The *lore and disorder discursive field* allows the debate over public order to connote racial meanings without necessarily referring to black people directly.

7. The local newspaper ran a story during the fieldwork period about a postman who had been "mugged" for the dole cheques that he was delivering to people out of work on the estate. The story quoted people from the area and the postman saying how they feared delivering in this area. The end result was that although local accounts were being produced they were also being reconstituted within the local media. The media version was in turn re-circulated in the area and supported by already existing racialized notions of black criminality.

8. The worst case of this was reported in a liberal journal where Southgate was characterized as being the centre for manufacturing "crack" cocaine. The publication carried a picture of the back of a young man in a hooded tracksuit walking towards a huge tower block. The story was untrue and what had in fact been "discovered" was a very small and (more importantly) failed attempt to manufacture drugs in one disused flat. Again the important point is that the discourses that define areas such as Southgate serve to make these claims believable.

9. Here I am borrowing heavily from Paul Gilroy's (1987: 236) notion of black social movements. Definitions of "blackness" are moments of closure. These closures are arbitrary in the sense that "race" has no essential meaning. However, socially constructed definitions of race occur in relation to a racist so-

ciety, or what Omi & Winant (1983a,b) refer to as "race formation". This constitutes a powerful way in which the experience of black communities is translated into political action. As Hall states: "All the social movements which have tried to transform society and have required the constitution of new subjectivities, have had to accept the necessary fictional, but also the fictional necessity, of the arbitrary closure which is not the end, but which makes both politics and identity possible" (Hall 1987: 45).

10. This notion of "outside" includes the development of racist images of the area in neighbouring working-class communities, the police stations and the local media.

11. There are some direct similarities between this discourse and the formulations recorded and analyzed in Chapter 2 for Riverview.

12. This is not merely a hypothetical situation; I have had similar conversations with this young man, although not in the context of the interview quoted here.

Chapter 6

1. This phenomenon is not confined to the South London context. Suttles (1968: 65) showed in his study of young people in Chicago that "jive talk" was operated by both blacks and whites. David Parkin (1977) has also documented multilingual adolescent peer groups in Nairobi.

2. Lexically, Creole use includes expletives such as *bahty* and *rass* (noun: meaning bottom), *bamba* (noun: female pudenda), *bambaclaht* and *pussyclaht* (noun: sanitary towel), *rassclaht* (noun: toilet paper). White Creole use can be confined to the use of "dangerous words" and expletives. This is referred to as "clahting". However, Creole is also used as a prestigious code to signify excellence and disdain and includes words such as *irie* (adjective: excellent/ prestigious), *dread* (adjective: excellent, highest prestige), *stylin* (verb: to have style), *facety* and *renk* (adjective: cheeky), *tarra* and *rateed* (exclamation that can be either positive or negative), *boom* (adjective: high prestige or the best), *cris* (adjective: high quality), *skank* (verb: to dance or to steal or deceive), *yard* (noun: home), *chaa* (exclamation of anger or disapproval). These exclamations and descriptions are often accompanied by "tooth sucking". This is a verbal click that is produced by sucking air through the teeth and lips, and denotes disapproval or surprise. Other descriptive Creole words are also operated by whites to refer to friends (*star* and *spar*) or movements such as to stop (*ress*), to leave (*chip*), to break (*mash*), to steal (*tief*) (adapted from Hewitt 1986).

3. These include a whole range of words, including prestigious terms such as *def* (adjective: the standard of excellence), *bus this* (very important, pay attention), *fly* (adjective: attractive), *fresh* (adjective: excellent and original), *slammin* (adjective: active, dynamic, excellent) and *Yo* (interjection: pay attention). Words relating to special relationships that define cultural insiders are also used such as *home* or *homeboy/girl*. Other words are used that signify contempt, such as *dis* (verb: disrespect, contemptible), *bite* (verb: to

steal) and *sucka* (noun: person who is easily duped), also *wax* (verb: to beat in a duel of wits). Phrases from black American argot are also being incorporated. The best example of this is "you know what I am saying", which is used as an emphasizing tag.

4. One of the key determinants in defining black London language is the subtlety of pronunciation, often manifested in the softening of consonant sounds. Intonation is also important. Roger Hewitt offers an analysis of the way "you know" as a tag phrase has taken on a black intonation and that white young people have adopted this phraseology (Hewitt 1986: 134).

5. In fact Hewitt questions whether or not black lexical items in this context should be viewed as "black" at all (Hewitt 1986: 104). However, as I will discuss in the following section, these semantic shifts are led by black young people and they retain black associations. White young people share access to the linguistic spaces where these words are adopted but they are not the innovators.

6. Ken Johnson (1972) has outlined a similar process at work within the urban black American context of Chicago in the 1960s. Here the most negative names were "the man", "blue-eyed devils" and "honky", and the most positive names were "blue-eyed soul brother" or "blue-eyed soul sister". Although Johnson does not pursue this, whites were intimately associated with black linguistic codes and musical cultures. "Soul" in this context referred to the essence of the black American condition (Hannerz 1968), and whites who operated black codes could be "soulful" and "righteous" (i.e. commanding respect in black terms of reference). This is best illustrated by the case where a white American duo were singing soul and gospel ballads in a club when a black Marine stood up and shouted from the crowd, "Man, you sing so righteous, brother!" From then on these blue-eyed soulsters were named the "Righteous Brothers". There is a genre of white soul music called "blue-eyed soul". The Righteous Brothers and another blue-eyed soul act called The Young Rascals were also popular in black communities. The message of this genre is captured in Vic Waters' musical answer to James Brown's "Say it Loud – I am Black and I am Proud". The tune is entitled "I am White and I am Alright" and its lyrics are unambiguous: "If you're black you'd better be proud / And if you are white you'd sure nuff betterbe alright!" There is evidence to suggest that within black and white musical cultures ambiguous inter-racial dialogues have been occurring since the 1920s (Hewitt 1983).

7. Debbie adopts some of the stereotypes that black people have of the white English. These include the idea that white people are not hygienic. Also, an often made comment is that white people do not clean and rinse their plates and knives properly. Debbie repeated an often made assertion that the white English are not hospitable. She went to great pains to say that, when you visit the white English, "they only put out a few biscuits on the plate".

8. This notion of race is close to what I identified in the previous chapter with regard to blackness. Here racial identity is expressed without an attendant ideology of racial superiority.

9. For the most part, young people in this area considered blackness to be a culturally defined concept that had a specific local expression. In these terms

of reference, Asian young people were not necessarily considered black. However, on two occasions I recorded interviews where young black people talked about the connection between their experience of racism and the harassment experienced by Asian communities in line with the definition of blackness as a political colour of opposition to racism.

10. I recorded many cases of black young people who were from Guyana, Trinidad or Barbados who spoke Jamaican Creoles as opposed to the language of their parents.

11. There are wide discrepancies in estimated frequency of Creole use amongst black British young people. Rosen & Burgess (1980) estimated in their study of Creole speech in London that only 10–20 per cent of black young people speak Creole, whereas others have estimated that 95 per cent of black youngsters speak some Creole (cited in Hewitt 1986: 103). Hewitt's study of black language in South London showed how this form of language functioned as a prestigious code. Hewitt, influenced by the approach adopted by Le Page (1985), stresses the importance of locating Creole use in the fluid and changing linguistic situation experienced by black young people.

Chapter 7

1. Jenny Williams has made it clear that "[t]here is no one to one relationship between the idea and the effect, the ideology and the material practice . . . I do not accept definitions of racism and institutional racism which conflate ideologies and practices, but agree that ideologies influence the development of institutions, can become systemic within them, and have material effects on the organisation of the institution" (Williams 1985: 335).

2. The Black Cockney is operating a linguistic code that is shared with working-class whites. Like other class-based forms of non-standard vernacular, it is comprehensible to middle-class people and as a result it is the form in which translations can take place.

Chapter 8

1. Important in this regard was a tour by the Fisk University Jubilee Singers to Britain in the early 1870s. This group was the first to perform spirituals on a public platform and to present black music as a mass entertainment (Gilroy 1991: 14; 1993a). In particular the Jubilee singers performed in East London at Hackney Juvenile Mission and this made such an impact that it prompted the manager of the mission, John Newman, to teach the children of the mission the songs the Jubilee singers had sung, and the East London Jubilee Singers of Hackney Juvenile Mission were formed.

2. Phillips points out that many Afro-Caribbean settlers bought large radiograms to service social events (Phillips 1982: 117).

3. According to legend, Duke Vin was the first to run a "sound" in Britain and

it is said that he first played his sound at his brother's wedding in 1956 (Bradshaw 1979). Other sounds to emerge in this period included Count Suckle, Savoy Sound, Boothe, Daddy Young, Ly Bird, CB, Ossie, Duke Reid and Sir Fonso.

4. The Roaring Twenties or "Twenties" was the most famous of the Soho clubs. With Count Suckle's departure, a string of sounds competed for the residency, but it was Lloyd Coxone who appeared and won the spot; Coxone has been a central figure in the sound system world ever since. He began as a DJ for Duke Reid's South London Sound. In 1969 he raised enough money to develop his own sound system and Sir Coxone Sound was born and later renamed "Sir Coxsone Outernational".

5. Evidence of the impetus and the degree of inter-racial dialogue during this time can be shown in the composition of the audience on the popular music television programmes. On 16 September 1966, Otis Redding, the seminal African American rhythm and blues performer, appeared on the music programme "Ready Steady Go" to a racially mixed studio audience.

6. In 1981 South East London sound systems included:
Jah Shaka the Spiritual Dub Warrior (Lewisham)
Tiffany's Hi-Fi (Lewisham)
T-W-J (Lewisham)
Moziah (Lewisham)
The Mighty Enforcers (Lewisham)
Jah Man (Lewisham/Peckham)
Admiral Ken of Peckham
Papa Viking Sound (Peckham)
His Imperial Gordon Gorgon Hi-Fi (Peckham)
Jah Revelation the Placid Rockers (Dulwich)
The Mighty Revolutionaries – South East A1 Sound (Deptford)
Jah Cesar (Deptford)
Rootsman Hi-Fi (Deptford)
Creator from Camberwell
Sanatone Hi-Fi the Cool Charm Rockers (Waterloo)
Trojan Hi-Fi (Woolwich)
Mighty Observer (West Croydon)
Papa Cass of Croydon
Youth Steppers (Thornton Heath)
Mighty Crusader (Downham)
Neville the Music Exchanger
Sir Royale Quadrophonic – the Sound of the South.

7. In 1981 the technology of Sir Coxone Outernational, one of the largest of South London sounds, consisted of:
Amplifiers:
Five pieces of 600 watts (valve) – weight
Four pieces of 600 watts (transistor) – treble
Use depends on venue – Brixton Town Hall determines three pieces of valve and one piece of transistor
Pre-amp with built-in equalizer to cover weight, treble, mid-range
HH Echo Unit and special percussion box

Speakers:
On average 19–20 bass speakers (other sounds may play around 50)
Many different horns in treble section and small speakers
Several thousand yards of cable
A 7 ton truck and a transit van

8. Tipper Irie, taken from Saxon Studio's live album *Coughing Up Fire*, released by UK Bubbler (Lockwood 1).

9. Equally they have participated in incidents where London rappers have come together to present a collective response. In 1989 the Cookies, London Rhyme Syndicate, Overlord X, Demon Boyz and She Rockers came together to form BROTHER (Black Rhyme Organisation To Help Equal Rights), which produced an anti-apartheid single "Beyond the 16th Parallel".

10. Quoted in Rose (1990: 158–9).

11. It should be noted that the racial equality found on the dancefloor was not translated to the culture industry that became interested in the movement. The West London nightclubs played the music but did not allow black DJs access to the clubs. The black DJ Trevor Nelson points out: "This is England. Here all the ground work has been done by people like us, for shops and the DJs. Behind every big white DJ there's always been the manipulation of a little black DJ" (*City Limits*, 5–12 November 1987).

12. Paradoxes are, however, always present in the participation of whites within these cultures. Particularly interesting is the American all-white rap group the Young Black Teenagers (YBT). When YBT played in Britain they received a mixed welcome. YBT member Tommy Never commented in the magazine *Blues and Soul* (April 1991): "London gave us a really hard time. They heard our name and everybody cheered, then they saw us and everyone started booing! They threw a pair of glasses at my DJ who put them on and carried on DJ-ing." There are parallels here with the account offered in Chapter 6 of white young people who identify with blackness in extreme ways. For a longer discussion of YBT and white hip hop see Stephens (1992).

13. Taken from BBC Radio 1, "Soul by the sea", 6 April 1991. Artists on the bill included: Rich Nice, Ziggy Marley, the Temptations, Lady Levi and Malira.

14. The emergence of Bengali sound systems was reported in the black arts magazine *Artrage* (Summer 1991), in an article by Hussain Ismail and Anthony Whynne Hong Lam.

15. The body without organs (BWO) is a difficult concept to summarize. What it constitutes is a state of fusional multiplicity, with indeterminate organs, or with temporary, transitory organs (Deleuze & Guattari 1984, 1986; see also Boundas 1993). The BWO needs a principle of production in order to achieve what they refer to as a zero intensity. Deleuze and Guattari list a number of examples, including the cold experienced by the drugged body (Deleuze & Guattari 1986: 153). In the context of what I have been describing, a zero intensity is achieved by music and the banishing of racism.

16. A generation of young scholars are breaking this silence. I would like to thank Ko Banerjea, who has helped me re-think many aspects of this chapter and whose work offers much-needed new insight into the history and cultural formation of Asian sound systems.

17. Quoted in Rose (1991: 42).

18. This point is taken from Isaac Julien's film "The Darker Side of Black" which is by far the best account of the sexual politics of dance-hall (broadcast 12 February 1994 in the Arena series on BBC2)

19. Isaac Julien's film pointed to the stark rise in violent attacks against gays and lesbians in South London during the early 1990s. It would be short-sighted merely to blame ragga DJs for this outbreak of aggressive homophobia, but the cheery vangardism of Cooper's reading needs to be seen alongside the following story from the writer and black gay Londoner David Dibosa quoted from the film: "In terms of my own personal experience music such as *Boom Bye Bye* has shouted homophobia from the roof tops. In terms of my living experience walking down the street, the experience I have had is to face homophobia – which I have had to face before – but on the sharp end where people have actually used the symbol of the gun pointing towards my head. I had an experience in the middle of June [1993], June the 4th to be precise – it is a day that I will never forget – where I walked down a street which I walked down a thousand times to be faced by physical and verbal abuse. Bottles were thrown at me. I was punched. I was kicked. I was pursued for some 20 yards, down a road by at least ten men. The horror was that then they were joined by others – ten, fifteen, twenty. I was lying in the middle of the road with my boyfriend being kicked, and kicked, and kicked as if I was a dog. I was surrounded by shoppers on a Friday, a very hot and sunny day in June. Nobody raised a hand to help us. Two women came out of a pub to ask what was actually taking place. Nobody even had the decency afterwards to ask: 'had we been hurt? Were we all right?' What in fact took place was that I and my boyfriend were hospitalised by people who I had felt had been my neighbours and my brothers."

20. Quoted in "The Darker Side of Black", Isaac Julien, BBC 2, 12 February 1994.

21. Quoted in "All Junglist: A London Somet'ing Dis", Rachel Seeley, Channel 4 Black Xmas series, 19 December 1994.

Chapter 9

1. Taken from Chocolate Milk's "Action Speaks Louder Than Words" (RCA, APL1–1188). Thanks to Paul Gilroy for this reference from his exhaustive "vinyl library".

2. In the South London borough of Southwark, the last three years of the 1980s saw an increase of 56 per cent in recorded cases of racial harassment (*The Independent*, 13 February 1990).

3. Speech by J. Enoch Powell, Trinity College, Dublin, 13 November 1964.

4. T. S. Eliot quoted in John Casey, "One Nation: The Politics of Race", *The Salisbury Review* (Autumn 1982). Also cited in Gilroy (1993b: 19).

5. I am thinking of Rushdie's intoxicated Indian film director "Whisky" Sisodia. Sisodia offers a corpus of statements that outline the pitfalls in Englishness. Through Sisodia, Rushdie comments: "The trouble with the Engenglish is that their hiss hiss history happened overseas, so they dodo don't know what it means" (Rushdie 1988: 343).

Bibliography

Abrahams, R. D. 1970. *Deep down in the jungle.* New York: Aldine.

Adorno, T. W. 1967. Perennial fashion-jazz. In *Prisms,* T. W. Adorno, London: Neville Spearman.

— 1978. On popular music. In *Literary taste, culture and mass communication,* P. Davidson, R. Meyersohn, E. Shils (eds), vol. 8, *Theatre and song.* Cambridge: Chadwyck Healey.

Allen, S. 1973. The institutionalisation of racism. *Race* 15(1), 99–106.

Anderson, B. 1983. *Imagined communities: reflections on the origins and spread of nationalism.* London: Verso.

Apte, M. L. 1985. *Humour and laughter: an anthropological approach.* London: Cornell University Press.

Arendt, H. (ed.) 1968. *Illuminations.* New York: Harcourt, Brace and World.

Arif Ali (ed.) 1979. *West Indians in Britain.* London: Hansib.

Back, L. 1988a. "Coughing up fire": sound systems and cultural politics in South East London. *New Formations* 5 (Summer), 141–52.

— 1988b. "Coughing up fire": sound systems and cultural politics in South East London [extended version]. *Journal of Caribbean Studies* 6(2), 203–19.

— 1990. *Racist name calling and developing anti-racist strategies in youth work.* Centre for Research in Ethnic Relations Research Papers No. 14, University of Warwick.

— 1991a. Social context and racist name calling: an ethnographic perspective on racist talk within a South London adolescent community. *European Journal of Intercultural Studies* 1(3), 19–39.

— 1993. "Gendered participation": masculinity and fieldwork in a South London community. See Bell et al. (1993).

Banton, M. 1970. The concept of racism. In *Race and racialism,* S. Zubaida (ed.). London: Tavistock.

— 1987. The battle of the name. *New Community* 14(1–2), 170–75.

Barker, M. 1981. *The new racism.* London: Junction Books.

Barth, F. 1969. *Ethnic groups and boundaries: the social organisation of cultural difference.* London: Allen & Unwin.

— 1989. The analysis of culture in complex societies. *Ethnos* 54(3–4), 120–42.

Barthes, R. 1973. *Mythologies.* London: Jonathan Cape.

271

Bastide, R. 1978. *The African religions of Brazil: towards a sociology of the interpretation of civilisations*. Baltimore and London: Johns Hopkins University Press.

Bateson, G. 1978. A theory of play and fantasy. In *Steps to an ecology of mind*, G. Bateson (ed.). London: Paladin Books.

Baumann, G. 1990. The reinvention of Bhangra, social change and aesthetic shifts in Punjabi music in Britain. *Journal of the International Institute for Comparative Music Studies and Documentation Berlin*, XXXII(2), 81–95.

Bradshaw, P. 1979. Music. See Arif Ali (1979)..

Bell, D., P. Caplan, W. Jahan Karim (eds) 1993. *Gendered field: women, men and ethnography*. London: Routledge.

Benedict, R. 1983. *Race and racism*. London: Routledge and Kegan Paul.

Benjamin, W. 1968a. The work of art in an age of mechanical reproduction. See Arendt (1968).

— 1968b. The storyteller: reflections on the work of Nikolai Leskov. See Arendt (1968).

Benson, S. 1981. *Ambiguous ethnicity: inter-racial families in London*. London: Cambridge University Press.

Bernstein, N. 1994. Goin' gangsta, choosin cholita: teens "claim" a racial identity. *Utne Reader*, March–April, 87–90.

Bhabha, H. K. 1990. Interrogating identity: the postcolonial prerogative. See Goldberg (1990).

— 1994. *The location of culture*. London: Routledge.

Bhachu, P. 1985. *Twice migrants: East African settlers in Britain*. London: Tavistock.

— 1991. Culture, ethnicity and class among Punjabi Sikh women in 1990s' Britain. *New Community* 17(3), 401–2.

Billig, M. 1978. *Fascists: a social psychological view of the National Front*. London: Academic Press.

Billig, M., S. Condor, D. Edwards, M. Gane, D. Middleton, A. Radley 1988. *Ideological dilemmas: a social psychology of everyday thinking*. London: Sage.

Blauner, R. 1972. *Racial oppression in America*. New York: Harper & Row.

Booth, C. 1902. *Life and labour of the people in London – Third series: religious influences 5*. London: Macmillan.

Boundas, C. V. 1993. *The Deleuze reader*. New York: Columbia University Press.

Bourne, J. 1980. "Cheerleaders and ombudsmen": the sociology of race relations in Britain. *Race and Class* 21(4), 331–52.

Bradshaw, P. 1979. Music. See Arif Ali (1979).

Brandt, G. 1984. British youth Caribbean Creole – the politics of resistance. Paper presented at the Conference on Languages Without a Written Tradition, Thames Polytechnic.

Breakwell, G. 1986. *Coping with threatened identities*. London: Methuen.

Brown, C. 1972. The language of soul. See Kochman (1972).

Carmichael, S. & C. V. Hamilton 1968. *Black power: the politics of liberation in America*. London: Jonathan Cape.

Cashmore, E. E. 1979. *Rastaman: the rastafarian movement in Britain*. London: Allen & Unwin.

— 1984. *No future*. London: Heinemann.

—1987. *The logic of racism*. London: Allen & Unwin.

Castells, M. 1977. *The urban question: a marxist approach*. Cambridge, Mass.: MIT Press.

— 1983. *The city and the grassroots*. London: Edward Arnold.

Centre for Contemporary Cultural Studies, 1982. *The empire strikes back*. London: Hutchinson.

Chambers, I. 1976. "A strategy for living": black music and white subcultures. See Hall & Jefferson (eds) (1976).

— 1985. *Urban rhythms: pop music and popular culture*. London: Macmillan Education.

Clark, K. B. & M. K. Clark 1947. Racial identification and preferences in negro children. In *Readings in social psychology*, T. Newcomb & E. Hartley (eds). New York: Holt, Rhinehart and Winston.

Clifford, J. 1986. Part truths. See Clifford & Marcus (eds) (1986).

— 1988. *The predicament of culture: twentieth century ethnography, literature and art*. Cambridge, Mass.: Harvard University Press.

— 1992. Travelling cultures. In *Cultural studies*, L. Grossberg, C. Nelson, P. Treichler (eds). London: Routledge.

Clifford, J. & G. E. Marcus (eds) 1986. *Writing culture: the poetics and politics of ethnography*. Berkeley: University of California Press.

Cochrane, R. & M. Billig 1984. "I am not National Front but . . .". *New Society* 68, 255–8.

Cohen, A. P. 1985. *The symbolic construction of community*. London: Tavistock.

Cohen, P. 1972. *Subcultural conflict and working class community*. Working Papers in Cultural Studies 2, University of Birmingham.

— 1986. *Rethinking the youth question*. Post sixteen Education Centre. London: University of London Institute of Education.

— 1988a. Popular racism, unpopular education. *Youth and Policy*, No. 24, 8–12.

— 1988b. "Tarzan and the jungle bunnies": class, race and sex in popular culture. *New Formations* 5 (Summer), 25–30.

— 1988c. The perversions of inheritance. See Cohen & Bains (1988).

— 1989. *Tackling common sense racism*. Cultural Studies Project Annual Report. London: University of London Institute of Education.

Cohen, P. & H. Bains (eds). 1988. *Multi-racist Britain*. London: Macmillan Education.

Conrad, J. [1899] 1990. *Heart of darkness and other tales*. Oxford: Oxford University Press.

Cooper, C. 1993. *Noises in the blood: orality, gender and the "vulgar" body of Jamaican popular culture*. London: Macmillan Caribbean.

Crapanzano, V. 1986. Hermes' dilemma: the masking of subversion in ethnographic description. See Clifford & Marcus (1986).

Crossick, G. 1978. *An artisan elite in Victorian society*. London: Croom Helm.

Daniel, S. & P. McGuire 1972. *The paint house: words from an East End gang*. Harmondsworth: Penguin.

Davey, A. G. 1983. *Learning to be prejudiced: growing up in multi-ethnic Britain*. London: Edward Arnold.

— 1987. Insiders, outsiders and anomalies: a review of studies of identities – a reply to Olivia Foster-Carter. *New Community* 13(3), 51–60.

Davey, A. G. & M. V. Norburn 1980. Ethnic awareness and ethnic differentiations amongst primary school children. *New Community* 8(1–2), 51–60.

Deleuze, G. & F. Guattari 1984. *Anti-Oedipus: capitalism and schizophrenia.* London: Athlone.

— 1986. *A thousand plateaus: capitalism and schizophrenia.* London: Athlone.

Dews, N. 1971. *The history of Deptford.* London: Conway Maritime Press.

Drake, C. 1987. *Black folks here and there.* Berkeley: University of California Press.

Dummett, A. 1973. *A portrait of English racism.* Harmondsworth: Penguin.

Dyer, R. 1988. White. *Screen* 29(4), 44–56.

Fanon, F. 1963. *The wretched of the earth.* London: Penguin.

— 1967. *Toward the African revolution.* New York: Monthly Review of Books.

— 1968. *Black skin, white masks.* London: MacGibbon & Kee.

Finnegan, R. 1970. *Oral literature in Africa.* Oxford: Oxford University Press.

Foucault, M. 1977. *Discipline and punish.* London: Tavistock.

Frith, S. 1986. Art versus technology: the strange case of popular music. *Media, Culture and Society* 8, 265–77.

Fryer, P. 1984. *Staying power: a history of black people in Britain.* London: Pluto.

Gamble, A. 1974. *The conservative nation.* London: Routledge & Kegan Paul.

Gilroy, P. 1982a. The myth of black criminality. *Socialist Register.* London: Merlin Press.

—1982b. "Steppin out of Babylon" – Race, class and autonomy. See CCCS (1982).

— 1985. Hip hop technology. In *World view*, P. Ayrton, T. Engelhardt, V. Ware (eds). London: Pluto Press.

— 1987. *There ain't no black in the Union Jack: the cultural politics of race and nation.* London: Hutchinson.

— 1988. Nothing but sweat inside my hand: diaspora aesthetics and black arts in Britain. See Institute of Contemporary Art (1988).

— 1988–9. Cruciality and the frog's perspective. *Third Text* 5 (Winter), 33–45.

—1990. "One nation under a groove": the cultural politics of "race" and racism in Britain. See Goldberg (1990).

— 1991. It ain't where you're from it's where you're at . . .: The dialectics of diasporic identification. *Third Text* 13 (Winter), 3–17.

— 1992. It's a family affair. In *Black popular culture*, G. Dent (ed.). Seattle: Bay Press.

— 1993a. *The black Atlantic: modernity and double consciousness.* London: Verso.

— 1993b. *Small acts: thoughts on the politics of black cultures.* London: Serpent's Tail.

— 1994a. "After the love has gone": bio-politics and etho-poetics in the black public sphere. *Public Culture* (Fall), 1–27.

— 1994b. Diaspora. *Paragraph* 17 (3), 207–12.

Gilroy, P. & E. Lawrence 1988. Two tone Britain: white and black youth and the politics of anti-racism. See Cohen & Bains (1988).

Gilroy, P. & J. Sim 1985. Law order and the state of the Left. *Capital and Class,* no. 25 (Spring), 15–55.

Glissant, E. 1992. *Caribbean discourse: selected essays*. Charlottesville: University Press of Virginia.

Goldberg, D. T. (ed.) 1990. *Anatomy of racism*. Minnesota: University of Minnesota.

Gramsci, A. 1971. *Selections from the prison notebooks*. London: Lawrence & Wishart.

Griffin, J. H. 1960. *Black like me*. Boston: Houghton Mifflin Company.

Gutzmore, C. 1978. Carnival, the state and the black masses in the United Kingdom. *The Black Liberator* 1 (December), 8–27.

Hall, S. 1978. Racism and reaction. In *Five views of multi-racial Britain*, Commission for Racial Equality (ed.). London: Commission for Racial Equality.

— 1980. Race, articulation and societies structured in dominance. In *Sociological theories: race and colonialism*, UNESCO. Paris: UNESCO.

—1982. The rediscovery of ideology: return of the repressed in media studies. In *Culture, society and the media*, M. Gurevitch, T. Bennett, J. Curran, S. Woolacott (eds). London: Methuen.

— 1987. Minimal selves. In *Identity*, Institute of Contemporary Art, Documents 6. London: ICA/BFI.

— 1988. New ethnicities. See Institute of Contemporary Art (1988).

— 1991a. The local and the global. See King (1991)..

— 1991b. Old and new identities, old and new ethnicities. See King (1991).

— 1992. The question of cultural identity. In *Modernity and its futures*, S. Hall, D. Held, T. McGrew (eds). Cambridge: Polity Press.

Hall, S. & T. Jefferson (eds) 1976. *Resistance through rituals*. London: Hutchinson.

Hall, S., C. Critcher, T. Jefferson, B. Roberts 1978. *Policing the crisis: mugging, the state and law and order*. London: Macmillan.

Hannerz, U. 1968. The rhetoric of soul identification in negro society. *Race*, 9(4), 453–65.

— 1969. *Soulside: inquiries into ghetto culture and community*. New York: Columbia University Press.

— 1980. *Exploring the city: inquiries towards an urban anthropology*. New York: Columbia University Press.

— 1987. The world in creolisation. *Africa* 57(4), 546–59.

— 1989a. Culture between centre and periphery: towards a macroanthropology. *Ethnos* 54(3–5), 200–216.

— 1989b. Five Nigerians and the global ecumene. Paper presented at the SSRC Symposium on Public Culture in India and its Global Problematics, Carmel, California, 26–30 April 1989.

— 1990a. Cosmopolitans and locals in world culture. *Theory, Culture and Society* 7, 237–51.

— 1990b. The cultural role of world cities. Paper presented at the International Symposium on the Age of the City: Human life in the 21st Century, Osaka, Japan, 27–30 March.

— 1990c. Stockholm: doubly creolizing. Paper presented at the International Conference on the Organisation of Diversity, Botkyrka, Sweden, 13–16 June.

— 1990d. The global ecumene as a network of networks. Paper presented at the

European Association of Social Anthropologists Session on Conceptualizing Societies, Coimbra, Portugal, 31 August–3 September.

Hebdige, D. 1974a. *Aspects of style in the deviant subcultures of the 1960's.* MA thesis, Centre for Contemporary Cultural Studies, University of Birmingham.

— 1974b. *Reggae, rastas and rudies: style and the subversion of form.* Stencilled paper 24, Centre for Contemporary Cultural Studies. Birmingham: University of Birmingham.

— 1979. *Subculture: the meaning of style.* London: Methuen.

— 1981. Skinheads and the search for a white working class identity. *New Socialist* (September), 38.

— 1983. "Ska tissue": the rise and fall of Two Tone. In *Reggae International*, S. Davis & P. Simon (eds). London: Thames & Hudson.

— 1987. *Cut 'n mix: culture, identity and Caribbean music.* London: Routledge.

Henriques, J. 1984. Social psychology and the politics of racism. In *Changing the subject*, J. Henriques, W. Holloway, C. Urwin, V. Walkerdine. London: Methuen.

Hewitt, R. 1982. White adolescent creole use and the politics of friendship. *Journal of Multi-lingual and Multicultural Development* 3(3), 217–32.

— 1983. Black through white: Hoagy Carmichael and the cultural reproduction of racism. *Popular Music* 3. Cambridge: Cambridge University Press.

— 1986. *White talk, black talk: inter-racial friendship and communication amongst adolescents.* London: Cambridge University Press.

— 1988a. *Social context and the Ludic elements in adolescent verbal interaction.* Working Papers in Adolescent Language Use. London: Institute of Education.

— 1988b. Youth, race and language: deconstructing ethnicity? Paper presented at the Conference on the Sociology of Youth and Childhood, Philipps University, Marburg, West Germany, 14–15 November.

— 1989. Creole in the classroom: political grammars and educational vocabularies. In *Social anthropology and the politics of language*, R. Grillo (ed.). Sociological Review Monographs. London: Routledge.

— 1990. A sociolinguistic view of urban adolescent relations. See Røgilds (1990).

— 1991. Language, youth and the destabilisation of ethnicity. Paper presented at the Conference on Ethnicity in Youth Culture: Interdisciplinary Perspectives, Fittjagard, Botkyrka, Sweden, 3–6 June.

Hind, J. & S. Mosco 1985. *Rebel radio: the full story of British pirate radio.* London: Pluto.

Hinds, D. 1980. The "Island" of Brixton. *Oral History* 8(1), 49–51.

Hiro, D. 1971. *Black British white British.* London: Eyre & Spottiswoode.

Hoare, I. 1975. Mighty, mighty spade and whitey: soul lyrics and black white crosscurrents. In *The soul book*, I. Hoare et al. (eds). London: Methuen.

Hoggart, R. 1958. *The uses of literacy.* London: Penguin.

Honeyford, R. 1989. *Integration or disintegration.* London: Claridge Press.

hooks, b. 1994. *Outlaw culture: resisting representations.* London: Routledge.

Howe, D. 1973. Fighting back: West Indian youth and the police in Notting Hill. *Race Today* 5 (11), 333–7.

Hraba, J. & G. Grant 1970. "Black is beautiful": a re-examination of racial preference and identification. *Journal of Personality and Social Psychology* 16,

398–402.

Institute of Contemporary Art 1988. *Black film/British cinema*. Documents 7. London: ICA/BFI.

Jackson, B. 1969. *Working class community*. London: Penguin.

Jackson, B. & P. Marsden 1966. *Education and the working class*. London: Pelican.

Jahan Karim, W. 1993. Epilogue: the nativised self and the native. See Bell et al. (1993).

James, A. 1986. Learning to belong: the boundaries of adolescence. In *Symbolising boundaries: identity and diversity in British cultures*, A. P. Cohen (ed.). Manchester: Manchester University Press.

James, W. 1986. A long way from home: on black identity in Britain. *Immigrants and Minorities* 5(3), 258–84.

Jarviluoma, H. (ed.) 1994. *Soundscapes: essays on Vroom and Moo*. Tampere: Tampere University.

Jeater, D. 1992. Roast beef and reggae music: the passing of whiteness. *New Formations* 18 (Winter), 107–21.

Jephcott, P. 1942. *Girls growing up*. London: Faber.

Johnson, K. 1972. The vocabulary of race. See Kochman (1972).

Johnson, L. K. 1976. Jamaican rebel music. *Race and Class* 17(4), 396–401.

Jones, S. 1986. *White youth and Jamaican popular culture*. PhD thesis for Centre for Contemporary Cultural Studies, Faculty of Arts, University of Birmingham.

— 1988. *Black youth, white culture: the reggae tradition from JA to UK*. London: Macmillan.

— 1990. Black music and young people in Birmingham. See Røgilds (1990).

Julien, I. 1991. Introduction. In *Diary of a young soul rebel*, I. Julien & C. MacCabe. London: British Film Institute.

Keil, C. 1972. Motion and feeling through music. See Kochman (1972).

Keith, M. 1993. *Race, riots and policing: lore and disorder in a multi-racist society*. London: UCL Press.

— forthcoming. Shouts from the street: identity and the spaces of authenticity. *Social Identities* 2.

Kelly, E. 1987. Pupils, racial groups and behaviour in schools. In *Racism in schools – new evidence*, E. Kelly & T. Cohn. Stoke: Trentham Books.

King, A. D. (ed.) 1991. *Culture, globalisation and the world system*. London: Macmillan.

Kochman, T. (ed.) 1972. *Rappin' and stylin' out: communication in black America*. Chicago and London: University of Illinois Press.

Labov, W. 1972. *Language in the inner city: studies in the black English vernacular*. Oxford: Basil Blackwell.

Lam, T. & C. Martin 1995. *The settlement of the Vietnamese in London: official policy and Vietnamese response*. Occasional Paper in Sociology and Social Policy, South Bank University.

Lawrence, E. 1981. White sociology, black struggle. *Multi-Racial Education*, 9 (Summer), 3–17.

— 1982. In the abundance of water the fool is thirsty: sociology and black "pathology". See CCCS (1982).

Le Page, R. B. 1985. *Acts of identity*. Cambridge: Cambridge University Press.

Levi-Strauss, C. 1976. *The savage mind*. London: Weidenfeld & Nicolson.

Levitas, R. 1986. *The ideology of the new right*. London: Polity Press.

Linebaugh, P. 1991. *The London hanged: crime and civil society in the eighteenth century*. London: Penguin Books.

Lord, A. 1958. *The singer of tales* Cambridge, Mass.: Harvard University Press.

Mac an Ghaill, M. 1988. *Young gifted and black: student teacher relations in the schooling of black youth*. Milton Keynes: Open University Press.

Macdonald, I., T. Bhavnani, L. Khan, G. John 1989. *Murder in the playground: the report of the Macdonald Inquiry into racism and racial violence in Manchester schools*. London: Longsight Press.

McRobbie, A. [1980] 1991. *Feminism and youth culture*. London: Macmillan.

— 1994. *Postmodernism and popular culture*. London: Routledge.

Malvery, O. C. 1907. *The soul market*. London: Hutchinson.

Marcus, G. E. 1986. Contemporary problems of ethnography in the world system. See Clifford & Marcus (1986).

Mason, D. 1982. After Scarman: a note on the concept of institutional racism. *New Community* 10(1), 38–45.

Mercer, K. 1987. Black hair/style politics. *New Formations* 3 (Winter), 33–56.

— 1988. Diaspora culture and the dialogic imagination. In *Blackframes: critical perspectives on black independent cinema*, M. Cham & C. Watkins (eds). Boston: MIT.

— 1990a. Welcome to the jungle: identity and diversity in postmodern politics. See Rutherfor (1990).

— 1990b. Black art and the burden of representation. *Third Text* 10 (Spring), 61–79.

— 1992. Back to my routes: a postscript on the 80s. *Ten* 8(2–3), 32–9.

— 1994. *Welcome to the jungle: new positions in black cultural studies*. London: Routledge.

Miles, R. 1978. *Between two cultures? The case of rastafarianism*. SSRC Working Papers in Ethnic Relations No. 10, University of Bristol.

— 1989. *Racism*. London: Routledge.

Miles, R. & A. Phizacklea 1979. *Racism and political action in Britain*. London: Routledge & Kegan Paul.

— 1984. *White man's country: racism and British politics*. London: Pluto Press.

Miller, D. 1991. Absolute freedom in Trinidad. *Man* 26, 323–41.

Milner, D. 1983. *Children and race: ten years on*. London: Ward Lock Educational.

Modood, T. 1988. "Black", racial equality and Asian identity. *New Community*, 14(3), 397–404.

Murdock, G. & B. Troyna 1981. Recruiting racists. *Youth in Society* 60, 3–15.

Myrdal, G. 1969. *Objectivity and social research*. London: Duckworth.

National Union of Teachers 1981. *Combating racism in schools*. London: National Union of Teachers.

Oliver, P. 1970. *Savannah syncopators*. London: Studio Vista.

Omi, M. & H. Winant 1983a. By the rivers of Babylon: race in the United States Part 1. *Socialist Review* 13(5), 31–65.

— 1983b. By the rivers of Babylon: race in the United States Part 2. *Socialist*

Review 13(6), 35–68.

Park, R. E. 1937. Introduction. In *The marginal man*, E. Stonequist. New York: Scribners.

Parker, D. 1995. *Through different eyes: the cultural identities of young Chinese people in Britain*. Aldershot: Avebury.

Parkin, D. 1977. Emergent and stabilised multi-lingualism: poly-ethnic peer groups in urban Kenya. In *Language, ethnicity and intergroup relations*, H. Giles (ed.). London: Academic Press.

Patrick, J. 1973. *The Glasgow gang observed*. London: Methuen.

Patterson, O. 1980. *Slavery and social death*. Cambridge, Mass.: Harvard University Press.

Pearson, G. 1976. Paki-bashing in a North East Lancashire town: a case study and its historical roots. In *Working class culture*, G. Mungham & G. Pearson (eds). London: Routledge & Kegan Paul.

Phillips, D. 1987. The rhetoric of anti-racism in public housing allocation. In *Race and racism: essays in social geography*, P. Jackson (ed.). London: Allen & Unwin.

Phillips, M. 1982. Thirty years of black Britain: language and originality. *Frontline* 2(2), 116–18.

Phizacklea, A. & R. Miles 1980. *Labour and racism*. London: Routledge & Kegan Paul.

Porter, R. 1994. *London: a social history*. London: Hamish Hamilton.

Potter, J. & M. Wetherall 1988. Accomplishing attitudes: fact and evaluation in racist discourse. *Text* 18, 51–68.

Powell Williams, A. 1972. Dynamics of a black audience. See Kochman (1972).

Pratt, M. L. 1992. *Imperial eyes: travel writing and transculturation*. London: Routledge.

Prescod, C. 1979. Black thought. *New Society* 48, no. 865 (3 May), 280–81.

Radcliffe-Brown, A. R. 1940. On joking relationships. *Africa* 13, 195–210.

— 1949. A further note on joking relationships. *Africa* 19, 133–40.

Rampton, M. B. H. 1987. *Uses of English in a multi-racial peer group*. PhD thesis, University of London, Institute of Education.

— 1989. *Evaluations of black language crossing and the local sociocultural order*. Adolescence and Language Use Working Paper No. 3, Institute of Education.

Rediker, M. 1987. *Between the devil and the deep blue sea: merchant seamen, pirates, and the Anglo-American maritime world*. Cambridge: Cambridge University Press.

Reicher, S. 1987. Crowd behaviour as social action. In *Rediscovering the social group: a self categorisation theory*, J. C. Turner (ed.). Oxford: Basil Blackwell.

Rex, J. & R. Moore 1967. *Race, community and conflict: a study of Sparkbrook*. London: Oxford University Press.

Røgilds, F. 1990. *Every cloud has a silver lining*. Studies in Cultural Sociology No. 28. Hostebro: Akademisk Forlag.

— 1991. Rhythm, racism & new roots: a bridge between blacks and whites? Paper presented at the Seminar on Modernity, Gender & Ethnicity, Centre for Youth Research, University of Gothenburg, Sweden, 17 April.

Roosens, E. E. 1989. *Creating ethnicity: the process of ethnogenesis*. London, Sage.

Rosaldo, R. 1989. *Culture and truth: the remaking of social analysis.* London: Routledge.

Rose, C. 1990. *Living in America: The Soul Saga of James Brown.* London: Serpent's Tail.

— 1991. *Design after dark: the story of dancefloor style.* London: Thames & Hudson.

Rosen, H. & T. Burgess 1980. *Languages and dialects of London school children.* London: Ward Lock Educational.

Ross, A. & T. Rose 1994. *Microphone friends: youth music and youth culture.* London: Routledge.

Roy, D. F. 1953. Work satisfaction and social reward in quota achievement: an analysis of piecework incentive. *American Sociological Review* 18, 507–14.

— 1960. "Banana time" job satisfaction and informal interaction. *Human Organisation* 18, 156–68.

Rushdie, S. 1988. *The satanic verses.* London: Viking.

Rutherford, J. (ed.) 1990. *Identity: community, culture, difference.* London: Lawrence & Wishart.

Said, E. W. 1978. *Orientalism.* London: Penguin.

— 1993. *Culture and imperialism.* London: Chatto & Windus.

Sartre, J. P. 1965. Portrait of an anti-semite. In *Existentialism from Dostoevsky to Sartre,* W. Kaufmann (ed.). Cleveland: Meridian Books.

Saunders, P. 1979. *Social theory and the urban question.* London: Hutchinson.

Sebba, M. 1983a. Code-switching as a conversational strategy. Paper presented at the York Creole Conference, University of York.

— 1983b. *Language change among Afro-Caribbeans in London.* Stencilled paper, Department of Language, University of York.

— 1986. London Jamaican and black London English. See Sutcliffe & Wong (1986).

Sebba, M. & Wooton, T. 1984. Code-switching as conversational strategy. Paper presented at the 5th Sociolinguistic Symposium, University of Liverpool.

Shafer, R. Murray 1977. *The tuning of the world.* New York: Knopf.

Sims Holt, G. 1972. "Inversion" in black communication. See Kochman (1972).

Sithole, E. 1972. Black folk music. See Kochman (1972).

Sivanandan, A. 1981–2. From resistance to rebellion: Asian and Afro-Caribbean struggles in Britain. *Race and Class* 23(2–3), 111–51.

Small, J. 1986. Transracial placements: conflicts and contradiction. In *Social work with black children and their families,* S. Ahmed, J. Cheetham, J. Small (eds). London: Batsford.

Solomos, J. & L. Back 1996. *Racism and society.* London: Macmillan.

Stacey, J. 1988. Can there be a feminist ethnography? *Women's Studies International Forum* 11, 21–7.

Stallybrass, P. & A. White 1986. *The politics and poetics of transgression.* London: Methuen.

Steele, J. 1993. *Turning the tide: the history of everyday Deptford.* London: Darwin Press.

Stephens, G. 1992. Interracial dialogue in rap music: call and response in a multicultural style. *New Formations* 16 (Spring), 62–79.

Stonequist, E. 1937. *The marginal man.* New York: Scribners.

Sutcliffe, D. 1982. *British black English*. Oxford: Blackwell.

Sutcliffe, D. & A. Wong 1986. *The languages of the black experience*. Oxford: Basil Blackwell.

Suttles, G. 1968. *The social order of the slum: ethnicity and territory in the inner city*. Chicago: University of Chicago.

Tajfel, H. & J. C. Turner 1979. *The social identity theory of intergroup conflict*. Monterey: Brook/Cole.

Tajfel, H. & J. C. Turner 1986. The social identity theory of intergroup behaviour. In *The psychology of intergroup relations*, S. Worchel & W. G. Austin (eds). Chicago: Nelson–Hall.

Tizard, B. & A. Phoenix 1989. Black identity and transracial adoption. *New Community* 15(3), 427–37.

Toop, D. 1984. *The rap attack: African jive to New York hip hop*. London: Pluto Press.

Troyna, B. 1979. Differential commitment to ethnic identity by black youth in Britain. *New Community* 7(3), 406–14.

Turkie, A. 1982. *Know what I mean?* Leicester: National Youth Bureau.

Turner, J. C. 1987. *Rediscovering the social group: a self categorisation theory*. Oxford: Basil Blackwell.

Turner, V. 1969. *The ritual process*. London: Routledge & Kegan Paul.

— 1984. Liminality and the performative genres. In *Rite, drama, festival, spectacle: rehearsals towards a theory of cultural performance*, J. J. MacAloon (ed.). Philadelphia: Institute for the Study of Human Issues.

van Dijk, T. A. 1984. *Prejudice and discourse: an analysis of ethnic prejudice in cognition and conversation*. Amsterdam: Benjamins.

— 1987. *Communicating racism: ethnic prejudice in thought and talk*. London: Sage.

— 1991. *Racism in the press*. London: Routledge.

Van Gennep, A. 1960. *The rites of passage*. London: Routledge & Kegan Paul.

Vaught, C. & D. L. Smith 1980. Incorporation and mechanical solidarity in an underground coal mine, *Sociology of Work and Occupations* 7(2), 159–87.

Wallerstein, I. 1974. *The modern world system*. New York: Academic Press.

Wallman, S. 1975–6. A street in Waterloo. *New Community* 4(4), 1–7.

— 1978a. The boundaries of "race": processes of ethnicity in England. *Man* 13(2), 200–17.

— 1978b. Race relations or ethnic relations? *New Community* 6(3), 306–9.

— (ed.) 1979. *Ethnicity at work*. London: Macmillan.

— 1983. Identity options. In *Minorities: community and identity*, C. Fried (ed.). Berlin: Springer-Verlag.

— 1984. *Eight London households*. London: Tavistock.

— 1986. Ethnicity and boundary process in context. In *Theories of race and ethnic relations*, J. Rex & D. Mason (eds). Cambridge: Cambridge University Press.

Wallman, S. et al. 1982. *Living in South London*. London: Gower/LSE.

Ward, R. 1979. Where race didn't divide: some reflections on slum clearance in Moss Side. In *Racism and political action in Britain*, R. Miles & A. Phizacklea (eds). London: Routledge & Kegan Paul.

Ware, V. 1992. *Beyond the pale: white women, racism and history*. London:

Verso.

Ware, V. & L. Back 1994. White/whiteness. *Paragraph* 17(3), 281–91.

Watson, J. L. 1977. *Between two cultures: migrants and minorities in Britain.* Oxford: Basil Blackwell.

Weeks, J. 1990. The value of difference. See Rutherford (1990).

Weinreich, P. 1975a. Conflict in identity and perception in ethnic groups. SSRC Research Unit on Ethnic Relations at the University of Bristol, mimeo.

— 1975b. Identity diffusion in immigrant and English adolescents. Paper presented at the British Psychological Society's Annual Conference at Nottingham; published in *Race, education and identity*, G. V. Verma & C. Bagley (eds). London: Macmillan.

— 1979. Ethnicity and adolescent identity conflicts. In *Minority families in Britain*, V. Saifullah Khan (ed.). London: Macmillan.

Wellman, D. T. 1977. *Portraits of white racism.* Cambridge: Cambridge University Press.

West, C. 1992. The new cultural politics of difference. In *Out there: marginalization and contemporary cultures*, R. Ferguson, M. Gever, T. Minh-ha, C. West (eds). Cambridge, Mass.:MIT Press.

— 1993. *Race matters.* New York: Beacon Press.

Wetherall, M. & J. Potter 1986. Discourse analysis and the social psychology of racism. *Newsletter of the Social Psychology Section of the British Psychological Society* 15, 24–9.

Williams, J. 1985. Redefining institutional racism. *Ethnic and Racial Studies*, 8(3), 323–48.

Willis, P. 1977. *Learning to labour.* London: Saxon House.

— 1978. *Profane culture.* London: Routledge & Kegan Paul.

Wilmott, P. 1966. *Adolescent boys in East London.* London: Routledge & Kegan Paul.

Wilson, A. 1984. "Mixed race" children in British society: some theoretical considerations. *British Journal of Sociology* 35(1), 42–61.

— 1987. *Mixed race children: a study of identity.* London: Allen & Unwin.

Wong, A. 1986. Creole as a language of power and solidarity. See Sutcliffe & Wong (1986).

Wulff, H. 1988. *Twenty girls: growing up, ethnicity and excitement in a South London microculture.* Stockholm: Stockholm Studies in Social Anthropology.

Young, M. & P. Wilmott 1957. *Family and kinship in East London.* London: Penguin.

Index